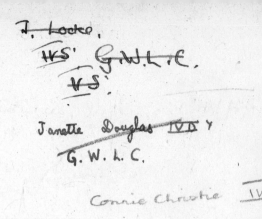

T. Locke.

HS' G.W.L.C.

HS'

Janette Douglas IVD y

G. W. L. C.

Connie Christie IVB

A CONCISE ENGLISH COURSE

A CONCISE
ENGLISH COURSE

BY

A. R. MOON
M.A.LOND., A.K.C.

LONGMANS, GREEN AND CO.
LONDON ▲ NEW YORK ▲ TORONTO

LONGMANS, GREEN AND CO. LTD.
39 PATERNOSTER ROW, LONDON, E.C.4
17 CHITTARANJAN AVENUE, CALCUTTA
NICOL ROAD, BOMBAY
36A MOUNT ROAD, MADRAS

LONGMANS, GREEN AND CO.
55 FIFTH AVENUE, NEW YORK
221 EAST 20TH STREET, CHICAGO
88 TREMONT STREET, BOSTON

LONGMANS, GREEN AND CO.
215 VICTORIA STREET, TORONTO

New Edition . . *December* 1939
New Impression . *February* 1941

CODE NUMBER 68151

Printed in Great Britain at THE DARIEN PRESS, *Edinburgh.*

PREFACE

In writing this Concise English Course I have concentrated upon the most important parts of the school syllabus in English composition, comprehension testing, and grammar. Believing that example is more important than precept I have been careful to offer the student standards on which to exercise his judgment. Although these standards are not far beyond his scope, for he is not asked to write a letter in the style of Charles Lamb, the further stimulus of good literature will often be found.

The chapter on punctuation is intentionally full, since faulty punctuation is one of the worst features of students' essays. Care has been taken to provide ample practice in expression before coming to the essay chapter.

In particular, after working through a number of these widely varied exercises, the reader should find he can turn even unpromising matter, such as apparently dull figures, into short but interesting paragraphs.

A special endeavour has been made to give adequate treatment to figures of speech.

Purposely, a consideration of syntax and of clause analysis has been left until late in the book as their influence is corrective rather than stimulating.

This book is not intended as a text-book for any particular examination, but it will be found useful for students preparing for Matriculation, School Certificate, Civil Service, R.S.A., and London Chamber of Commerce Examinations.

I wish especially to thank Dr P. Gurrey of the Institute of Education, London University, for valuable criticisms and suggestions.

ACKNOWLEDGMENTS

FOR kind and courteous permission to reproduce copyright material my thanks are due to the following authors, publishers, and examining bodies :—

Messrs J. M. Dent & Sons, Ltd, and the Author for short extracts from *Blow for Balloons* by W. J. Turner.

Mr William Heinemann Ltd, and the Author for an extract from *They Walk in the City* by J. B. Priestley.

Messrs Constable & Co., Ltd, and the Author's Trustees for an extract from *The Private Papers of Henry Ryecroft* by George Gissing.

The Author for a short quotation from George Bernard Shaw.

The Hogarth Press and the Author for extracts from *The Edwardians* by Miss V. Sackville-West.

Messrs Gerald Duckworth & Co., Ltd, and the Author's Executors for a passage from *The Silver Box* by John Galsworthy.

Mr Vyvyan Beresford Holland for the opening passages of *The Decay of Lying* by the late Oscar Wilde.

The Proprietors of *Punch* for a short extract.

Mr Clifford Bax for a quotation from his play *Square Pegs*.

Messrs Longmans, Green & Co., Ltd, and the Authors or their Executors for passages from Arthur Bryant's *The National Character*, Stella Gibbons' *Miss Linsey and Pa*, Cardinal Newman's *Apologia*, and Andrew Lang's *History of English Literature*.

Messrs Constable & Co., Ltd, and the Author for an extract from *Soliloquies in England* by Professor George Santayana.

Messrs W. Collins Sons & Co., Ltd, and the Authors for an extract from *Dead Man's Watch* by G. H. D. and Margaret Cole.

Messrs Jonathan Cape, Ltd, and the Author for an extract from *Naval Odyssey* by Thomas Woodrooffe.

Messrs William Heinemann Ltd, and the Author for a passage from *Faraway* by J. B. Priestley.

Messrs Macmillan & Co., Ltd, for statistics from *The Statesman's Year-Book*.

ACKNOWLEDGMENTS

Messrs Methuen & Co., Ltd, and the Authors for extracts from *My Friend the Chauffeur* by C. N. Williamson, and from *Harvest Home* by E. V. Lucas.

Messrs Macmillan & Co., Ltd, and the Authors or their Executors for extracts from *Views and Reviews* by W. E. Henley, *Political Economy* by W. S. Jevons, and *Lectures and Essays* by T. H. Huxley.

The Editor of *The Observer* for two extracts.

The Editor of *The Times* for a leading article and for an extract from another leading article.

The Editor of *The Evening Standard* for extracts from cables sent from Australia by Commander C. B. Fry and Neville Cardus.

The Editor of *The Lancet* for a passage from the supplement *On Writing for ' The Lancet.'*

The Editor of *The Daily Express* for a passage from Beachcomber's column.

The Editor of *John o' London's Weekly* and the Authors for extracts from ' Jackdaw ' and from an article by Richard Prentis.

The Editor of *The Manchester Guardian* for a leading article.

The Oxford and Cambridge Schools Examination Board and the Cambridge University Press for questions from School Certificate English papers.

The Royal Society of Arts for questions from papers set by the Society.

The Controller of H.M. Stationery Office and the Civil Service Commissioners for extracts from official examination papers published by H.M. Stationery Office.

The Northern Universities Joint Matriculation Board for some questions set in their School Certificate Examination Papers.

The University of London for some questions set by the University Examiners.

The London Chamber of Commerce for questions set in their Certificate Papers.

The Executors of the late Cynthia Stockley for a short extract from *The Claw*.

The Executors of the late Archibald Marshall for a short extract from *The Birdikin Family*.

CONTENTS

A Concise English Course

CHAPTER I

WORDS AND IDEAS

> I love words opalescent, cool and pearly,
> Like midsummer moths, and honied words like bees,
> Gilded and sticky, with a little sting.
>
> ELINOR WYLIE.

(1) *Words Rightly and Wrongly Used*

WORDS are the dress of thoughts. Overdressed thoughts may die of suffocation, choked by a surfeit of finery. Writing of Silas Marner, a student said :

> It is due to the effect which superstition has upon the interpretation by the villagers of Raveloe of what are really quite natural happenings, that Silas Marner is regarded as someone who has dealings with the supernatural.

A far more effective statement is

> The villagers of Raveloe, prone to superstition, magnify Silas Marner's natural actions until they seem to be significant evidence of necromancy.

or,

> The superstitious villagers of Raveloe misconstrue Silas Marner's natural acts into dealings with the supernatural.

Study and practice are needed before the student can realize the expressive power of words. Too many think power is the same thing as weight. They cram together many small words, perhaps in the belief that 'unity is strength,' or they produce long words, powerful only in their appearance but weak and shabby when unnecessarily or wrongly used.

Listen to this garrulous talk :—

If my tooth were aching I should go at once to the dentist's where the latter would either pull my tooth out, or else drill out the decayed part and refill the tooth with a substance like cement.

Even this is preferable to the pomposity of :—

It is undeniably to be deprecated that while many of our compatriots are unable to procure a modicum of nutrition, an unenlightened plutocracy may enjoy a maximum of luxurious indulgence. Surely this is an unwarrantable blemish on our much flaunted democratic institutions.

Probably the writer of the last paragraph felt proud of having at his beck and call such a fine array of words.   By far the commonest fault in essay writing is turgidity, a wearisome inflation of a few ideas, unnecessarily repeated, and over-emphasized.

Exercise

Rewrite the following so as to express the thoughts more effectively and concisely :—

1. Only a comparatively small proportion of the public avail themselves of the facilities for boating where any manual exercise is involved, with the result that, in some instances, boat letters who had hoped to let a good number of their boats when the fine weather set in found that they had registered boats in excess of the demand.

   (*Try to express this in fourteen words.*)

2. The governing body of the land would be entirely concerned with the welfare of the population which inhabited the country.

3. Chemists, scientists, and doctors, by their investigations have made many remarkable discoveries which have made modern life much easier than of yore.

This exercise should be followed by reading some of the essays of Robert Lynd, Max Beerbohm, Alpha of the Plough, or Hilaire Belloc. There is no padding, no over-elaboration of a few ideas, but a firm stride into the subject, a sense of development and finish. Instead of feeble inflation there is a sparkle of personality gleaming through each telling phrase. The style is the man.

As a contrast, read some of De Quincey's anecdotes, especially those embedded in his *Reminiscences of the Lake Poets*. The essay *Early Memorials of Grasmere* is an excellent illustration of how not to tell a story. Read this essay and make a list of its irrelevancies.[1] You will find Stephen Leacock's chapter on Story-Tellers and Story-Killers a useful counter-irritant.[2]

Exercise

Clarify the thoughts in the following sentences. Some of them may be recognized as perversions of proverbs or quotations

1. If a person has a bad reputation we are inclined to believe any ill that is spoken of him.

2. Fear of the unknown makes us endure known ills rather than seek remedies which may make matters worse.

3. On Hospital Sunday students are seen pushing their way through the crowds shaking cans which are nearly full up to capacity with coins of some value or other.

4. Year by year, the Americanization of England is becoming more evident ; and many believe that this will continue until England, who once called America her province, has developed into little more than a province of her erstwhile [3] subject-state.

---

[1] Everyman's Library, pp. 202-231.
[2] *Humour*, p. 184.
[3] *Former* is a better word to use. Why ?

Express more concisely the thoughts expressed in this essay on ' A Heat Wave.'

During August of this year the phrase ' Heat Wave ' was much discussed amongst the public. Most people who felt the heat unbearable scrambled to the nearest place where they could refresh themselves, whilst others who did not feel its effects so much simply threw off a few unnecessary clothes and took full advantage of the beneficial rays of the glorious sunshine.

Even trade was greatly affected by this phenomenon of the hot weather. A typical example of this is the extraordinary growth in this weather of the following trades which cater for the needs of a parched public, brewers, light-drink and ice-cream manufacturers. Conversely other occupations suffer in consequence of this weather, trades such as the providing of indoor amusements and the making of heavy articles of attire.

On the whole commerce is naturally affected because work of any kind under such conditions to ordinary people tends to lower their degree of concentration, and increased irritability does not incline workers to carry out their natural degree of efficiency.

The sudden exodus of workers to cooler parts of the countryside and seaside temporarily ruins the local trader.

In this country, however, heat waves are of such short duration that they are welcome to the major portion of the community.

(2) *Words Wrongly Used*

A study of vocabulary is desirable not only for concise expression, but also for correct expression. In a recent article Dean Inge pointed out that Carlyle confused *euphuism* and *euphemism*, Thomas Hardy used *predicate* for *predict*, and that Dickens has *trustful* for *trustworthy*, *complaisant* for *complacent*. That most misused of modern words, *hectic*, really means ' habitual ' or ' permanent ' ; a hectic flush is ' a usual symptom of the later stages of consumption.' [1]

---

[1] Article in the London *Evening News*, 8th May, 1935.

It is undesirable to press scientific or commercial terms into common usage. *Factor* and *asset* are repeatedly and unnecessarily used.[1] They add vagueness, not strength, to one's writing.

The Editor of *The Lancet* rightly says that even in a highly technical subject brevity and clarity of expression are most desirable. As an example he gives :—

> Though numerous instances have been recorded in the United States, examination of the literature with reference to idiopathic glandulosis suggests that this disorder is of relatively infrequent occurrence in this country. Up to the present time no consensus of opinion exists in connexion with the factors which may play an ætiological rôle in its causation ; and in view of their variety, taken in conjunction with certain abnormal characteristics involved in their symptomatology, it would appear that the following series of cases under the present author's observation may be of sufficient interest to warrant being placed on record.

Given time, we might translate it thus :—

> Though often reported in the United States, idiopathic glandulosis appears to be less common in this country. Its cause is still uncertain, and I am recording these cases because the disease is rare and some of the symptoms were unusual.

(3) *Ghost Words*

Often in writing there is a temptation to use words and phrases which seem satisfying at the time but which have little real meaning. They have been labelled ' ghost words ' : they are unsatisfying, for there is not much substance in them.

> These relics are now reposing in various museums, and their place is taken by mass-produced components which are identical *to an amazingly high degree of accuracy.*

[1] See H. W. Fowler, *Modern English Usage*, pp. 35, 65, 445. Fowler also points to the too frequent use of the word *case*. Recently an Oxford don, asked what he would do in the case of foreign students, replied, ' We do not keep foreign students in cases.' Notice the unnecessary words in : (In the case of) the motor-car owner (he) may have spent a week in cleaning and overhauling the car.

It is clearer to say ' which are *almost* identical.' The words *reposing* and *various* should also be discarded. By ' relics ' the student was referring to early makes of wireless valves, coils, and condensers.

Beware of such clumsy periphrases as ' come well to the fore ' ; ' in more favourable circumstances ' ; ' under similar conditions ' ; ' of an interesting nature ' ; ' with a modicum of enjoyment.' Be critical of your own work ; make a list of similar ghosts that stalk up and down your essays. Do not let these ghosts gibber.

Beachcomber once wrote an amusing illustration of the futility of certain fine-sounding phrases.

> The prophetic faculty enables me to anticipate the authoritative pronouncement (or, if you prefer it, the official communiqué) which will be issued to the Press after Mr Anthony Eden's visit to Rome.
>
> He will authorize it to be said that :—
>
> He is satisfied that considerable progress has been definitely made towards an amicable consideration of the possibility of effecting a working agreement concerning the undoubted willingness of all parties to approach the question of disarmament in a spirit that brooks no delay in the appreciation of the pressing problems which face all responsible statesmen to-day in their earnest and heartfelt desires on behalf of the peoples whom they represent, to smooth away all those difficulties, based on past misunderstandings, which shall be suffered no longer, in the light of experience, to complicate the frank attitude which is recognized to be essential towards the considerable progress which has been definitely made towards an amicable consideration of . . .
>
> —At this point the automatic device comes into operation and the record replays itself. ~The Adventures of Rupert~
>
> *The Daily Express.*

Mr St John Ervine once spoke of a fellow-critic who, asked for his opinion of the play he had just seen, said that it was ' definitely bad.' This, said Mr St John Ervine, was the most *indefinite* criticism he had ever heard.

The following sentence appeared in an advertisement. Does its meaning leap at once into the mind?

The minimum service cost continues these economies in inexpensive maintenance throughout all the years it serves you.

Try to express the above idea clearly.

William Cullen Bryant, the American poet, condemned the following words as ' utterly unworthy ' :—

aspirant, authoress, bogus, collide, darky, donate, humbug, jeopardize, loafer, locate, ovation, poetess, roughs, rowdies, taboo, talented.

Can you suggest why they should have been considered unworthy? Which three do you particularly dislike? What synonyms would you use to avoid them?

(4) *Synonyms*

The English language is fortunate in the richness of its synonyms. The words *calamity* and *harm*, although it is not obvious from their appearance, are both of the same origin. What is their difference in meaning? Words which often appear to be interchangeable are not absolutely synonymous. It is easy to frame sentences in which *catastrophe* can be replaced by *calamity*, but their difference was once cleverly illustrated on a political platform. It was mentioned that if Mr Blank, a very unpopular Cabinet Minister, fell off the end of a pier, it would be a catastrophe. ' Yes,' retorted an opponent, ' but if someone dived in and saved him it would be a calamity.'

What exactly is the difference between the words?

Exercise

Indicate by brief explanations, or by using the words in sentences, the distinctions between :—

enormous, abnormal

solicitous, administrative, ministerial

quixotic, capricious

sporadic, spasmodic

impudence, assurance

reticent, taciturn, laconic

plot, stratagem, machination

condone, condole

imply, implicate

meditate, cogitate, contemplate

(5) *Borrowings*

By its absorption of foreign words at different stages in history our language has become more flexible : it is rich in words to express shades of meaning.

As a result of contact between Saxons and Romans, we find some Latin borrowings in Old English. *Bishop, candle, clerk, mass, monk* are reminiscent of the conversion of the Anglo-Saxons to Christianity. *Camp, cheese, -chester* or *-caster, mint* (money), and *pile* (javelin) were probably used by the Ancient Britons and later absorbed by the English from the same Roman source.

The Norman Conquest enriched English with hosts of words, especially terms savouring of soldiering, religion, the law, and hunting :

> armour, assault, baron, captain, fealty, homage, lance, march, soldier, vassal ; altar, baptism, friar, homily, penance, prayer, relic, religion, sacrifice, saint ; assize, court, cause, dower, estate, felony, judge, jury, plaintiff, plea, statute, sue ; brace, chase, covert, falcon, forest, mews, quarry.

In the Middle English period, about 1150 to just before 1500, there was no printing press to preserve case-terminations and verb-endings. Caxton did not begin to print at Westminster until 1476, by which time, through belonging to the unaccented part of the word, many of the case-endings of nouns and adjectives had weakened to an unaccented *-e* and the nominative plural in *-s* had been levelled into the other plural case forms. Thus instead of O.E. *Nom.* stānas (stones), *Gen.* stāna, *Dat.* stānum, there was now the one form *stones*. The termination of the O.E. present participle in *-ende* and the verbal noun in *-ung* gradually weakened to a common ending in *-ing*.

> The boys were *swimming*. (Present participle.)
> *Swimming* helped the sailor to escape from the shark. (Verbal noun.)

Into Middle English were absorbed many words of Latin, Norman, and Old French origin. Towards the end of the Middle English period, owing to the Hundred Years' War and a re-awakened interest in seafaring, numbers of Flemish and Scandinavian words were borrowed. Many of these, like the Scandinavian word *wros* (corners), stayed but a short time. Others were later given up for their cognate forms in English.

Sergeant came from Anglo-French : the verbs *to raise*, *to cast* (into prison), *to spill* (*i.e.*, to destroy), and *to rayke* (to wander to and fro), *to sway* (to bend, in the term ' sway-backed,' used of a horse), the nouns *tow* (taken in tow), and *bloom* (of a flower), and the plural forms of the third person pronoun, *they*, *them*, *their*, were introduced from Scandinavian sources into Middle English.

Many Latin words which had been introduced into Old or Early Middle English gradually underwent such changes of spelling and pronunciation that, later, in the fifteenth and sixteenth centuries, they were again borrowed direct from the Latin. Such pairs of words are called ' doublets.' Often their meanings widely diverge. You will find an interesting list of doublets in Professor W. W. Skeat's *Etymological Dictionary*, p. 772 onwards. Thus, with *blaspheme* and *blame*, *tradition* and *treason*, *persecute* and *pursue*, the first word in each pair is the later borrowing coming from the Latin in Late Middle or Early New (Modern) English ; the second comes to us first through the French in Early Middle English times.

Exercises in Using the Dictionary

1. In section (*a*) are given some doublets. In (*b*) you will find some words related in origin although they are not doublets. Point out any differences in meaning between the words in each pair :

(*a*) cadence, chance ; assoil, absolve ; dainty, dignity ; journal, diurnal ; aggravate, aggrieve.

(*b*) haunch, hinge ; careful, chary ; chastise, castigate ; imply, implicate ; oration, orison.

2. Look up the exact meanings of the words in the following groups, and make notes on any interesting points of difference :—

accidental, casual, fortuitous ; break, void, hiatus, interval, schism ; subterfuge, quibble, chicanery ; compulsion, compunction ; concession, conciliation ; discomfiture, embarrassment, confusion.

3. M. Müller estimates that in modern English the classical element (words of Latin and Greek origin) is about 68 per cent. of our dictionary words, the Teutonic element about 30, and words from other sources only 2 per cent.

From which languages have we borrowed :—

almanac, checkmate, cipher, accolade, bivouac, apache, blasé, ambulance, bizarre, banshee, caber, plaid, targe, shantung, pekoe, brandy, catkin, clinker, bowsprit, bruin (*a bear*), paper, oasis, barouche, lager, zinc, botulism, collectanea, aphesis, coma, cassia, boanerges, shibboleth, chintz, jungle, cheetah, chit (*paper*), colleen, galore, pillion, aria, arsenal, balcony, buffoon, burlesque, caricature, brigantine, bravura, sequin, cartoon, casino, caddy (*tea*), cheroot, atoll, cachou, chocolate, tomato, yam, pemmican, moccasin, begum, scarlet, tambour, calabash, alpaca, llama, tattoo (*to mark the skin*), betel, alcove, albino, cobra, mandarin, marmalade, steppe, ukase, vodka, bodega, bastinado, bravado, caramel, sherry, vanilla, anchovy, apricot, embargo, cockroach, cocoa, barrack (*of spectators, to make loud and caustic comments*), aryan, bosh (*nonsense*), sherbet, kiosk, odalisque, horde, gorilla, chimpanzee, coach (*large vehicle*).

4. The following words have interesting etymologies. You should look them up in *The Shorter Oxford English Dictionary*.

aitch-bone, alopecia, anthologist, apron, assassin, awning, asphodel, auburn, bachelor, backgammon, blue-stocking, blunderbuss, book, buccaneer, burglar, buttery, cannibal, caterpillar, chancellor, chapel, chauffeur, chess*men*, coax, cockney, coco, codex, dismal, gossip, humble-pie, kerchief, lady, malinger, nickname, prose, twilight.

5. These words have been derived from names of places :—

argosy, artesian, astrakhan, axminster, baldachin, balmoral, bergamot, berlin, bezant, blarney, brussels, bunkum, canary, canter, coburg, gasconade, guinea, muslin, sardonic, solecism, worsted, chevaux de *frise*.

State with what each of the above words is associated, and give any interesting historical associations that you have noticed.

6. It is customary to blame American talking-pictures for the introduction of copious and even objectionable words into English. Before being too severely critical you should note the following, all of which have been adopted from America.

bogus, caption, to be ' a caution ' (*a funny fellow*), cut (*salary cut*), business man, graveyard, overcoat, law-abiding, once in a while, time and again, to be up against (*to have a difficult problem*), to take a chance, to be rattled, a census, a wisecrack, loafer, lengthy.

See if you can add to this list.

7. So far from American usage being a coarse or inferior kind of English, it can be shown that some equivalents to our words are really more grandiloquent. The following list was published in *John o' London's Weekly* last year :—

shorthand writer	stenographer
time table	schedule
spittoon	cuspidor
door-keeper	janitor
tap	faucet
street-crossing	intersection
gum	mucilage
any mortal thing !	proposition
undertaker	mortician

Comment upon the advisability of introducing some or all of the words in the right-hand column into English.

8. You may come to the conclusion that the English usages of the words in No. 7 will successfully resist the American invasion. If you study your dictionary carefully you will find that words, by analogy, powerfully influence each other. Look

up these words in *S.O.E.D.* and write notes on their origin and present form :—

> andiron, ante-room, aitch-bone, anythingarian, penthouse, argufy, sparrow-grass, bathetic, benignant, frontispiece, bloater, broider, levitate, choir, cockroach, squirearchy, sovereign, court-card, country-dance.

Which of the above words owe their origin to jocular usage ?

9. What differences can you detect between these pairs of expressions ?   Which of those in the right-hand column do you consider unnecessary in any circumstances ?

bright clothes	scintillating raiment
a tramp	a human derelict
foot	pedal extremity
sad thoughts	melancholy musings
inadvisable	highly inexpedient
burglar	nocturnal marauder
a pair of scissors	a glittering forfex
nose	olfactory organ
to placate	to adopt a conciliatory attitude
outside work	extraneous activity
prompt request	peremptory demand
ugly face	repulsive countenance
lack of knowledge	abysmal ignorance
unprepared	deluded by an unforeseen contingency

10. What is meant by the following expressions ?

> to be on the carpet ; to reckon without one's host ; to be in one's element ; a moral victory ; a Roland for an Oliver ; to be within an ace of ; to be on all fours with ; Dead Sea Fruit ; in apple-pie order ; to be armed to the teeth.

11. Use the following phrases in sentences to bring out their meaning. Which of these phrases are tolerated only in colloquial usage ?

> to sweep the board ; to be a catspaw ; to lose caste ; to be on short commons ; to compound a felony ; a coign of vantage ; to be in clover ; to show respect for the cloth ; to clinch an argument ; to be without benefit of clergy ;

to cap an anecdote ; to catch a Tartar ; to stand upon ceremony ; to bear the brunt ; to take the bull by the horns ; to burn the candle at both ends ; to burn one's boats ; chapter and verse ; cheek by jowl ; to ring the changes ; under colour of ; Hobson's choice ; Cimmerian darkness ; to argue in a circle ; a clean bill of health.

(6) *Prose Diction*

From the exercises you have worked through, and especially No. 9, you may have formed the opinion that you are to use only short simple words. The true distinction is not one of the length of words but whether they are clear and effective in expressing your meaning. As your thoughts become more expansive so should your vocabulary grow. Wordsworth's theory of poetic diction, the use of the simplest words, or 'the very language of men,' was not borne out in practice in his *Ode on the Intimations of Immortality*. So, too, you will feel disappointed if you are told *always* to use simple words and to show no advance in literary style from the essays you wrote five or six years ago. You should aim at straight speech and not permit cumbersome circumlocutions like those expressions you found to be unnecessary in the previous exercises.

You should also prefer concrete and particular words to abstract and general ones.

1. In proportion as the manners, customs, and amusements of a nation are cruel and barbarous, the regulation of their penal codes will be severe.

2. A large percentage of the villagers were unable to procure regular nutrition.

3. A loud burst of acclamation greeted the scorer's remarkable achievement.

Notice how more easily understood you will be if you say :—

1. According as men delight in battles, bullfights, and com-

bats of gladiators, so will they punish by hanging, burning, and crucifying.

2. Most of the villagers could not obtain regular supplies of food.

(*Sentence 2 is so vague that it can be expressed in a number of different ways.*)

3. The spectators applauded this clever goal.

Hasten away to the cricket field where Mr C. B. Fry and Mr Neville Cardus are describing an exciting game. The former, intentionally humorous, packs out his sentences with all manner of incongruous ideas and somehow conveys his meaning to us.

. . . and all the time young Badcock is exercising his bijou power-plant with squat aptitude in a miniature tornado of off-drives and square cuts.

It is a style not to imitate. You must remember that readers of sports columns are usually uncritical of literary style.

Mr Neville Cardus gives a serious psycho-analysis of the same batsman :

The innings had about it an air of complete control with its technique not a servant of the mind but the outward and swift manifestation of the mind itself. There were no falterings, not a single material obstruction between the stroke conceived and the stroke executed.

Here you have a single unit of thought well expressed in words. It is beside the point to say that so serious an analysis is out of proportion to a mere game of cricket. Mr Cardus sees a beauty, a grace, and an art in the way strokes are played. His words come at command and are adequate for his expression.

The following words were taken from the essays written by two hundred candidates at a recent examination. Few candidates had attained the age of sixteen. All the words were used correctly and effectively. From time to time you should practise using in sentences of your own construction words newly found in your reading.

altruistic
amicably
antipathy
appalling
appreciable
apprehension
aptitude
aptly
arbitrament
archaic
ascertain (v.)
assert (v.)
atrocity
audacity
automaton
autopsy
auxiliary
avert (v.)
basis
behest
beholden to (v.)
beneficent
bland
blatant
blithe
bluster (v.)
brusque
centenary
chafe (v.)
chide (v.)
churlish
circumvent (v.)
clandestine
clinic
coddle (v.)
collaborate (v.)
colleague
collusion
colonnade

commendation
commodity
complication
compunction
conceivable
conclave
condescending
condolence
congestion
consign (v.)
consolidate (v.)
conspicuous
contingency
co-operate (v.)
cope with (v.)
counteract (v.)
curb (v.)
defective
deficiency
degraded
depict (v.)
deter (v.)
dexterous
dilemma
discourtesy
dispense with (v.)
distinctive
distorting
distribute (v.)
drab (adj.)
drastic
elation
elegant
eliminate (v.)
emergency
enforcement
enhance (v.)
enmity
ensuing

ensure (v.)
estimate
estimation
exorbitant
fabulous
fallacy
fatality
festoon with (v.)
flaw
forthcoming
ghastly
hamper (v.)
immersion
immune
impede (v.)
imprudence
impulse
inadequate
inaugurate (v.)
incentive
inclement
incompetent
inevitable
infest (v.)
ingratiating
insecurity
inspiration
institute (v.)
insufferable
insurmountable
intense
intricate
irrelevant
lethargic
logical
mania
massive
materially
meander (v.)

menace
miniature
minimize (v.)
morally
mutilate (v.)
notorious
obligation
organization
penetrate (v.)
perpetual
plea
praiseworthy
precaution
precision
predominating
querulous

recklessness
relentlessly
reluctant
respite
restriction
rigidly
robot
routine
scrupulous
self-assurance
servility
shifty
sordid
spectacular
stolid
suavity

subconsciously
supervision
surmise (v.)
symptom
taunt
tenacity
timely
transept
twinge
ultimate
uncomplimentary
unfailingly
unrestricted
unsavoury
vital
wary

It is advantageous if you can readily draw from a copious stock of words when you are writing a précis, a paraphrase, a letter or an essay.

CHAPTER II

ECONOMY OF WORDS

But flee we now prolixitee best is,
. . . and lat us faste go
Right to th' effect.

CHAUCER.

IF, instead of saying *a final proposal or statement of terms, the rejection of which by another country may lead to a declaration of war*, you know and use the word *ultimatum*, you economize in words.

Exercises in vocabulary are valuable, since they not only teach new words but help you to appreciate and use many words gained from your reading.

Exercise

Substitute *one word* for each of the following italicized phrases or clauses. It may be necessary to make a few changes in sentence construction. (*E.g.*, This is a discrimination *likely to lead to ill-feeling*. This is an *invidious* discrimination.)

1. The young Warden's remarks were *in season and to the point*.

2. The dictator's latest decree has *reduced to nothing* all existing laws.

3. These articles on war are poisoning people's minds so much that the committee feels obliged to administer *something which will counteract the poison*. (You will have to introduce the indefinite article here.)

4. My friend is not an author; he is merely *one who publishes a collection of literary passages*. (Introduce the indefinite article.)

5. The whole community protested against the admission of the *one who had renounced his religious faith*.

6. The brewers declared they had never seen a cask *capable of holding* so *much*.

7. It was found necessary to *make new laws* to prevent such wholesale evasion of income-tax.

8. How do you propose *successfully* to *justify yourself for* your harshness ?

9. The young actress was most *lively and quick-spirited*.

10. Pope's friends were amazed at the *extreme bitterness* of his satires.

11. By some strange *deviation from the natural course of the law* the tourists were detained in prison while their passports were *examined with minute attention to detail*.

Use in sentences of your own construction the words you have found by doing this exercise.

Further Vocabulary Practice

1. Substitute adjectives ending in *-ive* for the phrases in italics. You may have to recast some of the sentences.

This battle was *the event which brought the war to an end*.

An actor could scarcely hope to have an audience more *sensitive to the value of his work*.

Until Janet learns to be less *swayed by sudden emotions* she will not make lasting friendships.

The employees' defiant attitude was not *likely to lead* to a peaceful settlement.

It was unnecessary for the men to be so *disposed to attack other people*.

All the music master's critical opinions were *characterized by a tendency to keep things unchanged*.

This is not a statement *proceeding from a competent person*.

Jones, I fear, is a kind of person *who prefers to keep himself too much to himself and to be unnaturally discreet*.

2. Express in a single word any *five* of the following :—

(*a*) One who always looks on the bright side of life.
(*b*) A group of stars.

(c) A dog of mixed breed.
(d) To pass the winter in sleep.
(e) A person who is recovering from an illness.
(f) A conversation between two people.
(g) A man eighty years old.
(h) A five-sided figure.

Royal Society of Arts, Stage I.

3. Replace each of the following phrases by an adjective ending in -*ious* :—

full of life and gaiety ; characterized by unsteadiness or fickleness ; bitter and caustic ; addicted to giving adverse critical opinions ; alluring by a false, glittering show ; given to falsehood ; given to the truth ; characterized by scrupulous attention to duty.

4. Replace the words, phrases, and clauses in italics by a single word ending in -*ary*, -*ery*, or -*ory* :—

(a) Robin Hood and his outlaws lived by making *plundering* raids on the neighbouring aristocracy.
(b) These factory hands have no knowledge *of even the very beginnings* of their work.
(c) The piano manufacturer was invited to be a member of the committee *that gives counsel and makes suggestions*.
(d) Most active people dislike work *which requires long continuance in a sitting posture* as they do not believe it is *conducive to health*.
(e) Tom's mother held up a finger *to give him warning*.
(f) This offence was so serious that it belonged to a different *class* of negligence ; it was criminal negligence.
(g) Although the shopkeeper had acted unwittingly, he had laid himself open to a charge of *having helped the criminal after he had committed* the crime. (Say *being an . . . to . . .*)
(h) In a voice *that brooked of neither question nor delay* Sir Anthony Absolute ordered his son to marry the lady.
(i) It is manifestly unfair to evade paying one's debts by resorting to *legal quibbles and subterfuges*.
(k) The rest of the committee will express their feelings to Mr Simmonds in a letter *which will tend to bring him solace and comfort*.

5. Give adjectives ending in *-al* for each of the following phrases :—

happening each year ; trivial and commonplace ; equally skilled in two languages ; pertaining to the soul ; pertaining to the body ; happening at uncertain times ; belonging to ordinary conversational usage ; of married life ; suited to a person's nature or disposition ; of uncertain disposition ; of enormous dimensions ; prejudiced in favour of one side or party ; pertaining to a current subject of discourse ; handed down from bygone days ; recurring every three years or lasting for three years ; existing everywhere ; worthy of being overlooked as a pardonable offence ; pertaining to spring.

6. Explain briefly the meaning of the following words and write six short sentences, each containing one of the words so as to bring out its meaning :—

bovine, volatile, clemency, beneficent, malignant, contentious, morose, callous.

7. Show that you understand the meaning of the following adjectives either by using them with appropriate nouns or by illustrative sentences :—

aquatic, beatific, bombastic, bucolic, caustic, chronic, erratic, neurotic, optimistic, pacific, platonic, strategic.

8. Give as briefly as you can the meaning of the following expressions. (*E.g.*, a storm in a teacup ; ' a trivial dispute.')

to bandy words ; to cross the Rubicon ; to buy a pig in a poke ; to hitch one's waggon to a star ; to be in a brown study ; a bull in a china shop ; a virtue of necessity ; a tower of strength ; a bird in the hand ; a castle in Spain.

9. Express the following colloquialisms in better English :—

to mean business ; butter-fingered ; to have an eye to the main chance ; to change one's tune ; once in a blue moon ; to set one's cap at ; to clap eyes on ; to bowl a person out ; to be caught napping ; to chip in ; to blow a person up.

10. Explain the meaning of the following picturesque words and expressions :—

a blue-stocking ; a blackleg ; blind man's holiday ; cagmag ; a capful of wind ; a chawbacon ; Clootie ; to be cock-a-hoop ; cheese-paring ; a free lance ; the sinews of war ; to be hand in glove with ; to curry favour ; to render yeoman service.

(You are advised to consult the *Shorter Oxford English Dictionary*.)

11. Give a synonym for each of the following words :—

conspicuous, bellicose, verbose, veracious, chaotic, bombastic, clandestine, supine, competent, affable, ostentatious, poignant.

Are the words you have chosen exactly synonymous with those in the above list ? Draw attention to any distinctions of meaning that you may have noticed.

12. Write sentences to illustrate the difference in meaning of the words in the following groups :—

(*a*) console, reconcile, conciliate.
(*b*) proposal, proposition, project, projectile.
(*c*) flimsy, sparse, frugal, scanty, attenuated, rarefied.
(*d*) acme, climax, crisis, zenith.
(*e*) efficient, effective, efficacious.
(*f*) belief, knowledge, supposition, opinion, fancy, conviction.

13. Explain the difference in meaning between the following pairs of words. Write one sentence for each word to illustrate your answer.

occur, happen	exceptional, exceptionable
illustrious, illustrative	mediate, mitigate
timidity, temerity	tend, tender (v.)
retrace, retract	insipid, incipient
idol, ideal	immunity, impunity

14. The following words are echoic or onomatopœic. Use them appropriately in sentences :—

babble, blurt, bluster, chatter, chink, chuckle, churr, clack, clang, clatter, cloop, climp, twitter, whizz, whuff, yap, yaffle, zip.

15. Write five sentences using words suitable to describe :—

(*a*) The sound of the wind in a wood.
(*b*) The movement of a rabbit.
(*c*) The appearance of the sky at night.
(*d*) The motion of a stream.
(*e*) A telescope.

Oxford and Cambridge School Certificate.

16. Distinguish the meanings of :—

clod, clot	lineal, collateral
meed, mead	inflammable, inflammatory
colonial, colonist	originate, inaugurate
various, variable	comment, commentary
flout, flaunt	partner, colleague, collaborator

17. Embody each of the following words in sentences so as to show clearly the meaning of each word :—

banter, barter	incompatible, incomparable
peak, pique (n.)	dominate, predominate
confer, collate	longevity, vivacity
intimate (v.), intimidate	continuity, contiguity
scholastic, scholarly	auricular, ocular, oracular

18. Distinguish the meanings of :—

unjust, injudicious	laudable, praiseworthy
cognisant, conversant	recrimination, discrimination
imply, implicate	circulate, circularize
partake, participate	purify, edify
limpid, lucid	aspersion, aspiration

19. (*a*) If you had to rewrite the following passage, which word would you choose from each bracket ? You need not write out the whole passage ; write only the words you choose together with the corresponding numbers.

One star may differ (1) $\begin{cases} \text{with} \\ \text{from} \\ \text{to} \end{cases}$ another in (2) $\begin{cases} \text{grandiloquence} \\ \text{greatness} \\ \text{magnitude} \end{cases}$, but no (3) $\begin{cases} \text{astronomer} \\ \text{astrologer} \\ \text{geologist} \end{cases}$ would be so

(4) $\left\{\begin{matrix}\text{proud}\\\text{haughty}\\\text{arrogant}\end{matrix}\right\}$ as to deny even the (5) $\left\{\begin{matrix}\text{smallest}\\\text{greatest}\\\text{brightest}\end{matrix}\right\}$ its place

in the solar system ; and you may be sure it is some

(6) $\left\{\begin{matrix}\text{efficiency}\\\text{deficiency}\\\text{detriment}\end{matrix}\right\}$ of culture, some narrowness of feeling in

yourself, if you are not (7) $\left\{\begin{matrix}\text{sensible}\\\text{sensuous}\\\text{sensitive}\end{matrix}\right\}$ to the poetry of

Cowper, for example, or Pope. Longfellow, again, is too

often (8) $\left\{\begin{matrix}\text{subjected}\\\text{ejected}\\\text{rejected}\end{matrix}\right\}$ by (9) $\left\{\begin{matrix}\text{superfluous}\\\text{superstitious}\\\text{superior}\end{matrix}\right\}$ minds because

he makes a more general appeal than Donne.

(*b*) In any **three** instances give the reasons why you have
rejected the two words you have not chosen.

Joint Matriculation Board, School Certificate.

20. Point out exactly the difference in meaning between the
words in each of the following pairs, and write sentences in
illustration :—

compiled, complied ; convivial, jovial ; visitor, visitant ;
dramatist, tragedian ; petulance, acrimony ; coherence,
cohesion ; cognizance, recognition ; precocity, preciosity.

21. The following are examples of **antonomasia**, *i.e.*, the
substitution of an epithet, or the name of an office or dignity,
for a person's proper name [1] :—

(*a*) To whom do these refer :—
The Iron Duke ; the Little Corporal ; the Lady with
a Lamp ; the Swedish Nightingale ; the Merry
Monarch ; the Pocket Chancellor ; the Iron
Chancellor ; the Sick Man of Europe ?

(*b*) By what titles or phrases do we sometimes refer to
Queen Victoria ; Queen Elizabeth (*d.* 1603) ; William
Shakespeare ; King Edward the First ; Joan of Arc ?

[1] This is the definition in the *Shorter Oxford English Dictionary*.

2

22. Express in fewer words each of the following phrases :—

Obstinately wedded to a creed or opinion ; a writer of the life-story of another ; offensively self-conceited ; to get one's own way by promises and flattery ; impossible to calculate ; quick to take offence ; collective slaughter of men in battle ; sepulchral monument in honour of a person whose body is elsewhere ; that which takes possession of the mind to the exclusion of everything else ; one belonging to the same country as oneself ; a sudden turn of the mind without apparent motive ; the body of voters who elect a representative member of a public body ; passing from an ancestor to a descendant ; brilliancy of reflected light ; conformity to established rules and customs, especially of behaviour ; place at a school or college where meals are served ; a letter or certificate of recommendation ; a form of society impracticably ideal ; an angry or noisy dispute.

23. Illustrate the meanings of the following phrases by including them in sentences :—

to look askance ; to have an axe to grind ; to break the back of ; to save one's bacon ; to be on the beam ends ; to bring to bear on ; to take the bit between one's teeth ; to breed bad blood ; to run in the blood ; to restore in blood ; to blow hot and cold ; the blue riband of the Atlantic ; Blue-water school ; to sweep the board ; to body forth ; a bone of contention ; without more bones ; to bring to book ; the boot is on the other leg ; to draw the long bow ; to make one's bow ; to bow to the inevitable.

CHAPTER III

CONTINUITY OF THOUGHT—LINKING UP SENTENCES AND PARAGRAPH STRUCTURE

> Fit words are better than fine ones.
> FELLTHAM.

(1) *Monotony*

IT was a fine day. I decided to go for a picnic. My sister declared she would come with me. We boarded a bus. It took us to Epping Forest. We arrived. We had our lunch. We rambled among the trees and bracken. We returned tired and happy.

If this were the opening paragraph of a long essay you would not wish to read the next ten pages. There is a dull monotony like the repeated thuds of a woodman's axe. The sentences are similar in length and structure. Five of them begin with the same word.

It is easy to avoid this dullness :

We rambled among the trees and bracken.

Among the trees and bracken was an ideal place for a ramble.

There, under the trees and bracken, my sister and I roamed at will.

Rambling beneath the trees, and with bracken all around us, my sister and I were lost in the wonder of it all.

The cool shade of the trees standing loftily above the ferns impelled us to leave the open road with its dust and heat.

Few joys could compare with our ramble among the ferns which grew right up to the tree-trunks.

Write three more sentences expressing the same idea.

(2) *Emphasis*

In writing it is usually desirable to give prominence to the chief idea of a sentence, or to stress certain words. The beginning and end of the sentence are the emphatic positions, but you should be sparing in your use of inversions.

In the forest I met a fool. The king's jester he had once been. On him all eyes were turned when at the court he made merry in the days of his prosperity. Downcast was this fool now. Slow was his gait. Melancholy was his countenance.

Thus you see an effective literary device, when occasionally used, becomes first obtrusive and then monotonous if used too frequently.

Exercise

Stress the words indicated in brackets by altering the order of the words in the sentences below. You may add words or make changes in the construction of the sentence. Be careful, however, not to keep to one method. You may use the interrogative or exclamatory form of the sentence where you can do so effectively.

The passengers complained of the huger liner's vibration. (Complained.)

Complaints were made about the huge liner's vibration.

1. In his last novel R. Roberts introduces some amazing situations. (R. Roberts.)
2. The pirates halted dejectedly at the mouth of the cave. (Dejectedly.)
3. You may not have noticed how calm your friend is. (Calm.)
4. Battleships which have become obsolete in design are to be replaced at once. (Obsolete.)
5. Inch by inch the temporary bridge was lowered into position by a handful of quite unskilled engineers. (Handful.)
6. It is a scientist's duty to probe the secrets of nature. (Nature.)

(3) *Combination of Sentences*

Just as it is desirable to attain variety in the sentence, so it is pleasing to give paragraphs more unity by subordinating unimportant thoughts. Relatively unimportant ideas do not require to be set out in clauses ; often participial phrases or even one word will be sufficiently expressive.[1]

1. Our first acquaintance with Munich was disappointing. The suburban streets were dark and dingy.
   Approaching Munich, we were disappointed with the dark, dingy streets of its suburbs.
2. The sea was placid. *The Hurrying Angel* sped merrily on. *The Hurrying Angel* sped merrily on over a placid sea.
3. You made no attempt to catch the train. The reason is obvious.
   Obviously you made no attempt to catch the train.

Sentences may be effectively linked together :—

1. by using CONJUNCTIONS. You should be sparing in the use of *and*. You should take care to observe unity : do not link incongruous ideas.

   My uncle is a retired sea-captain and she is going to gather primroses.

A common mistake is to use *but* where no notion of excepting is intended.

   I was lucky to be able to read morse, but I had learnt it in the Scouts. (*But* is wrong here. Improve this sentence.)

2. by using the RELATIVE PRONOUNS *which, what, that, who, whom, whose.* Here you will subordinate one or more clauses to a main clause and introduce them by one or other of the above relative pronouns.

   My uncle is a retired sea-captain for whom a little girl often gathers primroses.

[1] This is especially desirable when you are writing a description of some process or narrating the progress of a continuous action, or working out the development of an argument.

3. by using ADVERB CLAUSES.

This is a most effective form of linking. The commonest adverbial conjunctions are *after, although, as, because, consequently, for, if, nor, since, so that, unless, until, while.*

Be careful with *while*. It is not merely a convenient substitute for *and* ; it contains the notion of time. Do not write :

✱   The Dean read the lessons *while* the Bishop preached the sermon.

4. by REPLACING CLAUSES BY PHRASES.
   The bank shut its doors. It refused payment. There were bitter protests from the crowd outside.
   The bank, *having refused payment*, shut its doors *in spite of bitter protests from the crowd outside.*

5. by using PARTICIPLES. As you have seen in the previous example, *having refused payment* is made dependent on the main clause, *The bank shut its doors.*

This construction is so common that there is a danger of resorting to it too frequently. Improve the following passage by introducing more variety in linking the sentences :

Catching an early train at Waterloo, John and I soon arrived at Southampton. Missing our friends, we decided not to wait for them, so that, embarking on the tender, we were quickly interested in the numerous ships plying to and fro.

Leaving the quay, the tender, after an hour's journey, brought us alongside the huge liner *Europa*. On approaching, we heard the ship's band strike up a merry tune, filling us with high spirits. Looking up many feet above us, I could just discern the band conductor's white cap.

Having boarded this famous ship, we were soon part of a long queue waiting to be allotted our cabins and our places at table. These formalities having been satisfactorily completed, we took the lift to the promenade deck, the ship in the meantime, having weighed anchor, was swiftly passing the floating forts just off Portsmouth.

6. by giving attention to PUNCTUATION. This is so important a topic that it must be treated more fully later. Effective use of the semicolon is strangely absent from essays written by candidates even at the School Certificate stage.

Study the following passages :—

(a) Having got thus far, Mr Stiggins looked about him again, and sighed grievously ; with that, he walked softly into the bar, and presently returning with a tumbler half full of pineapple-rum, advanced to the kettle which was singing gaily on the hob, mixed his grog, stirred it, sipped it, sat down, and taking a long and hearty pull at the rum and water, stopped for breath.

Here you see the comma effectively used to link up a series of actions. What is the effect of the comma after *again* ?

(b) When Milton first rose, he heard a chapter in the Hebrew Bible, and then studied till twelve ; then took some exercise for an hour ; then dined ; then played on the organ, and sang, or heard another sing ; then studied to six ; then entertained his visitors till eight ; then supped ; then, after a pipe of tobacco and a glass of water, went to bed.

Rewrite the above passage, avoiding the too frequent use of *then*.

Combine the sentences given at the beginning of this chapter and, in the light of what you have since read, avoid all trace of monotony.

Further Practice in Joining Sentences

1. Combine the following sentences in *three* ways as different from each other as possible :—

Tom had now left the office. He had never been happy there.

2. Combine the following simple sentences into one complex sentence, without altering the sense :—

I left the crowded drawing-room. I went into the beautiful old garden. The garden was fragrant with the scent of roses. The roses scattered their petals on the lawn. The lawn was dewy. The garden was musical with the voice of blackbirds. The blackbirds called to one another.

University of London, Matriculation.
(This is the first part of a question.)

3. Combine the following sentences in three different ways. When you have finished, say which you consider your most effective effort, and try to say why this should be so.

Savonarola was nervous. He had a highly strung constitution. His constitution was weakened. Asceticism had weakened it. He was anxious. He shrank from physical pain. He never abandoned his duty. He had always been haunted. Fear of personal violence haunted him. Under torture he had confessed his errors. He now retracted these confessions.

Here is an essay written by a boy of fourteen. Criticize it (*a*) from the standpoint of unity of paragraph structure, and (*b*) from the way in which the sentences are joined together.

Rewrite it, or correct it orally, drawing attention to any necessary changes in punctuation.

An Adventure

Sidney decided to run away to sea. As Sidney walked down the cliff road the wind sang in his ears so loudly as almost to deafen him, and he was continually suspicious that someone would clap a heavy hand on his shoulder, and stop him going. During his journey to the harbour he looked round nervously twenty times at least.

He went down the steps to the pier and he could not see anybody. He walked along the pier and on turning the corner he thought he saw a man waiting for him but it was only a capstan. The spray flew up and fell upon him and a biting wind was blowing.

He caught sight of a boat called the *Princess* ; clambering quickly aboard he hid himself as comfortably as he could.

When he awoke in the morning the ship was moving and he felt frightened. Suddenly he felt a bump and water poured into the hold. When he got on deck the boats had already deserted the ship as they did not know anybody else was on board. One of the boats saw him and got him off just as the ship sank. When he got back to land he vowed he would never go back to sea again.

Reproduction

Read the passage first. Close the book and write out the anecdote or incident in your own words. Do not go beyond the limit of a single paragraph. When you have finished, compare your version with the one in the book. Does your account contain any ugly or ineffective joinings? Does it proceed smoothly so as to retain a listener's interest? Many people spoil a good story by telling it badly. Stephen Leacock gives amusing illustrations of this in his book on *Humour*.

When you have finished, give each passage as attractive a title as possible.

1. A famous lawyer, who prided himself on the effective use of irony, was once prosecuting a burglar caught red-handed on the roof of a house. In his final address to the jury this learned counsel remarked, ' If you consider, gentlemen of the jury, that the accused was on the roof of the house for the purpose of enjoying the midnight breeze, and, by pure accident, happened to have about him the necessary tools of a housebreaker, with no dishonest intention of employing them, you will, of course, acquit him.' The simple sons of Wessex who formed the jury nodded complacently at counsel and, accepting his invitation, acquitted the prisoner.

2. Some years ago the Curator of a famous museum noticed two old ladies who regularly sat for some considerable time in front of a mummy. On being spoken to, they said that their interest was not in Egyptology, but that when they wanted to make a momentous decision they always asked the mummy, and, if the answer was favourable, it would nod its head. After they had gone, the Curator, much amused, examined the

mummy. He found that the bone at the nape of
the mummy's neck, although resting on a support,
was just swinging clear of the bottom of the casket.
Further inspection showed that in front of the case
there was a loose floorboard, and that pressure upon
it slightly shook the case and caused the mummy's
head to move up and down. It is said that, to this
day, the old ladies abide steadfastly by the mummy's
decisions, for the Curator had not the heart to dis-
illusion them.

3. Two brothers, the elder of whom suffered from asthma,
called late at night at an inn in the country. No
bedroom accommodation being available, they were
given a bed in the drawing-room. During the night,
the elder brother woke up gasping. He implored his
brother to open the window. The younger, by groping round, discovered the window but was unable to
locate any catch so as to open it. At last, in despera-
tion, he broke a pane. The sufferer soon began to
feel better. While it was still dark, however, he had
another attack. There still seemed to be no way of
opening the window, so that, to save his brother's life,
the younger smashed all the remaining panes. This
effected the desired remedy ; both brothers slept well
on into the morning. As soon as they awoke they
observed the window still shut tight ; in the corner of
the room stood a china cabinet with its glass hopelessly
shattered and strewn about the floor.

(4) *Paragraphs*

In which of these stories did you feel prompted to use
more than one paragraph ? How would this improve the
telling of the story ? Does the use of paragraphs merely
divide a passage into more easily digestible parts ?

Paragraphs show how a theme is being developed.
Various parts have to be amplified and illustrated. To-
day, when there is a great call for concise and well-ordered
expression, paragraphs tend to become shorter and more
manageable. In the Earl of Clarendon's *History of the
Great Rebellion*, written between 1670 and 1674, are two

sentences, each of which contains about 400 words. In Smollett's *Roderick Random*, first published in 1748, you will find numerous instances of paragraphs filling two pages, and one where a paragraph extends for nearly eight pages.[1]

Length, however, is no criterion in measuring the effectiveness of a paragraph. A writer, carried away by his subject, will launch out into copious illustrations ; he will wish to reveal many aspects of his theme ; he will see that each of these little points has its bearing on the logical unity of his paragraph. Unity, therefore, is what you are to look for in your reading and to strive for in your writing.

Notice how Mr J. B. Priestley handles the topic of coldness. Rose Salter, a young girl from Yorkshire, takes a post as parlourmaid at a large house in Cumberland Square, near Hyde Park.

What she chiefly remembered afterwards of those first few days in Cumberland Square was that she felt cold all the time. During her first interview with Lady Holt-Ibstock, in that wooden cubby-hole, she had felt cold, and Lady Holt-Ibstock had looked cold. Once inside the Holt-Ibstock house, she felt colder still. Rose and her family had always lived in small rooms, and those rooms, if they were downstairs, had good big fires in them from September to the end of May. The Salters believed in being snug. They did not mind being over-warm, and sometimes they and their guests fairly sweated in the glare of the roaring coals ; but they always took every possible precaution against the cold, from filling the coal cellar to buying plenty of thick woollen blankets. Now, for the first time, Rose had stepped out of this hearty snug tradition. She was so far removed from any familiar cosiness that she might almost be living at the bottom of the sea. Although it was hardly winter yet, these were bitterly raw days. But the square outside was no colder than the house, and possibly a bit warmer in the early afternoon. The house had been recently redecorated and partly refurnished ; its predominating shades were cream and pale blue ; and there was a good deal of unpainted wood about ; and very few carpets.

[1] See pp. 260-267 in the Everyman's Library edition.

Nearly everything she saw there gave Rose the shivers. There was a little white statue of a naked girl on the first landing that made Rose ache. It was better, of course, down in the basement, where the servants had a little sitting-room —sometimes referred to as the ' servants' hall '—opposite the kitchen. The kitchen itself, with its big stove, was warm enough, but Rose did not often find her way in there, because her work was upstairs in the dining-room or the butler's pantry, and also because the cook, Mrs Penner, did not like people to go uninvited into her kitchen. As for Rose's bedroom on the top floor, a room she shared with the second housemaid, Eva, it was a little ice-house, and the bedclothes failed miserably to keep out the cold. Eva said that she and the last parlourmaid (who had left to get married and warm again) used to cram themselves into one bed, just for warmth ; but Rose, who did not much like the look of Eva, a messy sort of girl, was having none, and preferred to shiver alone. Downstairs, there were plenty of fires, but somehow they never seemed big and fierce enough even to take the chill off the large rooms. And all the stairs and landings, which had some secret but direct connection with the arctic regions, were permanently glacial.

J. B. PRIESTLEY : *They Walk in the City*.

This is a good illustration of how interest can not only be sustained but heightened in a long paragraph, provided that there is unity. There is also development, for, although the story may appear to halt, the coldness of the house emerges and becomes so penetrating that we are learning a good deal about the people who live in it.

Exercise

1. The owners of the large house about which you have just read are frigid and aloof. Write two paragraphs, the first, descriptive of Lady Holt-Ibstock, and the second, of her husband, Sir Edwin. When you have finished, criticize your work from the aspect of its having unity.

2. Write paragraphs describing and developing one or more of the following :—

    (i) *Quietness :* (*a*) in the woods ; (*b*) in a large town on Sunday.

(ii) *Heat :* (*a*) a hot day (read Leigh Hunt's essay [1]) ; (*b*) on a ship passing through the Red Sea (read Chapter Thirteen of H. M. Tomlinson's *Gallion's Reach*).

(iii) *Enthusiasm :* (*a*) the wind on a boisterous day ; (*b*) a closely contested House-match at your school.

(iv) *Gloom :* (*a*) a dingy railway station ; (*b*) a sea-fog creeping over the moors.

(v) *Gaiety :* (*a*) a party of schoolgirls on reaching England after three weeks' holiday abroad ; (*b*) a droll comedian.

(vi) *Dust :* (*a*) the lumber-room ; (*b*) an untidy show-room.

(vii) *Colour :* (*a*) the garden at the vicarage ; (*b*) the interior of a new cinema. Do not spoil the effect by introducing every colour. Show, if you can, why Nature's profusion of colour is never garish.

If you have read Priestley's *Angel Pavement*, you will recall his description of the sumptuousness of a ' super-cinema.'

3. Write a suitable consecutive paragraph to the one you have just written. Do not make it of the same length. Consider the last sentence in your first paragraph ; see if it lends itself to a further development of the main theme. If not, then you can easily present some entirely new aspect, either by introducing a character [in vii (*a*) the vicar himself can appear], or by leading to an anticlimax [in iii (*a*) the storm can blow itself out], or up to a climax, or by stating some point of view opposed to your own [in vi (*b*) the futility of having a fetish for tidiness].

(5) *Connexion*

Notice how these two passages go straight to the point. The sentences are not overloaded but lead the thought on logically and attractively. You will not find ' odds and ends,' ghost words, or clumsy circumlocutions. There is a crispness and a simplicity about these two paragraphs, although the subject-matter may seem complex.

The Englishman is no missionary, no conqueror. He prefers the country to the town, and home to foreign parts. He is rather glad and relieved if only natives will remain natives and strangers strangers, and at a comfortable dis-

[1] See p. 266 of W. Peacock's *Selected English Essays*.

tance from himself. Yet outwardly he is most hospitable and accepts almost anybody for the time being ; he travels and conquers without a settled design, because he has the instinct of exploration. His adventures are all external ; they change him so little that he is not afraid of them. He carries his English weather in his heart wherever he goes, and it becomes a cool spot in the desert, and a steady and sane oracle amongst all the deliriums of mankind. Never since the heroic days of Greece has the world had such a sweet, just, boyish master. It will be a bad day for the human race when scientific blackguards, conspirators, churls, and fanatics manage to supplant him.

GEORGE SANTAYANA : Soliloquies in England.

What is a Fair Day's Wages ? It is a favourite saying that a man should have a fair day's wages for a fair day's work ; but this is a fallacious saying.   Nothing, at first sight, can seem more reasonable and just ; but when you examine its meaning, you soon find that there is no meaning at all. It amounts merely to saying that a man ought to have what he ought to have.   There is no way of deciding what is a fair day's wages.   Some workmen receive only a shilling a day ; others two, three, four, or five shillings ; a few receive as much as ten, or even twenty shillings a day ; which of these rates is fair ?   If the saying means that all should receive the *same* fair wages, then all the different characters and powers of men would first have to be made the same, and exactly equalized.   We have seen that wages vary according to the laws of supply and demand, and as long as workmen differ in skill, and strength, and the kind of goods they can produce, there must be differences of demand for their products.   Accordingly, there is no more a fair rate of wages than there is a fair price of cotton or iron.   It is all a matter of bargain ; he who has corn or cotton or iron or any other goods in his possession, does quite right in selling it for the best price he can get, provided he does not prevent other people from selling their goods as they think best.   So, any workman does quite right in selling his labour for the highest rate of wages he can get, provided that he does not interfere with the similar right of other workmen to sell their labour as they like.   W. S. JEVONS : *Political Economy.*

CHAPTER IV

DIRECT AND INDIRECT SPEECH

THIS is a chapter introductory to Précis-writing. When you read a newspaper you at once notice that full reports are rarely given, that there is considerable compression of a speaker's remarks, and that minor points raised in a debate or a discussion are barely mentioned, *e.g.*, *Mr Thorpe then alluded to the development of Little Pudlington*, or *Mr Thomas expressed disagreement with the last speaker's views*.

A. W. Kinglake uses this kind of compression in an amusingly effective way to point the contrast between oriental effusiveness and English bluntness :

> PASHA. The ships of the English swarm like flies ; their printed calicoes cover the whole earth, and by the side of their swords the blades of Damascus are blades of grass. All India is but an item in the ledger-books of the merchants whose lumber-rooms are filled with ancient thrones !— whirr ! whirr ! all by wheels !—whiz ! whiz ! all by steam !
>
> DRAGOMAN. The Pasha compliments the cutlery of England, and also the East India Company.

On the other hand, it is often important to have on record a full report of the speaker's words, such as during the hearing of a case in court. Nothing must be omitted : the rendering of the words spoken must be exact. You must aim at this exactness of reproduction when you are told to turn a passage into Indirect or Reported Speech. Keep closely to the original words, unless, as in a Précis, you are instructed to give a more concise rendering.

Compare the following :—

1. Professor Helzenforz said, ' I always seem gayer when I am abroad than when I am in my own country.'
2. Professor Helzenforz here interposed the remark that he always seemed gayer when he was abroad than when he was in his own country.

Which words were changed ? What parts of speech were they ? Why were there no inverted commas in the second passage ?

Notice the further changes made in the following :—

MRS MICAWBER. ' I am convinced, myself, and this I have pointed out to Mr Micawber several times to-day, that things cannot be expected to turn up of themselves. We must, in a measure, assist to turn them up. I may be wrong, since I formed this opinion only yesterday.'

DAVID COPPERFIELD. ' Hear, hear ! '

MRS MICAWBER. ' Very well. Then what do I recommend ? Here is Mr Micawber with a variety of qualifications—with great talent—— '

MR MICAWBER. ' Really, my love ! '

MRS MICAWBER. ' Pray, my dear, allow me to conclude. It appears to me that, from to-morrow, what Mr Micawber has to do is to throw down the gauntlet to society.'

Adapted from Dickens's *David Copperfield.*

Mrs Micawber declared that she herself *was* convinced and that she *had* pointed *that* out to Mr Micawber several times *that very day* that things *could* not be expected to turn up of themselves. *They* must, in a measure, assist to turn them up. She *might* be wrong, since she *had* formed *that* opinion only *the previous day.*

Here David Copperfield *showed his cordial approval,* whereupon Mrs Micawber *expressed satisfaction* and continued by asking what then *did she* recommend ? *There was* Mr Micawber with a variety of qualifications—with great talent——

At this point she was interrupted by a mild but affectionate remonstrance from her husband. She prayed him, her dear husband, to allow *her* to conclude. It *appeared* to *her* that, from the *next day* onwards, what Mr Micawber *had* to do *was* to throw down the gauntlet to society.

Direct Speech puts the characters before you much more vividly. Mannerisms of speech tend to become lost when Reported Speech is used.

The principal alterations necessary in changing Direct Narration into Indirect Narration are :—

Verbs

shall, will into	should, would [1]	can	into could
may ,,	might	is	,, was
has, have ,,	had	are	,, were
have been ,,	had been	was, were ,,	had been

Pronouns

I, me   become he or she, him or her.
We, us   ,,   they or them.
You becomes he, she, him, her, they, or them.

Notice that since all pronouns thus become Third Person there is some danger of ambiguity. When this occurs you can either repeat the nouns which refer to those persons or things, or use expressions like *the former, the latter*.

Adjectives and **Adverbs** referring to things or to times close at hand are changed into corresponding Adjectives and Adverbs expressing remoteness. You should change

this into	that	now	into then
these ,,	those	today	,, that day
here ,,	there	to-morrow	,, the next day or the
hither ,,	thither		following day
hence ,,	thence	yesterday	,, the previous day, or
			the day before

The following hints should be found helpful. Study how they were put into practice in the example worked above.

(*a*) Be conservative in changing words. (You gain nothing by changing *assist* into *help*, or *allow* into

---

[1] Exercise care in changing these words. *Shall* does not automatically change into *should*. See p. 206.

permit. You have quite sufficient to do to make the necessary changes without volunteering unnecessary ones.)

(*b*) Avoid ambiguity.   (He asked him to pass his testimonials.   Reintroduce the relevant nouns, *e.g.*, *The manager* asked *the applicant* to pass his testimonials.)

(*c*) Be careful in coping with commands, interruptions, and hesitations.   Try to interpret their significance.

(*d*) You will also have to be careful in handling asides and exclamations.   Notice how this was done in the example given.

(*e*) There is no need to change infinitives.   (John remarked, ' I do not wish to go to Brighton.' John remarked that he did not wish to go to Brighton.)

Exercises

Convert the following passages from Direct to Indirect Speech :—

1. I am truly sensible how unequal I have been to the expression of my own ideas.   To develop the latent excellences, and draw out the interior principles of our art, requires more skill and practice in writing, than is likely to be possessed of by a man perpetually occupied in the use of the pencil and the palette. It is for that reason, perhaps, that the sister art has had the advantage of better criticism.   Poets are naturally writers of prose.   They may be said to be practising only an inferior department of their own art, when they are explaining and expatiating upon its most refined principles.   But still such difficulties ought not to deter artists who are not prevented by other engagements from putting their thoughts in order as well as they can, and from giving to the public the result of their experience.

Sir Joshua Reynolds : *Fifteen Discourses on Art.*

2. *Scene* : A meeting in the Parish Hall of Lesser Muddle-
ton. Some parents have met to protest against their
children being obliged to attend a new school three
miles from their homes.

SPOKESMAN. Unless the Education Committee can provide
travelling facilities for our children it will be impossible
for them to make these long journeys to and fro.

CHAIRMAN OF THE EDUCATION COMMITTEE. Your notion is
preposterous.   When I was a little fellow all the boys of our
village would walk five miles to school in the morning.   You
cannot say that it did us any harm.   Look at me, eighty-six
years of age, and still strong as a lion.

VOICE FROM THE BACK. Where are the others ?

3. I am a poor ignorant fellow, bred to a mean trade, yet I
have sense enough to know that all pretences of foretelling by astrology are deceits, for this manifest reason ;
because the wise and the learned, who can only judge
whether there be any truth in this science, do all
unanimously agree to laugh at and despise it ; and
none but the poor ignorant vulgar give it any credit,
and that only upon the word of such silly wretches as I
and my fellows who can hardly write or read. . . . As
to foretelling the weather, we never meddle with that,
but leave it to the printer who takes it out of any
old almanac as he thinks fit ; the rest was my own
invention, to make my almanac sell, having a wife
to maintain and no other way to get my bread ; for
mending old shoes is a poor livelihood.
      JONATHAN SWIFT : *The Bickerstaff Papers.*

Be careful with the pronouns in the above passage.

4. ' It is not the first time that you have thought proper to
make very offensive remarks, Mr Biggs ; and as you
appear to consider yourself ill-treated in the affair
of the trousers—for I tell you once that it was I who
brought them on board—I can only say,' continued
our hero, with a very polite bow, ' that I shall be most
happy to give you satisfaction.'
      ' I am your superior officer, Mr Easy,' replied the
boatswain.

'Yes, by the rules of the service; but you just now asserted that you would waive your rank—indeed, I dispute it on this occasion; I am on the quarter-deck, and you are not.'

CAPTAIN MARRYAT: *Mr Midshipman Easy.*

Be careful to avoid ambiguity in the above passage.

5. Read the following passage carefully and then give the actual words the Chairman used in his speech :—

In opening the new promenade at Purlington-on-Sea yesterday, Sir Richard L—— said that anyone who had visited that popular resort ten years ago would see that it had grown to something almost beyond belief. Those engineers who had done the work had helped Nature to an extent that was scarcely imaginable. They had conserved a beauty spot from the sea's incessant encroachments, created a noble promenade, and redeemed what was once a gloomy waste. Purlington was showing an example of the way in which to cater for the health of the community. Both health and amusement were to be thought of.

Why was it that the Englishman seemed gayer abroad than at home? Is it because foreign countries did more to cater for his amusement? Sir Richard thought that legislation in this country cramped them in providing amusements that were to be enjoyed only abroad. Of all English resorts he had ever visited, Purlington appeared to him to come nearest to the Continental ideal. He had much pleasure in declaring the new promenade open and hoped from that day forth that town would maintain its position at the head of health resorts and that they, the members of the Council then listening to him, would ever fulfil their claim of providing a holiday that was different from any previously enjoyed.

6. Write the following note so as to avoid the third person as much as possible :—

'THE PLANTAINS,'
FAIRLAWN DRIVE,
ENDALE,
8th June, 19~~

Is Mr Braddon aware of the inconvenience caused Mr Ashley by Mr Braddon's having had that unsightly shed erected immediately against his garden fence? Why did not Mr Braddon ask Mr Ashley's permission before taking it upon himself to nail part of the superstructure to Mr Ashley's fence ?

Does Mr Braddon realize that he has no right to erect anything within three feet of Mr Ashley's fence and that he is therefore to remove the offending eyesore to the new position indicated within seven days, failing which Mr Ashley will seek legal advice.

If, however, it is not Mr Braddon's wish to cause a breach in the friendship which has hitherto existed between himself and Mr Ashley, the latter suggests that they should meet for a discussion at a time convenient for Mr Braddon. To ensure that the meeting shall be in a friendly spirit, Mr Ashley asks Mr Braddon's permission to withdraw the words *unsightly* and *eyesore*. He regretfully insists on regarding the shed as *very* bizarre.

R. ASHLEY.

(*a*) What kind of person do you imagine Mr Ashley to be ?
(*b*) Write a reply, in the third person, to the above note.
(*c*) Rewrite this reply in the first person. Do not forget to be tactful.

7. Rewrite the following passage from Charles Dickens's *Oliver Twist* as it would appear if played on the stage.

' Silence there ! ' cried the jailer.

' What is this ? ' inquired one of the magistrates.

' A pick-pocketing case, your worship.'

' Has the boy ever been here before ? '

' He ought to have been, a many times,' replied the jailer. ' He has been pretty well everywhere else. *I* know him well, your worship.'

' Oh ! you know me, do you ? ' cried the Artful, making a note of the statement. ' Wery good. That's a case of deformation of character, anyway.'

Here there was another laugh, and another cry of silence.

' Now then, where are the witnesses ? ' said the clerk.

' Ah ! that's right,' added the Dodger. ' Where are they ? I should like to see 'em.'

The wish was immediately gratified, for a policeman stepped forward who had seen the prisoner attempt the pocket of an unknown gentleman in a crowd, and indeed take a handkerchief therefrom, which, being a very old one, he deliberately put back again, after trying it on his own countenance. For this reason, he took the Dodger into custody as soon as he could get near him, and the said Dodger, being searched, had upon his person a silver snuff-box, with the owner's name engraved upon the lid. This gentleman had been discovered on reference to the Court Guide, and being then and there present, swore that the snuff-box was his, and that he had missed it on the previous day, the moment he had disengaged himself from the crowd before referred to. He had also remarked a young gentleman in the throng, particularly active in making his way about, and that young gentleman was the prisoner before him.

' Have you anything to ask this witness, boy ? ' said the magistrate.

' I wouldn't abase myself by descending to hold no conversation with him,' replied the Dodger.

' Have you anything to say at all ? . . ."

' No,' replied the Dodger, ' not here, for this ain't the shop for justice, besides which, my attorney is a-breakfasting this morning with the Wice-President of the House of Commons ; but I shall have something to say elsewhere, and so will he, and so will a wery numerous and 'spectable circle of acquaintance as'll make them beaks wish they'd never been born, or that they'd got their footmen to hang 'em up to their own hat-pegs, afore they let 'em come out this morning to try it on upon me, I'll—— '

' There ! He's fully committed ! ' interposed the clerk. ' Take him away.'

' Come on,' said the jailer.

(a) Which words in the above passage does the Dodger wrongly use ? He almost gets them right.

(b) Put the Dodger's last speech into Reported Speech, using correct English.

REVISION PAPER 1

1. Give a verb (or verbs) corresponding to each of the following :—

accent (2), climate, grand, guile, calumny, captive, cheap, solid (2), noble, sign.

2. Form nouns corresponding to :—

abet, abhor (2), absent (2), appeal (2), pay (3), brag, brief (2), gird (2), celebrate (3), civil (2), command (2), commend, compile, complain (2), conform, consult (2), grieve (2), portray (2), tragic, prosper, scan, pervert, pleasant (2).

3. Give abstract nouns corresponding to the following :—

abnormal, acclaim, acquire (2), acquit, adhere, admit (2), allege, apprentice, augur, bankrupt, baron, bigot, bless (2), break, bribe, broad, buffoon, candidate, casual, champion, coin, grand, diplomat, supreme, unequal, warm, preach, knight, tidy, rail (the *verb* rail).

4. Form adjectives corresponding to :—

abdomen, abuse, academy, awe (2), axiom, bone, bother, brass (2), cabal, cat, chaos, character, choler, choir, churl, circuit, circumstance, clan, exception (2), prose, sympathy, metal, elegy, homily, obtrude, whim, caprice, fallacy.

5. Form adjectives from the following names :—

Aristotle, Bacon, Bodley, Cromwell, Brobdingnag, Byron, Charles, Descartes, Charterhouse, Chaucer, Cicero, Ceylon, Circe, Draco, George, Homer, James, Manchester, Quixote, Rabelais, Saturn, Shakespeare, Tantalus, Venice, Wagner, York.

Place after each adjective a noun with which the adjective may be appropriately used.

6. Show the meaning of the prefix in :—

anticlimax, asymmetrical, antenatal, awash, attribute, byword, catastrophe, circumscribe, cohesion, connexion, elude, beguile, autograph, aversion, descend, insecure, imminent, imposition, ignoble, misconstrue, monologue, obtrude, perception, periscope, polytechnic, retrospect, sinecure, subterfuge, trimeter, telepathy, twilight, un-equal, ultramarine.

7. What is the effect of the suffix in each of the following words ? Give other examples of the use of each suffix.

bargee, brewster, bassoon, circlet, bannock, cellule, witling (a word used by Pope), briquette, canticle, babble, existence, assessor, accompanist, visible, cheapen, bovine, cadaverous, schism, brackish, bucolic, fortitude.

8. Write sentences to illustrate the difference in meaning of the words in the following groups :—

tyrant, despot, autocrat, aristocrat, dictator ; adept, adapt, adopt, addict ; comrade, companion, compatriot, accomplice ; abeyance, obedience, obeisance ; misogamist, misogynist, misanthrope ; comparative, comparable, compatible ; adventurous, venturesome, adventitious.

9. Construct sentences to illustrate the *idiomatic* use of the following words when used with the prepositions indicated :—

(a) *to break* away, down, forth, in, off, out, through, up.
(b) *to bring* about, down, forth, forward, in, off, on, out, over, round, through, under, up.
(c) *to buy* in, off, out, over, up.
(d) *to call* for, on, down, forth, in, off, out, over, up.
(e) *to carry* away, forward, off, on, out, over, through, up.
(f) *to cast* aside, away, about, back, down, forth, in, off, out, up.
(g) *to close* down, on, upon, round, with, up.
(h) *to come* about, across, by, into, to, under, upon, in, in for, off, on, out, out of, out with, up.

10. By using the *Shorter Oxford English Dictionary* or a similar large work of reference look up the idiomatic use of prepositions with the following verbs : look, put, prevail, intercede, originate, qualify, rail, rule, triumph, work, write.

11. Compose sentences using the following words as different parts of speech :—appropriate, articulate, base, blind, brave, brood, brook, cashier, coach, compact, force, grace, hinder, lumber, material, pall, school, score, stave, telescope, vice, wing.

12. Comment on the movement of the following passage. By linking up a number of the sentences, see how far you have been able to speed up the passage or to make its movement more smooth.

You take wheat to cast into the Earth's bosom : your wheat may be mixed with chaff, chopped straw, barn-sweepings, dust and all imaginable rubbish ; no matter : you cast it into the kind just Earth ; she grows the wheat—the whole rubbish she silently absorbs, shrouds *it* in, says nothing of the rubbish. The yellow wheat is growing there ; the good Earth is silent about all the rest—has silently turned all the rest to some benefit too, and makes no complaint about it ! So everywhere in Nature. She is true and not a lie ; and yet so great, and just, and motherly, in her truth. She requires of a thing only that it *be* genuine of heart ; she will protect it if so ; will not, if not so. There is a soul of truth in all the things she ever gave harbour to. Alas, is not this the history of all highest Truth that comes or ever came into the world ? CARLYLE : *The Hero as Prophet.*

13. Rewrite the following passage as Reported Speech, giving careful attention to wording and punctuation :—

SIR OLIVER SURFACE (*who is visiting his nephew, Charles, but gives himself out to be Mr Premium, a broker*).

. . . But there is one portrait which you have always passed over.

CARELESS. What, that ill-looking fellow over the settee ?

SIR OLIVER. Yes, sir, I mean that ; though I don't think him so ill-looking a fellow, by any means.

CHARLES SURFACE. What, that ? Oh ; that's my uncle Oliver ! 'Twas done before he went to India.

CARE. Your uncle Oliver ! Then you'll never be friends, Charles. That, now, to me, is as stern a looking rogue as ever I saw ; and unforgiving eye, and a disinheriting countenance ! An inveterate knave, depend on't. Don't you think so, little Premium ?

SIR OLIV. Upon my soul, sir, I do not ; I think it is as honest a looking face as any in the room, dead or alive. But I suppose uncle Oliver goes with the rest of the lumber ?

CHAS. SURF. No, hang it ! I'll not part with poor Noll. The old fellow has been very good to me, and I'll keep his picture while I've a room to put it in.

RICHARD BRINSLEY SHERIDAN :
The School for Scandal.

CHAPTER V

PRÉCIS-WRITING

A PRÉCIS is the clear presentation, in one's own words, of the salient points of a passage. It is usually stipulated that a précis shall be written in the third person and in the past tense. More important than this, however, is the style in which you write.

A précis leaves no scope for adornments such as similes and metaphors nor is it a mere stringing together of phrases lifted bodily from the original. If there is no cohesion there will be *vagueness*, a common yet unpardonable fault.

Example

Make a précis (about one-third of the present length) of the following passage :—

When a visitor came to London in the middle of Queen Victoria's reign, he noticed that there were Bibles chained up on lecterns in the waiting-rooms of all our railway stations. The English Sunday, that strange plantation of the sunny Oriental Sabbath in our cloudy northern clime, served a valuable end. It gave a breathing space, a rallying ground for the English energies before resuming their terrific task of harnessing the forces of the world to the chariot of their wealth. ' That day is not lost,' wrote Macaulay. ' While industry is suspended, while the plough lies in the furrow, while the Exchange is silent, while no smoke ascends from the factory, a process is going on quite as important to the wealth of nations as any process which is performed on more busy days. Man, the machine of machines, the machine compared with which all the contrivances of the Watts and the Arkwrights are worthless, is repairing and winding up, so that he returns to his labours on the Monday with clearer intellect, with livelier spirits, with renewed corporal vigour.' And lest any dangerous earthly pleasure or indulgence should distract our fathers during this necessary day of idleness, almost all activity was forbidden. ' The shops are shut, the streets almost deserted ; the aspect is that of an immense and well-ordered cemetery. The few passers-by under their umbrellas, in the desert of squares and streets, have the look of uneasy spirits who have risen from their graves ; it is appalling.'

Slightly adapted from ARTHUR BRYANT'S
The National Character.

A STUDENT'S ATTEMPT

The Purpose of the Victorian Sabbath

During Queen Victoria's reign a visitor to London would have noticed Bibles chained up in railway waiting-rooms. This idea was invaluable as it afforded a respite for English energies in their terrific task of harnessing Nature's forces to the chariot of their wealth. When machinery was stopped no time was more adaptable than Sunday. To ensure that he should work well the Englishman had to have time in which to build up that necessary strength of mind and body. So strong was this belief that all dangerous earthly activity was forbidden. On Sunday one saw only people who were obliged to look like uneasy spirits.

NOTES

1. There is little coherence. You have only a series of isolated statements.

2. Too much haste has resulted in an imperfect understanding of the passage. *No time was more adaptable* contradicts the central thought of the original. *All dangerous earthly activity* is a misinterpretation : the word *dangerous* was used ironically, and in a moral, not a literal sense.

3. A weak dependence on the original words is another result of imperfect comprehension. *Harnessing Nature's forces to the chariot of their wealth* is not a natural way for a student to express himself : no attempt has been made to interpret the thought in more concise terms.

4. A good attempt is made to supply a title, but although the one given does express the central thought of the passage, there is no indication whether the extract came from a speech, a book, or a letter.

PRÉCIS OF A PASSAGE FROM ARTHUR BRYANT'S ' THE NATIONAL CHARACTER,' DESCRIBING THE VALUE OF THE VICTORIAN SUNDAY.

In the middle of Queen Victoria's reign a visitor to London noticed Bibles chained to lecterns in railway waiting-rooms.

Sunday observance was stricter in those days. A halt was called in the task of turning Nature's forces to monetary advantage. Man became mentally revitalized and physically restored so that he returned to work with renewed energy and a clearer intellect. Accordingly Sunday became a day when almost all activity was forbidden. Then one saw only sombre, deserted streets with a few guilty-looking stragglers.

1. Usually a précis is written in a single paragraph. Here, since there is no close connexion between the first sentence and the rest of the passage, they have been separated.

2. The passage has been digested and understood before being set out in the student's own words except where it was impossible to effect an improvement. *Desks* is a poor substitute for *lecterns* : *almost all activity was forbidden* cannot be expressed more simply.

Revision—Practice in Concise Expression

Express the thoughts in the following passages more concisely and in your own words :—

1. I am not, however, totally destitute of such pleasures as an inland country may pretend to.

COWPER : *Letters.*

2. The advantages that my little charges will gain from the converse of my esteemed employers, while engaging in the healthful exercise of perambulation, would be beyond my powers to impart.

ARCHIBALD MARSHALL : *The Birdikin Family.*

3. If we contrast the present habit of going unarmed, with the dire necessity of those days, when his weapons were a man's constant companions, we can see how far the race has travelled the road to peace.

4. The time is not opportune for definite decisions of this nature since such arrangements must be considered as essential factors in a scheme of closer association among the constituent bodies of our large and extremely powerful union. *Criticize the style.*

5.
Aberalva Harbour

Beneath us, to the left hand, is the quay-pool, now lying dry, in which a dozen trawlers are lopping over on their sides, their red sails drying in the sun, the tails of the trawls hauled up to the topmast heads ; while the more handy of their owners were getting on board by ladders to pack away the said red sails ; for it will blow to-night. In the long furrows which their keels have left, and in the shallow muddy pools, lie innumerable fragments of exenterated maids (not human ones, pitiful reader, but belonging to the order Pisces, and the family Raia), and some twenty non-exenterated ray-dogs and picked dogs (Anglice, dogfish), together with a fine basking shark, at least nine feet long, out of which the kneeling Mr George Thomas, clothed in pilot-cloth patches of every hue, bright scarlet, blue, and brown (not to mention a large square of white canvas which has been let into that part of his trousers which is now uppermost), is dissecting the liver, for the purpose of greasing his ' sheaves ' with the fragrant oil thereof.

CHARLES KINGSLEY : *Two Years Ago.*

(a) Notice that the style here is diffuse. What is the writer's aim ? Is this diffuseness contributory to the effect he seeks ?

(b) In your summary steer through this mass of detail and concentrate only on those points which serve the writer's chief purpose.

A Few Principles to Notice

It is not true that the longer the passage the more difficult will it be to write a précis. In a fairly long piece of narrative the events are usually in chronological order. The chief care will be to observe proper proportion, that is to say, not to be leisurely expansive over the first few paragraphs and incoherently abrupt in rounding off.

In a descriptive passage, consider the main effect; see that you leave it standing out clearly. Again a sense of proportion will help you.

In a series of letters almost inevitably there will be repetition. Do not begin to write until you are clear about the main points at issue. Keep strictly to chronological order: keep the central theme to the fore: show clearly which person contributes most to the end in view.

A précis of a speech or of an argument is the most difficult. The matter is already concisely expressed. You may feel reluctant to leave anything out; everything seems tightly interwoven and logical. It is usual to prescribe fewer than a hundred words for the précis. Find the main theme: incorporate it in your title. Then select three or four of the chief stages in the development of this theme. Do not leave them as isolated statements, but link them to preserve a sense of continuity.

Whatever form the passage may take, read it through first to find its aim.

Supply a title. See that it really applies to the passage and is not a vague, useless thing.

Underline the main points, using thick strokes for indispensable topics. Roughly apportion the words you have at your disposal.

Write the précis, bearing in mind that it does not matter so much about gathering facts as giving them adequate, proportioned, and coherent expression. Have you understood the passage or are you merely juggling with words?

Finally, read your précis. Have you successfully avoided the four commonest and most grievous errors ?

(*a*) Misrepresentation of the facts of the original.
(*b*) Too close an adherence to the wording of the original.
(*c*) Vagueness instead of conciseness.
(*d*) Exceeding the number of words prescribed.

Always work up to the number of prescribed words. It *is* possible to summarize in forty or fifty words a passage you have been told to put into 150 words. A severely restricted précis serves an altogether different purpose from the one you have in hand. You gain nothing and omit much when you reduce the scope of your work.

Passages for Précis

1. Many years ago there was a poor village schoolmaster in Germany named Johann Maria, who was very badly paid and had a great fight every week to make both ends meet. He was very fond of Gretchen, the beautiful daughter of a wealthy miller in the village, and he believed she returned his affection, but her father had other plans for his daughter and forbade the young man his house.

One evening the door of the poor lover's cottage flew open, and a traveller, booted and spurred, with his long coat covered with mud, entered hastily, and, seating himself without ado by the fire opposite the astonished schoolmaster, demanded : ' Why do you never sign your surname, but only your Christian names ? '

' Because,' answered the schoolmaster, rather angrily, for he was annoyed by the stranger's rude entrance, ' because it pleases me to do so.' He held himself upright and gave the stranger a haughty stare.

' I know the reason well enough,' said this cool visitor with a laugh. ' It is because your father died a bankrupt. You think your name is covered with dishonour. But your father's bankruptcy was caused less by his fault than by his misfortune.'

He spoke so confidently that the schoolmaster was interested. ' What are you driving at ? ' he demanded.

' I come,' said the visitor, ' to offer you the restitution of your father's name, and in addition an income of 300 thalers (about £45) a year. At the end of five years you will obtain possession of the capital sum from which this income is derived.'

The schoolmaster, who felt he was being duped by some dream, asked : ' What do you ask of me in exchange for this money ? '

' Two things : that you marry within a fortnight and that you undertake that each of your boy children shall bear the same Christian names as your own, Johann Maria.'

' Are there any other conditions ? '

' Only this. Every day you must devote about six hours to writing your full signature, Johann Maria Farina, on certain little papers which I shall send you.'

' To what purpose will you put these little papers ? '

' None that you need fear, my dear sir.'

At that moment the silence of the winter night was broken by the sound of a horse galloping and the furious turning of wheels. A post chaise approached the thatched cottage, pulled up with great suddenness, and a man, springing out, rushed up to Johann Maria, exclaiming breathlessly : ' Heaven grant, for your sake and mine, that I have arrived in time. Have you signed anything ? Good. How much does this gentleman offer you ? '

' Three hundred thalers a year,' replied the astonished schoolmaster.

The newcomer laughed and offered three times that sum.

Then followed between these two visitors a fierce duel in bidding, each mounting above the other's last offer with a substantial sum, until the new arrival reached the highest point. He offered to pay then and there a sum of money which would produce an annual income of 3,000 thalers, and moreover to give the schoolmaster an additional 1,000 thalers as a gratuity.

' Now learn,' said the generous stranger, ' that you are the last descendant of Johann Maria Farina. This name, signed by your hand at the foot of the labels placed on the bottles of Eau-de-Cologne invented by the famous chemist who was your great-grandfather, and of whose recipe I am the sole owner—these names, I say, signed in full, in your own handwriting upon my bottles will reduce the opposition manufacturers like yonder gentleman to the position of forgers of trade marks. I shall give them the choice of respecting my monopoly or of being brought before the criminal court. There shall be no mistake in future as to which is the genuine Eau-de-Cologne.'

On the very next day Johann Maria asked the rich miller's consent to his engagement, and this was easily obtained.

> Make a summary, not more than 200 words in length, of the above passage. Write at the end of your summary the number of words you have used.
>
> *Civil Service Commission.*

In writing the above précis remember the hints given you about preserving due proportion. Do not reproduce the opening paragraphs almost verbatim and then hasten over or omit the reason why Johann's signature was in such demand. You will not use quotation marks since you are summarizing the speeches. Be definite : do not say, ' The speaker told a tale about bankruptcy.'

2. Write a connected summary of the following passage in not more than 150 words. Provide a suitable title.

One remark I must not omit, That royal or parliamentary grants of money are by no means the chief thing wanted ! To give our Men of Letters stipends, endowments and all furtherance of cash, will do little towards the business. On the whole, one is weary of hearing about the omnipotence of money. I will say rather that, for a genuine man, it is no evil to be poor ; that there ought to be Literary Men poor, —to show whether they are genuine or not ! Mendicant Orders, bodies of good men doomed to *beg*, were instituted in the Christian Church ; a most natural and even necessary development of the spirit of Christianity. It was itself founded on Poverty, on Sorrow, Contradiction, Crucifixion, every species of worldly Distress and Degradation. We may say that he who has not known those things, and learned from them the priceless lessons they have to teach, has missed a good opportunity of schooling. To beg, and go barefoot, in coarse woollen cloak with a rope round your loins, and be despised of all the world, was no beautiful business ; nor an honourable one in any eye, till the nobleness of those who did so had made it honoured of some ! . . . Who will say that a Johnson is not perhaps the better

3

for being poor ? It is needful for him, at all rates, to know that outward profit, that success of any kind is *not* the goal he has to aim at. Pride, vanity, ill-conditioned egoism of all sorts, are bred in his heart, as in every heart ; need, above all, to be cast out of his heart—to be, with whatever pangs, torn out of it, cast forth from it, as a thing worthless. Byron, born rich and noble, made out even less than Burns, poor and plebeian. Who knows but, in that same ' best possible organization ' as yet far off, Poverty may still enter as an important element ? What if our Men of Letters, men setting up to be Spiritual Heroes, were still *then*, as they now are, a kind of ' involuntary monastic order ' ; bound still to this same ugly Poverty,—till they had tried what was in it too, till they learned to make it too do for them ! Money, in truth, can do much, but it cannot do all. We must know the province of it, and confine it there ; and even spurn it back, when it wishes to get farther.

THOMAS CARLYLE : *Heroes and Hero Worship.*

(*a*) You should have no difficulty in finding the central theme. This was delivered as part of a lecture : usually in lectures there is some repetition to help the audience to grasp essential points. You will therefore find it advisable to arrange the salient thoughts of this passage so as to show the development of Carlyle's theme.

(*b*) You will attempt none of Carlyle's rhetorical flights nor imitate his habit of over-punctuation.

3. Make a précis of the following letter bringing out those points in which the recipient would most naturally be interested. Do not exceed 150 words :—

For the Honourable William Lenthall, Esquire, Speaker of the Parliament of England : These.

WORCESTER,
4th September 1651.

SIR,

I am not able yet to give you an exact account of the great things the Lord hath wrought for this Commonwealth and for His People : and yet I am unwilling to be silent ; but, according to my duty, shall represent it to you as it comes to hand.

This Battle was fought with various success for some hours, but still hopeful on your part ; and in the end became an absolute victory—and so full an one as proved a total defeat and ruin of the Enemy's Army ; and a possession of the Town, our men entering at the Enemy's heels, and fighting with them in the streets with very great courage. We took all their baggage and artillery. What the slain are, I can give you no account, because we have not taken an exact view ; but they are very many : and must needs be so ; because the dispute was long and very near at hand ; and often at push of pike, and from one defence to another. There are about Six- or Seven-thousand prisoners taken here ; and many Officers and Noblemen of very great quality : Duke Hamilton, the Earl of Rothes, and divers other Noblemen, I hear, the Earl of Lauderdale : many Officers of great quality ; and some that will be fit subjects for your justice.

We have sent very considerable parties after the flying Enemy ; I hear they have taken considerable numbers of prisoners, and are very close in the pursuit. Indeed, I hear the Country riseth upon them everywhere ; and I believe the forces that lay, through Providence at Bewdley, and in Shropshire and Staffordshire, and those with Colonel Lilburn, were in a condition, as if this had been foreseen, to intercept what should return.

A more particular account than this will be prepared for you as we are able. I hear that they had not many more than a thousand horse in their body that fled : and I believe you have near four-thousand forces following, and inter-posing between them and home ;—what fish they will catch, Time will declare. Their Army was about Sixteen-thousand strong ; and fought ours on the Worcester side of the Severn almost with their whole, whilst we had engaged about half our Army on the other side but with parties of theirs. Indeed it was a stiff business ; yet I do not think we have lost Two-hundred men. Your new-raised forces did per-form singular good service ; for which they deserve a very high estimation and acknowledgement ; as also for their willingness thereunto,—forasmuch as the same hath added so much to the reputation of your affairs. They are all despatched home again ; which I hope will be much for the ease and satisfaction of the Country ; which is a great fruit of these successes.

The dimensions of this mercy are above my thoughts. It is, for aught I know, a crowning mercy. Surely, if it be not, such a one we shall have, if this provoke those that are concerned in it to thankfulness ; and the Parliament to do the will of Him who hath done His will for it, and for the Nation ;—whose good pleasure it is to establish the Nation and the Change of the Government, by making the People so willing to the defence thereof, and so signally blessing the endeavours of your servants in this late great work. I am bold humbly to beg, That all thoughts may tend to the promoting of His honour who hath wrought so great salvation ; and that the fatness of these continued mercies may not occasion pride and wantonness, as formerly the like hath done to a chosen Nation ; but that the fear of the Lord, even for His mercies, may keep an Authority and a People so prospered, and blessed, and witnessed unto, humble and faithful ; and that justice and righteousness, mercy and truth may flow from you, as a thankful return to our gracious God. This shall be the prayer of,

Sir,
Your most humble and obedient servant,
OLIVER CROMWELL.

4. Make a précis of the following passage reducing it to one-third of its present length :—

It is because rulers do not pay sufficient attention to the stages of this great movement, because they underrate its force, because they are ignorant of its law, that so many violent and fearful revolutions have changed the face of society. We have heard it said a hundred times during these discussions, we have heard it said repeatedly in the course of this very debate, that the people of England are more free than ever they were, that the government is more democratic than ever it was ; and this is used as an argument against reform. I admit the fact ; but deny the inference. It is a principle never to be forgotten, in discussions like this, that it is not by absolute, but by relative misgovernment that nations are roused to madness. It is not sufficient to look merely at the form of government. We

must look also to the state of the public mind. The worst
tyrant that ever had his neck wrung in modern Europe
might have passed for a paragon of clemency in Persia or
Morocco. Our Indian subjects submit patiently to a
monopoly of salt. We tried a stamp duty, a duty so light
as to be scarcely perceptible, on the fierce breed of the old
Puritans ; and we lost an empire. The government of
Louis the Sixteenth was certainly a much better and milder
government than that of Louis the Fourteenth ; yet Louis
the Fourteenth was admired, and even loved, by his people.
Louis the Sixteenth died on the scaffold. Why ? Because,
though the government had made many steps in the career
of improvement, it had not advanced so rapidly as the
nation. Look at our own history. The liberties of the
people were at least as much respected by Charles the First
as by Henry the Eighth, by James the Second as by Edward
the Sixth. But did this save the crown of James the
Second ? Did this save the head of Charles the First ?
Every person who knows the history of our civil dissensions
knows that all those arguments which are now employed by
the opponents of the Reform Bill might have been employed,
and were actually employed, by the unfortunate Stuarts.
The reasoning of Charles, and of all his apologists, runs
thus :—' What new grievance does the nation suffer ? What
has the king done more than what Henry did ? more than
what Elizabeth did ? Did the people ever enjoy more
freedom than at present ? Did they ever enjoy so much
freedom ? ' But what would a wise and honest counsellor,
if Charles had been so happy as to possess such a counsellor,
have replied to arguments like these ? He would have
said, ' Sir, I acknowledge that the people were never more
free than under your government. I acknowledge that
those who talk of restoring the old constitution of England
use an improper expression. I acknowledge that there has
been a constant improvement during those very years during
which many persons imagine that there has been a constant
deterioration. But, though there has been no change in
the government for the worse, there has been a change in
the public mind which produces exactly the same effect
which would be produced by a change in the government
for the worse. Perhaps this change in the public mind is

to be regretted. But no matter : you cannot reverse it. You cannot undo all that eighty eventful years have done. You cannot transform the Englishmen of 1640 into the Englishmen of 1560. It may be that the simple loyalty of our fathers was preferable to that inquiring, resisting spirit which is now abroad. It may be that the times when men paid their benevolences cheerfully were better times than these, when a gentleman goes before the Exchequer Chamber to resist an assessment of twenty shillings. And so it may be that infancy is a happer time than manhood, and manhood than old age. But God has decreed that old age shall succeed to manhood, and manhood to infancy. Even so have societies their law of growth. As their strength becomes greater, as their experience becomes more extensive, you can no longer confine them within the swaddling bands, or lull them in the cradles, or amuse them with the rattles, or terrify them with the bugbears of their infancy. I do not say that they are better or happier than they were ; but this I say, that they are different from what they were, that you cannot again make them what they were, and that you cannot safely treat them as if they continued to be what they were.' This was the advice which a wise and honest minister would have given to Charles the First. These were the principles on which that unhappy prince should have acted. But no. He would govern, I do not say ill, I do not say tyrannically ; I only say this ; he would govern the men of the seventeenth century as if they had been the men of the sixteenth century ; and therefore it was, that all his talents and all his virtues did not save him from unpopularity, from civil war, from a prison, from a bar, from a scaffold.

LORD MACAULAY : *Speech on Parliamentary Reform*,
16th December 1831.

5. Make a précis of the following passage, reducing it to about 100 words :—

Is there, at this moment, any boy of twenty, fairly educated, but without means, without help, with nothing but the glow in his brain and steadfast courage in his heart, who sits in a London garret, and writes for dear life ? There must be, I suppose ; yet all that I have read and heard of late years about young writers, shows them in a very different aspect.

No garretteers, these novelists and journalists awaiting their promotion. They eat — and entertain their critics — at fashionable restaurants ; they are seen in expensive seats at the theatre ; they inhabit handsome flats—photographed for an illustrated paper on the first excuse. At the worst, they belong to a reputable club, and have garments which permit them to attend a garden party or an evening ' at home ' without attracting unpleasant notice. Many biographical sketches have I read, during the last decade, making personal introduction of young Mr This or young Miss That, whose book was—as the sweet language of the day will have it— ' booming ' ; but never one in which there was a hint of stern struggle, of the pinched stomach and frozen fingers. I surmise that the path of ' literature ' is being made too easy. Doubtless it is a rare thing nowadays for a lad whose education ranks him with the upper middle class to find himself utterly without resources, should he wish to devote himself to the profession of letters. And there is the root of the matter ; writing has come to be recognized as a profession, almost as cut-and-dried as church or law ; a lad may go into it with full parental approval, with ready avuncular support. I heard not long ago of an eminent lawyer, who had paid a couple of hundred per annum for his son's instruction in the art of fiction—yea, the art of fiction—by a not very brilliant professor of that art. Really, when one comes to think of it, an astonishing fact, a fact vastly significant. Starvation, it is true, does not necessarily produce fine literature ; but one feels uneasy about these carpet-authors. To the two or three who have a measure of conscience and vision, I could wish, as the best thing, some calamity which would leave them friendless in the streets. They would perish, perhaps. But set that possibility against the all but certainty of their present prospect—fatty degeneration of the soul ; and is it not acceptable ?

GEORGE GISSING : The Private Papers of
Henry Ryecroft.

6. Write a connected summary of the following newspaper article. You should not exceed 100 words.

The Government decision denying women entrance to the Consular and Diplomatic services is a precious piece of obscurantism. Since at this time of day the older sex-prejudice cannot be defended openly, the process known to psychologists as ' rationalization '—the finding of respectable reasons for not-respectable emotions—has clearly been at work. The result, in the language of the statement, is sometimes unconsciously funny. A consul, we are told, may have to cope with ' a number of matters '—what delicate reticence !—which it would be ' difficult ' for ' the average woman to handle.' But, as Lady Snowden points out, ' the average woman ' (whoever she may be) would neither want nor be able to enter the Consular Service. No one suggests that a woman should be appointed to a particular post unless she be as fit for that post, mentally and physically, as a man. As for women diplomats, it is said that ' in a large number of countries ' the ' innovation would not be welcomed.' But if the Grand Cham of Hindo-Kosh has an ineradicable distaste for discussing affairs of State with a woman there seems no pressing reason why a woman need be sent to his Court. There are plenty of more civilized countries where her services would be welcomed. For the Government to use the few countries with a barbarous attitude to women as an excuse for a general bar is really not good enough. The crowning irrelevance, if it does not deserve a worse name, is the blandly expressed doubt whether the admission of women to these services ' would contribute any special advantage to the State.' Must woman, then, plead that their employment would be of such ' special advantage ' before they are entitled to the barest measure of equality with men ? This extraordinary claim is perhaps more revealing of the Government's general attitude than anything else in the statement. Has it come to this : that before a woman worker can expect fair treatment she must prove not that she can do a job as well as a man but that she can do it better ?

The Manchester Guardian.

7. The following is an extract from the court scene in Galsworthy's play, *The Silver Box*. Write a connected summary of the passage bringing out the essential points in the case against the prisoner Jones. Keep to the central theme, avoid unnecessary repetition of names, and ignore what appear

to you to be irrelevant facts and comments. Try not to exceed 100 words.

MAGISTRATE. Now, you have heard the male prisoner's story, what do you say to that ?

JACK [1] (*turning to the* MAGISTRATE, *speaks suddenly in a confident straightforward voice*). The fact of the matter is, sir, that I'd been out to the theatre that night, and had supper afterwards, and I came in late.

MAGISTRATE. Do you remember this man being outside when you came in ?

JACK. No, sir. (*He hesitates.*) I don't think I do.

MAGISTRATE (*somewhat puzzled*). Well, did he help you to open the door, as he says ? Did *any* one help you to open the door ?

JACK. No, sir—I don't think so, sir—I don't know.

MAGISTRATE. You don't know ? But you must know. It isn't a usual thing for you to have the door opened for you, is it ?

JACK (*with a shamefaced smile*). No.

MAGISTRATE. Very well, then——

JACK (*desperately*). The fact of the matter is, sir, I'm afraid I'd had too much champagne that night.

MAGISTRATE (*smiling*). Oh ! you'd had too much champagne ?

JONES. May I ask the gentleman a question ?

MAGISTRATE. Yes—yes—you may ask him what questions you like.

JONES. Don't you remember you said you was a Liberal, same as your father, and you asked me wot I was ?

JACK (*with his hand against his brow*). I seem to remember——

JONES. And I said to you, ' I'm a bloomin ' Conserva*tive*,' I said ; an' you said to me, ' You look more like one of these 'ere Socialists. Take wotever you like,' you said.

JACK (*with sudden resolution*). No, I don't. I don't remember anything of the sort.

JONES. Well, I do, an' my word's as good as yours. I've

---

[1] Son of Mr Barthwick, M.P., owner of the silver box.

3 A

never been had up in a police court before. Look 'ere,
don't you remember you had a sky-blue bag in your 'and——

(BARTHWICK *jumps*.)

ROPER.[1] I submit to your worship that these questions are
hardly to the point, the prisoner having admitted that he
himself does not remember anything.[2] (*There is a smile on
the face of Justice.*)   It is a case of the blind leading the blind.

JONES (*violently*). I've done no more than wot he 'as.   I'm
a poor man.   I've got no money an' no friends—he's a toff
—he can do wot I can't.

MAGISTRATE. Now, now ! All this won't help you—you
must be quiet.   You say you took this box ?   Now, what
made you take it ?   Were you pressed for money ?

JONES. I'm always pressed for money.

MAGISTRATE. Was that the reason you took it ?

JONES. No.

MAGISTRATE (*to* SNOW[3]). Was anything found on him ?

SNOW. Yes, your worship.   There was six pounds twelve
shillin's found on him, and this purse.

(*The red silk purse is handed to the* MAGISTRATE.   BARTHWICK
     rises in his seat, but hastily sits down again.)

MAGISTRATE (*staring at the purse*). Yes, yes—let me see——
(*There is silence.*)   No, no, I've nothing before me as to the
purse.   How did you come by all that money ?

JONES (*after a long pause, suddenly*). I declines to say.

MAGISTRATE. But if you had all that money, what made
you take this box ?

JONES. I took it out of spite.

MAGISTRATE (*hissing, with protruded neck*). You took it
out of spite ?   Well now, that's something !   But do you
imagine you can go about the town taking things out of spite ?

JONES. If you had my life, if you'd been out of work——

MAGISTRATE. Yes, yes ; I know—because you're out of
work you think it's an excuse for everything.

---

[1] The solicitor employed by the Barthwicks.
[2] This admission had been made by the prisoner shortly before
our extract begins.   The solicitor's interruption is timely, for Jones
really remembers too much.
[3] A detective.

8. Write a summary of the following passage. Try not to exceed 75 words.

Freedom of opinion and freedom of the expression of opinion are necessary to the mental well-being of mankind on four distinct grounds :

First, if any opinion is compelled to silence, that opinion may, for aught we can certainly know, be true. To deny this is to assume our own infallibility.

Secondly, though the silenced opinion be an error, it may, and very commonly does, contain a portion of truth ; and since the general or prevailing opinion on any subject is rarely or never the whole truth, it is only by the collision of adverse opinions that the remainder of the truth has any chance of being supplied.

Thirdly, even if the received opinion be not only true, but the whole truth ; unless it is suffered to be, and actually is, vigorously and earnestly contested, it will, by most of those who receive it, be held in the manner of a prejudice, with little comprehension or feeling of its rational grounds. And not only this, but, fourthly, the meaning of the doctrine itself will be in danger of being lost, or enfeebled, and deprived of its vital effect on the character and conduct : the dogma becoming a mere formal profession, inefficacious for good, but cumbering the ground, and preventing the growth of any real and heartfelt conviction, from reason or personal experience.

J. S. MILL : *Liberty.*

9. Write a summary, in reported speech, of the following passage :—

What is it that constitutes and makes man what he is ? What is it but his power of language—that language giving him the means of recording his experience—making every generation somewhat wiser than its predecessor—more in accordance with the established order of the universe ?

What is it but this power of speech, of recording experience, which enables men to be men—looking before and after and, in some dim sense, understanding the working of this wondrous universe—and which distinguishes man from the whole of the brute world ? I say that this functional difference is vast, unfathomable, and truly infinite in its consequences ; and I say at the same time, that it may depend upon structural differences which shall be absolutely inappreciable to us with our present means of investigation. What is this very speech that we are talking about ? I am speaking to you at this moment, but if you were to alter, in the minutest degree, the proportion of the nervous forces now active in the two nerves which supply the muscles of my glottis, I should become suddenly dumb. The voice is produced only so long as . . . certain muscles contract with exact equality ; and that again depends on the quality of action of those two nerves I spoke of. So that a change of the minutest kind in the structure of one of these nerves, or in the structure of the part in which it originates, or of the supply of blood to that part, or of one of the muscles to which it is distributed, might render all of us dumb. But a race of dumb men, deprived of all communication with those who could speak, would be little indeed removed from the brutes. And the moral and intellectual difference between them and ourselves would be practically infinite, though the naturalist should not be able to find a single shadow of even specific structural difference.

THOMAS H. HUXLEY : *Lectures and Essays.*

10.[1] The possibilities of radio-activity are not dreams. There is . . . a certain quality of permanence about scientific discovery. Points of view may change, but the framework of the structure, the experimental fact round which ideas are built, is too well and truly laid to fear demolition. The building will go on. More than that, science—or shall we say the scientific man ?—feels that though the road to absolute knowledge, as to the absolute truth, stretches into a distance that may be approached, but for ever recedes, yet he knows the direction the road takes. Science has acquired the sense of direction. If that be not an immodest claim then new responsibilities fall on those who make it. Science cannot stand aloof from a world into which it introduces weapons of staggering possibilities. Could there from the cosmical standpoint be any greater crime than to bring into existence a weapon to make war more destructive ? Should science give to men a new source of energy, if that energy is not to benefit every

---

[1] Further passages suitable for précis will be found on pp. 110-119.

man who lives in the world, but is to enrich a few ? Is it not the task of science to help in removing the social injustices, the social inequalities, the social evils which disfigure life ? Is it not even the duty of the scientific mind to furnish man, if it may, with what the late Silvanus Thompson called ' a not impossible religion ' ?

E. S. Crew (from an article in *The Observer*).

1. Give a title to this extract and write a summary of it in 70 words.

2. What is meant by ' absolute truth ' ?

3. Use ideas from the extract to counter the statement that in our generation science has evolved long-range guns, bombing airplanes, and poison gas, but has failed to cope with the problems of consumption, rheumatism, and cancer.

4. What are the chief duties of science according to the above article ?

5. Explain what is meant by ' the cosmical standpoint,' ' a staggering possibility,' and ' social inequalities.'

6. What would be some of the chief tenets of the ' not impossible religion ' ?

CHAPTER VI

ARRANGEMENT AND PRESENTATION

(1) *Arrangement and Expansion of Notes*

WRITING from notes or making a short speech from a synopsis is an important part of work in English. At first sight it seems easy to ' fill in the gaps,' but if the essay or speech is to hold interest it must have continuity and must give prominence to one or two central ideas. If, for instance, you are writing a short biography of David Livingstone you should stress his long struggle against the slave-traders. Here are the main facts of his life. Arrange them in suitable order for an essay, indicating the chief paragraph divisions. You may find it necessary to discard some of these facts : if so, give reasons for your omissions.

DAVID LIVINGSTONE—came of Highland stock—lived and died to destroy slavery in Africa—his great-grandfather was killed at Culloden, 1746, fighting for Bonny Prince Charlie —David Livingstone born 1813 near Glasgow—parents were poor—he worked in a cotton mill from 6 A.M. to 8 P.M. and learnt Latin in his spare time !—at age 20 vowed to carry the Gospel among the heathens—was thrifty— saved enough to go to Glasgow University in the winter— in summer went back to work in the mill. 1840 took his medical diploma at Glasgow—was ordained and sent to Africa by the London Missionary Society—landed at Algoa Bay—went up-country by bullock waggon—built himself a home—one day was badly wounded in the arm by a lion— 1844 married the daughter of a colleague—with his wife crossed the Kalahari desert—began task of converting the savages—in order to open up the interior to influences more enlightened than those of the slave traders he followed up the line of the River Zambesi first to its mouth and then back to its source—it was thus that he discovered the Victoria Falls. After ten years' absence he returned to England where honours awaited him. In 1858 he returned to Africa as British Consul. Had to face grave difficulties— Portuguese undid his work by giving open encouragement to slave traders—his wife died. In 1866 he accepted commission of the Royal Geographical Society—penetrated to Lake Tanganyika—went east along one of the chief tributaries of the Congo, the Luabula—further evidences of success of the slave traders—robbed and deserted by his followers—he was found by H. M. Stanley, an American journalist, at Ujiji—refused to return with Stanley— Livingstone wished to explore the territory between the Nile and the Congo—took fever—died in a little hut near Lake Banguelo, May 1873. He is buried in Westminster Abbey. His body was identified by the injury inflicted by the lion many years before.

Write short articles on some of the following topics, giving prominence to the points specified in the brackets. There is no need to moralize too heavily ; you are writing short biographies, not seeking occasions to edify or threaten.

The *Dictionary of National Biography* should be your first mine of information. At the foot of each monograph you will see a short bibliography. You will not be able to read them all, but, bearing in mind the main topic you are to advance and by consulting the indexes of some of these books you should be able to acquire sufficient information for an essay of 400 words.

You must resist the temptation to try to put in everything. Read over your finished work to see if a real human being emerges. Perhaps you had better spend several days in collecting (and discarding) material.

G. K. CHESTERTON (versatility).
SIR CHRISTOPHER WREN (evolution of a genius).
LORD NELSON (' Glory's Favourite Son ').

DAVID GARRICK (versatility).
ANNE BOLEYN (the irony of fate).
CAPTAIN R. F. SCOTT (perseverance and endurance).
FLORENCE NIGHTINGALE (humanity).
SIR THOMAS MORE (wit, simplicity, piety).
ROBERT RAIKES (philanthropy).

The words in brackets are not intended as labels : greatness refuses to be put into categories. They are intended to suggest points to which prominence should be given.

Here are some thoughts on the topic, ' A Famous Spa.' Arrange these ideas into a more convincing order, then group them into five or six paragraphs, discarding those which interfere with the unity or balance of the subject. Thus, if you think too much space is given to amusements that can easily be procured elsewhere you should limit or even omit references to them.

> the palatial baths
> the Casino
> first impressions . . . the really sick and the merely jaded
> the band
> consultation with the local doctors
> progress of the cure
> efficacy of the waters
> what the waters taste like
> a particularly vigorous masseur (or masseuse)
> gradual increases in the ' dose '
> bubbling up of the warm springs
> control of the springs in marble, font-like erections
> an outdoor evening entertainment . . . spa grounds illuminated by arc lamps . . . items announced by loud-speakers
> improvement in health and final recovery
> friendships made with other patients

In planning out an essay or a speech do not scorn details. Often an original thought or impression proves irresistibly attractive to the reader or listener. In the above subject ' a particularly vigorous masseur ' may well provoke an excellent piece of description.

Plan essays or short articles on some of the following subjects. They are intentionally more difficult than the subjects on which you usually write so that you should spend some time in collecting and arranging your material.

> The Coming of Electricity ; The Work of Rivers ; The Fight Against Tropical Diseases ; William Herschel ; The Aeroplane ; A People's Theatre ; Science and the Housewife ; Birds in Legend and Folklore ; Autocrats ; Letters of Horace Walpole ; Carols ; Contemporary British Dramatists ; Humour and Humorists ; Fools in Fiction ; Julian Huxley ; Miracle Plays ; The Drama of Animal Life ; John Masefield's Novels ; History on the Stage ; Educational Films ; Vitamins ; Modern Fashions ; Colour in the Home.

Vagueness is probably the commonest fault of essays written in school. Therefore be on the look-out for interesting details or anecdotes to give point and illustration to your theme.

(2) *Observation of Detail*

Describe each of the following in not more than ten lines. Do not try to say everything that comes to your mind but try to give the thing you are describing some individuality. No two shoes are exactly alike.

1. an island, a public recreation-ground, a town hall.
2. a ship, a triumphal arch, a saxophone.
3. a forest glade, a hand-embroidered dress, a fire-screen.
4. a bazaar, a barber's shop, a hideous ornament.

In describing people be careful not to confuse details of dress with aspects of character.

Write short sketches of some of the following :—

1. a sleeping baby, a precocious child, my favourite cousin.
2. a bewildered porter, a shrewd salesman, an open-mouthed countryman.
3. the captain of the fire-brigade, a retired sailor, a bore.
4. a street musician, a clown, a jovial detective.

Keeping to the spirit of the following passage, add another paragraph of about the same length. You may not have seen the Dardanelles ; where will you be able to find out about them ?

The sea was an intense blue. The creamy wake of the cruiser stretched away like a gigantic streamer. At sunset the sea turned colour to emerald green, and one or two stars were shining before the sun, an orange ball of phosphorescence which gilded the side of the cruiser with its last rays, had disappeared. Cape Matapan stood up white against the blue ; arid-looking islands, brown and low, jumped up and sank away astern. Then, one Sunday morning, she was steaming up to the entrance to the Dardanelles.

THOMAS WOODROOFFE : *Naval Odyssey.*

(3) *Accuracy in Description—Definitions*

Much careless writing results from a failure to understand the purport of a subject. You often hear people talking at cross-purposes, especially at election times when slogans and catchphrases are in vogue. Thus ' effete legislation ' when dispassionately examined may mean ' reluctance to effect sweeping changes.' Since abstract ideas are controversial it is better first to practise on concrete things.

Criticize the following definition :—

A screen is a piece of household furniture, sometimes composed of two or more hinged leaves, covered with some air-resisting material, and placed round a doorway or a window to exclude the draught or to hide a fireplace in summer.

Write definitions of :—

(*a*) a valley	(*b*) bombast	(*c*) prejudice
a granary	wit [1]	nationalization
a certificate	superstition	culture
an axiom	a platitude	intuition
a balcony	a slogan	morality

[1] Some of the above you will find difficult. If you read Chapter Ten of R. W. Jepson's *Clear Thinking* you will realize why.

It was in a cynical mood that Ambrose Bierce, the American writer, defined a novel as ' A short story padded ' and peace as ' A period of cheating between two periods of fighting.'

One of the most famous of definitions occurs in Cardinal Newman's *Apologia pro vita sua* :

It is almost the definition of a gentleman to say he is one who never inflicts pain ; he is tender towards the bashful, gentle towards the distant, merciful towards the absurd.

(4) *Systematic Presentation of Descriptive Matter*

Ability to grasp the meaning and structure of a literary passage or the purport of a schedule of facts is valuable in helping you to arrange and develop your own thoughts.

Notes made at lectures or during the delivery of a speech show not merely the chief points raised but their development and their relation to the subject. Systematic presentation of facts is essential in preparing reports whether *descriptive*, such as an account of an exhibition or of a social function, *critical*, as, for instance, a summary of the reasons for the revival or the depreciation of trade, or *scientific*, such as an account of investigations into cheaper methods of production or distribution.

Care must be taken (*a*) not to confuse the issue by introducing irrelevant detail, (*b*) to provide proper sub-headings as each new division of the topics is approached, (*c*) to include all important points and to see that all ' afterthoughts ' are fitted into their proper places, (*d*) to arrange the matter logically, and (*e*) to use concise language.

Exercises

1. Add a further ten lines to each of the following descriptive passages :—

    (*a*) We had nearly threaded the wood, and were approaching an open grove of magnificent oaks on the other side, when sounds other than of nightingales burst on our ear, the deep and frequent strokes of the woodman's axe ; and on emerging from the Pinge we saw the havoc which that axe had committed.

Above twenty of the finest trees lay stretched on the velvet turf. There they lay in every shape and form of devastation ; some bare trunks, stripped ready for the timber carriage, with the bark built up in long piles at the side ; some with the spoilers busy about them, stripping, hacking, hewing ; others with their noble branches, their brown and fragrant shoots, all fresh as if they were alive—majestic corses, the slain of today.

Notice that the detailed parts of the description are reserved for a separate paragraph.

(*b*) There sits the yeoman at the end of his long room, surrounded by his friends. Glasses are filled, and a song is the cry, and a song is sung well suited to the place ; it finds an echo in every heart—fists are clenched, arms are waved, and the portraits of the mighty fighting men of yore, Broughton and Slack and Ben, which adorn the walls, appear to smile grim approbation, whilst many a manly voice joins in the bold chorus :

' Here's a health to old honest John Bull,
    When he's gone we shan't find such another,
  And with hearts and with glasses brim full,
    We will drink to old England his mother.'

(*c*) . . . The enclosed enchanted little landscape, then, is Strawberry Hill ; and I will try to explain so much of it to you as will help to let you know whereabouts we are when we are talking to you,—for it is uncomfortable in so intimate a correspondence as ours not to be exactly master of every spot where one another is writing or reading or sauntering.

This view of the castle is what I have just finished, and is the only side that will be all regular. Directly before it is an open grove, through which you see a field, which is bounded by a serpentine wood of all kinds of trees and flowering shrubs and flowers. The lawn before the house is situated on the top of a small hill, from whence to the left you see the town and church of Twickenham encircling a turn of the river, that looks exactly like a seaport in miniature. The opposite shore is a most delicious meadow, bounded by Richmond Hill, which loses itself in the noble woods of the park to the end of the prospect on the right, where is another turn of the river, and the suburbs of Kingston as luckily placed as Twickenham is on the left; and a natural terrace on the brow of my hill, with meadows of my own down to the river, commands both extremities.

Is not this a tolerable prospect? You must figure that all this is perpetually enlivened by a navigation of boats and barges, and by a road below my terrace, with coaches, post-chaises, wagons, and horsemen constantly in motion, and the fields speckled with cows, horses, and sheep.

Now you shall walk into the house . . .

This is from a letter by Horace Walpole to Sir Horace Mann, 12th June 1753. His letters abound in passages suggestive, as Thackeray tells us, of ' a brilliant, jigging, smirking Vanity Fair.'

2. Write three descriptive paragraphs on each of the following subjects :—

(a) a tastefully furnished room; (b) your home's water supply; (c) the lumber room; (d) an attractive shopwindow; (e) safety-first methods adopted in your district; (f) a local celebrity.

3. You have just taken an American friend to see his first county cricket match. He is surprised to learn that the game will last three days, that it is possible to score runs behind the wicket, and that a batsman can often remain at the crease for half an hour without making a scoring stroke. Your friend explains that a baseball game is usually over in less than two hours, that the striker does not receive more than three balls during an innings, and that his object is to hit the ball hard in front of him, and that when three men are out, the side is out. ' Cricket is an intolerably slow game,' is your friend's conclusion.

Write, in three paragraphs, a reasoned defence of cricket,

using some of the following ideas, which, of course, may be more effectively arranged :—

> team-spirit ; variety (weather, strokes made, positions in the field) ; importance of the time limit ; encourages a more friendly spirit since the players do not come into physical contact ; the bowlers' wiles ; scope for a captain who is a clever tactician.

4. Plan out a similar defence of another sport in which you are interested.

(5) *Drawing Conclusions from Tabulated Facts*

When you have studied the following tables, first put down your observations, then arrange them before writing them up in the form of a short report. This report should have a proper heading as in the first example given.

An Article on Traffic Accidents

The Home Office has issued its preliminary traffic-accident figures for 1933. They are disturbing. The number of accidents has gone up, and the number of deaths, rising in disproportionate ratio to the total, exceeded 7,000—or nearly twenty a day. If twenty persons were killed, and thirty times that number injured, in a railway accident or an air disaster, the most searching inquiry into its causes and the means of preventing its repetition would follow. But the deaths and injuries of road travel are scattered throughout the length and breadth of the country, and there is no systematic investigation by a competent authority.

Two things are clear. The first is that the effects of the new Road Traffic Act, the increased sense of responsibility which it gave to both motorists and pedestrians, are evaporating. True the 1933 figures do not equal the grim record of 1930 ; but they are creeping up, and it is no answer to say that the volume of traffic is increasing. The effects of a satisfactory traffic law would be cumulative, not evanescent.

Secondly, the accident figures bear a direct ratio to the volume of traffic. Saturday is the worst day, and August the worst month. This incontrovertible fact casts an ominous significance over the future. There is no doubt that the volume of traffic is increasing. If nothing is done, every day will soon be a Saturday and every Saturday will bring its holocaust. The substance of the case for vigorous and immediate action is that accidents have increased, are increasing, and ought to be diminished.

Make a précis (about 70 words) of the above passage.

PARTICULARS OF STREET ACCIDENTS IN THE CITY OF ELBERTON, EREWHON, FROM 1929 to 1937 INCLUSIVE

Year	Total Number of Fatal Accidents, Adults and Children	Total Number of Fatal Accidents to Children	Total Number of Persons Injured, Adults and Children	Total Number of Children Injured	Percentage of Children to Persons Killed	Percentage of Children to Persons Injured
1929	638	221	20,263	5,348	34·64	26·39
1930	571	185	22,647	5,913	32·40	26·11
1931	675	233	25,547	6,609	34·52	25·87
1932	668	210	30,333	7,333	31·44	24·17
1933	844	231	35,065	8,179	27·37	23·33
1934	840	219	39,186	8,810	26·07	22·48
1935	1,003	233	46,036	9,528	23·23	20·70
1936	1,056	221	48,049	10,040	20·93	20·90
1937	1,237	259	54,461	11,031	20·94	20·25

From the above figures, draw up a report after the manner of the one printed above. Comment fully upon the main points, first drawing your ideas from suggestions in the above passage, and then give consideration to questions such as :

(a) The increase in the total number of fatal accidents. (Is there any sign of a decrease ?)
(b) The increase in the total number of people injured.
(c) The decreasing percentages of children to the number of persons killed and injured.

(*d*) Why should there be more adults than children killed and injured ?

Assign what appear to you to be suitable reasons for the changes these figures indicate.

Further Exercises

Comment as fully as you can upon the figures given in the following tables and deduce as many points of significance as you can. When you have finished, arrange these particulars in a suitable order, and state for what purposes such an order of presentation would be desirable.

1. Argentina's Merchandise Trade from 1928 to 1935 inclusive :

Calendar Year	Millions of Paper Pesos	
	Imports	Exports
1928 . . .	1,902	2,397
1929 . . .	1,959	2,168
1930 . . .	1,680	1,396
1931 . . .	1,174	1,456
1932 . . .	836	1,288
1933 . . .	897	1,121
1934 . . .	1,110	1,438
1935 . . .	1,175	1,569

2. A few years ago an American newspaper published the following table showing the allocation of columns to different interests in various newspapers representative of four great countries :—

	America	England	France	Germany
Business . .	21	17	9	30
Sports . .	15	17	3	3
Amusement .	15	1	21	8
Politics . .	10	9	6	11
Police News .	10	6	8	3
Foreign News .	7	23	30	35
Arts . . .	4	5	5	3

If you have access to a number of foreign newspapers, compare the above results with present-day ones. Failing this, take five or six of most widely circulated English newspapers, draw up a similar table, and give a short account of your deductions.

3. *With the aid of the data printed below, review the progress of British civil aviation during the years 1919-1926. (The figures take no account of the movements of the Royal Air Force or of private owners : they refer only to British aircraft carrying goods and passengers for hire on regular air-routes.)*

Year	Number of Flights	Mileage Flown	Passengers	Cargo in Tons	Accidents	Killed	Injured
1919	467	104,000	870	30	2	3	3
1920	2,854	644,000	5,799	137	2	4	2
1921	993	225,000	5,256	19	...	...	...
1922	2,891	717,000	10,393	215	2	2	2
1923	2,559	943,000	15,552	328	3	5	3
1924	2,794	936,000	13,601	543	1	8	...
1925	2,891	862,000	11,193	550	...	...	...
1926	2,879	840,000	16,775	679	...	...	...

Civil Service Commission.

4. Value of the imports and exports of merchandise (excluding bullion and specie and foreign merchandise transhipped under bond) of the United Kingdom for five years :

Year	Total Imports	Exports of British Produce	Exports of Foreign and Colonial Produce	Total Exports
	£	£	£	£
1931	861,252,638	390,621,598	63,867,549	454,489,147
1932	701,670,061	365,024,008	51,021,256	416,045,264
1933	675,016,119	367,909,052	49,080,727	416,989,779
1934	731,413,783	395,985,521	51,243,347	447,228,868
1935 [1]	765,936,175	425,921,343	55,265,376	481,186,719

Quoted from p. 55 of *The Statesman's Year-Book.*

[1] Provisional figures.

5. On 25th October 1936, *The Observer* published the following table compiled from records kept at the Royal Observatory, Greenwich. These figures show the number of ' warm ' days (maximum shade temperature 70 degrees or above) and ' hot ' days (80 degrees or above) from April to October 1936, together with the respective averages over the period 1841-1933 :

| Month | 1936 | | Average | |
	Warm Days	Hot Days	Warm Days	Hot Days
April . . .	0	0	1	0
May . . .	7	0	7	1
June . . .	15	3	16	3
July . . .	17	0	22	6
August . . .	18	7	21	4
September . .	8	1	9	1
October . .	0	0	1	0

Comment upon (1) the weather during these months in 1936 compared with the average figures ; (2) the desirability of altering the schools' long summer vacation from August to June ; (3) the desirability of dividing the school year into four terms of ten weeks each with three weeks' vacation at the end. In considering the last point, you can give effect to topics other than those arising from the weather.

You will find interesting tables of figures upon a wide variety of topics if you consult *The Times* (Annual Financial and Commercial Review).

CHAPTER VII

FIGURES OF SPEECH AND LITERARY TERMS

Oh, for a man who'd write through tears, all swimmily,
And woo me with grand metaphor and simile !
CLIFFORD BAX : *Square Pegs.*

FALSTAFF. . . . 'Sblood, I am as melancholy as a gib cat or a lugged bear.
PRINCE. Or an old lion, or a lover's lute.
FAL. Yea, or the drone of a Lincolnshire bagpipe.
PRINCE. What sayest thou to a hare, or the melancholy of Moorditch ?
FAL. Thou hast the most unsavoury similes, and art indeed the most comparative, rascalliest, sweet young prince.
WILLIAM SHAKESPEARE : *Henry IV*, Part I.

You have seen that an author's style arises from his personality. His style is as much an expression of himself as is his taste in music, art, or painting. He will often draw on his experiences in these and other interests to make his style either more homely, more vigorous, or more picturesque. His thoughts are not merely bald statements concisely expressed but come to you as part of his life sustained and quickened by what he has seen and imagined. Until you have learnt the lesson to write deliberately and tersely you will do well to consider as a whole the work of great writers and not seek to concentrate on details. Literary style is more than a succession of echoes.

An author draws upon his experiences to increase the range and power of his writing. Unexpected, but telling comparisons are made. At times an epigrammatic terseness pervades his writing, especially when he uses metaphorical expressions.

Figures of speech are not embellishments superimposed on style : they rise or should rise naturally. You can often determine when a writer is striving for effect ; his similes become obscure or far-fetched. He cheapens the use of rhetoric. The delicate vein of irony may thicken into the grossest sarcasm.

Striving for effect is therefore a sign of the decadence of style. The bold language and powerful flights of fancy of the Elizabethans were too often followed by the laboriously hammered-out conceits of their successors.

Figures of speech, then, may be judged from their effective or ineffective use, their vividness or obscurity. In writing you should be careful to avoid worn-out notions. Proverbs, it is true, stand the test of time because their application is not limited to only a few situations : for instance, a host of different circumstances can be imagined in which ' Too many cooks spoil the broth ' is an apt comment. It is trite and not effective to speak of the woods being *clothed* in fresh greenery or being *carpeted* with fallen leaves.

You have seen that a proverb is used to comment upon or compare one situation in the light of another. Proverbs, however, are not regarded as figures of speech. Moreover, there are scores of idioms, drawn from common experiences, to compare with fresh situations. Thus, you speak of *feathering your nest ; beating about the bush ; making hay while the sun shines ; striving against the stream ; putting the break on ; striking while the iron is hot ; wasting powder and shot ;* and *not crying over spilt milk.* In addition to these comparisons are others, some of which begin to border upon similes : *as tall as a tree ; as hungry as a hunter ; as happy as a sand-boy ; as miserable as sin ; as mute as an oyster ; as pleased as a dog with two tails ;* and *as hard as nails.* These expressions are so familiar that no longer do they call up any feelings of delight or even interest. It is arguable whether they add anything at all to a description.

Simile : If you accept Dr Johnson's dictum that 'a simile, to be perfect, must both illustrate and ennoble the subject,' you should inquire whether the simile is appropriate or not.

A simile explicitly acknowledges a comparison between things that for the most part differ. The justification for bringing them together in a simile is to add clarity and vigour. When Mr P. G. Wodehouse describes a man so fat as if he had been poured into his clothes and had forgotten to say ' When,' you have, from the comparison of pouring grain into a sack or water into a rubber hot-water bottle, the notion of wobbling, uneven swelling and grotesque disproportion. A note that is both homely and humorous is struck, because it recalls an everyday experience. It is humorous partly because of your surprise at this novel association of two ideas.

If you say, ' I met a woman with untidy hair,' a friend will have only a general or outlined idea of her appearance ; Miss Edith Sitwell describes such a woman as having ' a dusty parting in her hair like a towpath the day after Bank Holiday,' a description which conveys a far more vivid impression. Perhaps Miss Sitwell mars the effect somewhat by adding, ' Nobody would have been surprised to find sandwich papers in it.' [1]

Sometimes a simile fails to impress. A person was described as having a face ' like Stonehenge in a blizzard.' For most of us this means nothing, except, perhaps, a feeling of gauntness and dreariness. No clear picture is left in the mind.

Consider these similes and comment upon their vigour and their suitability :—

When you try to be witty you are like a cart-horse in tights.

For when you are extremely tall it is not all rapture to sit for hours with your length huddled beneath you, like an idol of Buddha.   C. Stockley : *The Claw.*

[1] Quoted from *The Morning Post*, 16th September 1935.

The moon peered through the trees like a ghost that had lost its soul. *Ibid.*

An hour later the sun shot past the horizon like a red-hot cannon ball aimed at the other side of the world. *Ibid.*

A kingfisher flew past like a piece of the blue sky.
R. L. STEVENSON.

The lights and shadows played softly at hide-and-seek, like dumb children over the grass, among the pillars of the little cloister, over the tomb itself.
C. N. WILLIAMSON : *My Friend the Chauffeur.*

The road went curving up as gracefully and easily as a swan makes for water. *Ibid.*

" Bump ! " went the car, as he finished his explanation, and then we began to wade jerkily through a thick layer of loose stones that had been spread on the road like hard butter over stale bread. *Ibid.*

There was Mrs Levison, with her raucous voice and her hair like a yellow sponge.
V. SACKVILLE-WEST : *The Edwardians.*

People were lying about on the grass, many of them looking as if they had been dropped there, exhausted, almost lifeless, out of aeroplanes. They made her feel tired.
J. B. PRIESTLEY : *They Walk in the City.*

She was the narrowest woman William had ever seen : her head, features, neck, shoulders, all looked as if they had been compressed, ceaselessly, ruthlessly, since childhood ; she was like an image in a distorted mirror.
J. B. PRIESTLEY : *Faraway.*

And now she lowered her voice, and her eyes, which sat so close to her long thin nose that they were like two berries on a stalk, gleamed with secret satisfaction.

Ibid.

And suddenly, behind a hill, through branches of pine-trees, rose the moon, red, enormous, and as if benumbed with sleep.
GUY DE MAUPASSANT.

SUSTAINED SIMILE: Sometimes you have a sequence of beautiful similes, as for instance in *The Song of Songs*. You should consult Miles Coverdale's version on p. 569 of Miss Rose Macaulay's *The Minor Pleasures of Life*. More often, however, especially in poetry, you meet similes of considerable length : such similes are called ' sustained ' or ' Homeric.' The beauty or picturesqueness of what he is describing carries the poet into a simile of considerable length.

> Charm'd with this heat, the king his course pursues,
> And next the troops of either Ajax views :
> In one firm orb the bands were ranged around,
> A cloud of heroes blacken'd all the ground.
> Thus from the lofty promontory's brow
> A swain surveys the gathering storm below ;
> Slow from the main the heavy vapours rise,
> Spread in dim streams, and sail along the skies,
> Till black as night the swelling tempest shows,
> The cloud condensing as the west-wind blows.
> He dreads the impending storm, and drives his flock
> To the close covert of an arching rock.
> Such, and so thick, the embattled squadrons stood,
> With spears erect, a moving iron wood :
> A shady light was shot from glimmering shields,
> And their brown arms obscured the dusky fields.
>
> ALEXANDER POPE : *The Iliad.*

> Meanwhile the Adversary of God and man,
> Satan with thoughts inflam'd of highest design,
> Puts on swift wings, and towards the gates of Hell
> Explores his solitary flight ; sometimes
> He scours the right hand coast, sometimes the left,
> Now shaves with level wing the deep, then soars
> Up to the fiery concave towering high.
> As when far off at sea a fleet descri'd
> Hangs in the clouds, by equinoctial winds
> Close sailing from Bengala, or the isles
> Of Ternate and Tidore, whence merchants bring
> Their spicy drugs . they on the trading flood

Through the wide Ethiopian to the Cape
Ply stemming nightly toward the Pole. So seem'd
Far off the flying Fiend : at last appear
Hell bounds high reaching to the horrid roof,
And thrice three-fold the gates ; three folds were brass,
Three iron, three of adamantine rock,
Impenetrable, impal'd with circling fire,
Yet unconsum'd.

JOHN MILTON : *Paradise Lost*, Book II.

METAPHOR : 'A transfer '—often you use metaphors unconsciously. For instance, you may speak of ' the reins of government.' You are really transferring the notion of guiding a horse to that of ruling a country. There is an implied comparison : *the area of authorship ; a baptism of fire ; to run atilt at death*.

Aptly chosen metaphors tend to conciseness and picturesqueness of style, but they should be used sparingly as a reader cannot be expected to follow a rapid sequence of transferred notions. Indeed, you may easily fall into that venial and amusing blunder, the *mixed metaphor*.

' It is true that what this book offers is very tough meat and much spadework will be needed.'

It is best to avoid meat so tough that a spade is required to eat it.

Punch, on 21st October 1936, produced an amazing collection of mixed metaphors. Here is a brief selection from one of the sentences :

. . . what citizen whose judgment is not warped by bats in the belfry can fail to observe that these men who rode the high horse into office on the undertaking that they would make a silk purse out of a sow's ear have let the cat out of the bag to see which way it will jump, and admit that, by barking up the wrong tree, they have got the wrong sow by the ear ?

Here are some good examples of the effective use of metaphors. Charles Lamb speaks of a candle as ' a mild viceroy of the moon.' Good metaphors have the charm of spontaneity [1] :

> He played bo-peep with the Scripture. (Tyndale.)
> The unemployed are the human spare parts of the economic machine.
> The necessary notes below drive the text into the garrets of the page. (Andrew Lang.)

Lamb, in a playful moment, shows his skill in inventing metaphors :

> A poor relation—is the most irrelevant thing in nature,—a piece of impertinent correspondency,—an odious approximation,—a haunting conscience,—a preposterous shadow, lengthening in the noontide of our prosperity,—an unwelcome remembrancer,—a perpetually recurring mortification,—a drain on your purse,—a more intolerable dun upon your pride,—a drawback upon success,—a rebuke to your rising,—a stain in your blood,—a blot on your 'scutcheon,—a rent in your garment,—a death's head at your banquet,—Agathocles' pot,—a Mordecai in your gate,—a Lazarus at your door,—a lion in your path,—a frog in your chamber,—a fly in your ointment,—a mote in your eye,—a triumph to your enemy, an apology to your friends,—the one thing not needful,—the hail in harvest,—the ounce of sour in a pound of sweet.

SUSTAINED METAPHOR : Consider the following examples where the metaphor is continued for several lines :

> Chaucer . . .
> Our morning star of song, that led the way
> To welcome the long-after coming beam
> Of Spenser's lights, and Shakespeare's perfect day.
> THOMAS CAMPBELL.

---

[1] The difference between a live metaphor and a dead one is not always obvious. In the *Dictionary of Modern English Usage* Fowler speaks of ' moribund metaphors.' There appears to be little point in classifying metaphors, for to one person ' the reins of government ' may suggest a vivid, though implied, comparison ; while another person would not realize that he had used a figure of speech at all.

These growing feathers pluck'd from Cæsar's wing
Will make him fly an ordinary pitch,
Who else would soar above the view of men
And keep us all in servile fearfulness.

SHAKESPEARE : Julius Cæsar.

He that hath suffer'd this disorder'd spring
Hath now himself met with the fall of leaf ;
The weeds that his broad-spreading leaves did shelter,
That seem'd in eating him to hold him up,
Are pluck'd up root and all by Bolingbroke ;
I mean the Earl of Wiltshire, Bushy, Green.

SHAKESPEARE : Richard II, III, iv.

ALLEGORY : An allegory may be regarded as an extended metaphor. Usually it takes the form of a story in which the characters are symbolic and represent real people, or, more commonly, virtues and vices. Chaucer and his followers were especially fond of allegorizing. Stephen Hawes (? 1475-1523), in his poem, *The Passetyme of Pleasure*, allegorizes music, geometry, and arithmetic. You should read *Pearl*, a fourteenth-century poem about religion and the future life, Chaucer's *The Parlement of Foules*, Langland's *Piers Plowman*, Spenser's *Færie Queene*, Book I, and Bunyan's *Holy War*. It is assumed that you have read parts of Swift's *Gulliver's Travels* and Bunyan's *Pilgrim's Progress*.

Nowadays it appears that ' the novel with a purpose ' has superseded the allegory.

FABLE : A short story that conveys a moral lesson. Often, especially where animals are introduced as speaking characters, there is a strong current of sarcasm. Not always does virtue triumph, as you will find in Æsop's fables of the Fox and the Crane, and the Wolf and the Lamb.

METONYMY : A figure in which some attribute or associated idea is used instead of the thing meant.

The Crown for *governmental authority ; the cloth* for *the clerical profession ; to take silk* for *to attain the rank of King's Counsel ; the stage* for *the theatrical profession.*

SYNECDOCHE is a kind of metonymy in which the association of ideas is even closer. Thus the part may be taken for the whole, or the whole for the part.

Send for *buttons* at once ! (A page-boy whose uniform has two long rows of buttons on the tunic.)

A factory may announce vacancies for twelve *hands* : we hear of a fleet of thirty *sail*. When the shooting season begins we read that a party of eight *guns* sets out.

But when we read that *England* drew with *New Zealand*, we are considering the whole instead of the part.

TRANSFERRED EPITHET, or HYPALLAGE, is a figure of speech in which there is an interchange, usually of a descriptive word, from one substantive to another.

> . . . then like hedge-hogs, which
> Lie tumbling in my *bare-foot* way . . .
> SHAKESPEARE : *The Tempest.*

(The *way* is not bare-foot : this epithet applies to the speaker, Caliban.)

> The friends drank a *cheerful* glass.
> To right, to left, the *dexterous* lance I wield. POPE.

ANTONOMASIA : Reference to this will be found in Chapter II, p. 23. *Swan of Avon, Iron Duke etc*

PROLEPSIS : The use of an epithet before it is appropriately applicable. Thus the expression, ' the *doomed* army ' may be used while the soldiers, on their way to disaster, are at present safe.

The Shorter Oxford English Dictionary gives the example ' to hang his poison in the *sick* air.' The air would not be ' sick ' until the poison were hung in it.

ZEUGMA is a figure in which a single word is connected with a pair of words or clauses, although, grammatically, it does not belong to both of them. *Zeugma* is connected etymologically with our verb ' to yoke.'

When Fluellen exclaims, in *Henry V*, IV, vii, ' Kill the poys and the luggage ! ' the verb he uses fails to give sense with *luggage*.

SYLLEPSIS : A figure of speech similar to zeugma.

She was at the back of the house, washing clothes *with* happiness and a bar of Sunbright soap.

The prisoners were *in* fetters and a state of drunkenness.

The dismissed servant left the house *in* high dudgeon and a taxi-cab.

He retired *on* a pension and an anecdote.

She *recovered* her powder-puff and her equanimity.

The sentences are grammatically correct, but the humorous effect arises from the words in italics being used in a different sense with each of the pair of words that follow.

ANTITHESIS : This consists of a close placing together of opposing ideas.

Penny wise and pound foolish.

> Our pains are real things, and all
> Our pleasures but fantastical.
> SAMUEL BUTLER.

> Some few in that, but numbers err in this,
> Ten censure wrong for one who writes amiss ;
> A fool might once himself alone expose,
> Now one in verse makes many more in prose.
> POPE.

Prosperity is not without many fears and distastes ; and adversity is not without comforts and hopes.　　BACON.

Antitheses appeal to the ear as well as the mind. There is a pleasing anticipation of the contrast. Many a fine passage from the Bible remains implanted in the memory by virtue of the sonorous power and grace of an antithesis.

CHIASMUS is best described as a cross order of words and phrases. The inversion attracts because it seems more concise than a normal antithesis.

> In good roast-beef my landlord sticks his knife,
> The capon fat delights his dainty wife,
> *Pudding our Parson eats, the Squire loves hare,*
> But white-pot thick is my Buxoma's fare.
> GAY.

All are but parts of one stupendous whole,
Whose body Nature is, and God the soul.   POPE.

A fop their passion, but their prize a sot.   POPE.

EPIGRAM : A shrewd observation that has the appearance of spontaneity.   Often there is an unexpected antithesis or the sharp bite of sarcasm.

The parson knows enough who knows a duke.
COWPER.

War is a fool's game but the military virtues are still worth having.

One would need to be a god to decide who are the failures and who the successes of life.

A cigarette—that eleventh finger of bliss.
G. W. STONIER.

Freedom consists in the recognition of one's limitations.

Obedience is freedom from the intolerable burden of thought.   G. BERNARD SHAW.

(Where no indication is given I have been unable to trace the source of the epigram.)

A PARADOX is a statement that opposes a commonly accepted opinion.   The effect is to administer a sudden shock and to provoke a challenge.   Further reflection shows the truth of the paradox.

It is only shallow people who do not judge by appearances.
OSCAR WILDE.

Whatever is worth doing at all is worth doing badly.
G. K. CHESTERTON.

A paradox is thus often a cynical reaction against a complacent acceptance of platitudes.

OXYMORON : A sharp contrast.   The word is derived from two Greek words, *oxos*, sharp, and *moros*, dull.   It presents a more pointed contrast than the paradox because it is compressed usually into consecutive words.

I like a smuggler.   He is the only honest thief.   LAMB.

Their traitorous trueness and their loyal deceit.
FRANCIS THOMPSON.

Tennyson, wishing to convey the idea of Sir Lancelot's mind alternating between love for Queen Guenivere and loyalty to King Arthur, says :

> His honour rooted in dishonour stood,
> And faith unfaithful kept him falsely true.

HYPERBOLE : The term literally means ' throwing or shooting over the mark.' It is used to produce a required effect by exaggerating.

When Hamlet leaps into Ophelia's grave he cries :

> Now pile your dust upon the quick and dead,
> Till of this flat a mountain you have made,
> To o'er-top old Pelion or the skyish head
> Of blue Olympus.

A few lines later he shouts :

> I lov'd Ophelia : forty thousand brothers
> Could not, with all their quantity of love,
> Make up my sum.

Gray, speaking of the simple country folk, says :

>   . . . nor circumscribed alone
> Their growing virtues, but their crimes confined ;
> Forbad to wade through slaughter to a throne,
> And shut the gates of mercy on mankind.

LITOTES (also named MEIOSIS) : this figure of speech achieves its effect by restraint, by deliberate understatement. Sir James Barrie's *My Lady Nicotine* is a clever piece of sustained meiosis. Antony deliberately understates his powers when he declares :

> I am no orator, as Brutus is ;
> But, as you know me all, a plain blunt man, . . .

Often, however, a statement implying a strong affirmative is given in the form of a mild negative.

> 'Twas God's high will the victors to divide,
> And turn the event, confounding human pride :
> Some he destroy'd, some scatter'd as the dust
> (Not all were prudent, and not all were just).

POPE.

Princes and peers, attend ; while we impart
To you the thoughts of no inhuman heart.

POPE.

EUPHEMISM : The word means ' speaking well.' It means the avoidance of unpleasantly direct terms. In Pope's translation of Homer, from which we have quoted above, it is not easy to distinguish euphemisms from mere circumlocutions. To avoid the sudden abruptness of ' He's dead ! ' people prefer, ' He has passed away,' or the nobler language of John Drinkwater's announcement of the death of Abraham Lincoln, ' He is with the ages.'

Falstaff pleads

' . . . when thou art king, let not us that are squires of the night's body be called thieves of the day's beauty : let us be Diana's foresters, gentlemen of the shade, minions of the moon. . . .'

Anything, that is to say, that sounds better than ' thief.'

In *The Wealth of Nations*, Adam Smith refers to people who ' may sometimes ruin their fortunes by an excessive consumption of fermented liquors.'

Trollope apparently considered the word ' trousers ' indelicate, so in *Barchester Towers* he writes :

In truth, Mrs Proudie was all but invincible ; had she married Petruchio, it may be doubted whether that arch wife-tamer would have been able to keep her legs out of those garments which are presumed by men to be peculiarly unfitted for feminine use.

PERSONIFICATION is the endowment of an abstract idea or quality with the powers of life and movement.

The name of Cassius honours this corruption,
And chastisement doth therefore hide his head.

SHAKESPEARE.

These shall the fury Passions tear,
   The vultures of the mind,
Disdainful Anger, pallid Fear
   And Shame that skulks behind ;

Or pining Love shall waste their youth,
Or Jealousy with rankling tooth
That inly gnaws the secret heart,
And Envy wan, and faded Care,
Grim-visaged comfortless Despair,
    And Sorrow's piercing dart. ———— GRAY.

Three times they breathed and three times did they drink,
Upon agreement, of swift Severn's flood ;
Who then, affrighted with their bloody looks,
Ran fearfully among the trembling reeds,
And hid his crisp head in the hollow bank
Bloodstained with these valiant combatants.
               SHAKESPEARE : 1 *Henry IV*.

APOSTROPHE : Here the abstract idea or quality is addressed as if it were present. Sometimes an absent person is called on in the same way.

               Age, thou art shamed !
Rome, thou has lost the breed of noble bloods !

             O error soon conceived,
Thou never comest unto a happy birth
But kill'st the mother that engendered thee.

Milton ! thou shouldst be living at this hour.

RHETORICAL QUESTION : A form of emphasis that should be used sparingly. No answer is expected, for the speaker assumes that his audience is in full sympathy with him.

Do ye see nothing in our holidays ? of the which very few were made at the first, and they to set forth goodness, virtue, and honesty : but sithens, in some places, there is neither mean nor measure in making new holidays, as who should say, this one thing is serving of God, to make this law, that no man may work. But what doth the people in these holidays ? Do they give themselves to godliness, or else ungodliness ? See ye nothing, brethren ? If you see not, yet God seeth.   HUGH LATIMER.

Bad times come. He sees the wife whom he loves grow thinner and paler every day. His little ones cry for bread, and he has none to give them. Then come the professional agitators, the tempters, and tell him that there is enough

and more than enough for everybody, and that he has too
little only because landed gentlemen, fundholders, bankers,
manufacturers, railway proprietors, shopkeepers have too
much. Is it strange that the poor man should be deluded,
and should eagerly sign such a petition as this ?

LORD MACAULAY (from a speech made in 1842).

Shall the blessed sun of heaven prove a micher and eat
blackberries ? a question not to be asked.

SHAKESPEARE: 1 *Henry IV.*

CLIMAX: A sequence of thoughts expressed in increasing
importance or intensity.

Your brother and my sister no sooner met, but they
looked ; no sooner looked, but they loved ; no sooner
loved, but they sighed ; no sooner sighed, but they asked
one another the reason ; no sooner knew the reason, but
they sought the remedy : and in these degrees have they
made a pair of steps to marriage.

SHAKESPEARE : *As You Like It.*

A curse shall light upon the limbs of men ;
Domestic fury and fierce civil strife
Shall cumber all the parts of Italy ;
Blood and destruction shall be so in use,
And dreadful objects so familiar,
That mothers shall but smile when they behold
Their infants quartered with the hands of war.

SHAKESPEARE : *Julius Cæsar.*

ANTICLIMAX, or BATHOS : A descent, sometimes very
sudden, from lofty or serious style to the ridiculous. In
Mr D. B. Wyndham Lewis's *The Stuffed Owl* are some
good examples of unintentional bathos.

Where are my friends ? I am alone ;
    No playmate shares my beaker ;
Some lie beneath the churchyard stone,
    And some—before the Speaker.

Thackeray's poem *Timbuctoo* has as its dominant note,
' Africa for the Africans.' In a vision he declares :

I see her sons the hill of glory mount
And sell their sugars on their own account.

As chaos which, by heavenly doom,
Had slept in everlasting gloom,
Started with terror and surprise,
When light first flash'd upon her eyes :
So London's sons in nightcap woke,
    In bedgown woke her dames.
For shouts were heard mid fire and smoke,
And twice ten hundred voices spoke,
        " The Playhouse is in flames."
                JAMES and HORACE SMITH : *Rejected Addresses.*

PUN : This is, somewhat unkindly, called the lowest form of wit.[1]   It consists in using a word in two or more different senses, or in the use of two or more words of almost identical sound so as to produce a humorous effect. Thus, in the first example of bathos given above, there is a pun on the word *lie.*

As he was standing in the entrance hall of the Haymarket Theatre after a performance, Sir William Gilbert was mistaken for an attendant by a man whose appearance did not appeal to him.   Said the man :
    ' Call me a cab.'
    ' Certainly,' replied Gilbert ; ' you're a four-wheeler.'
    ' How dare you !   What do you mean ? '
    ' Well, you asked me to call you a cab, and I couldn't call you " hansom." '

        All you that are too fond of Wine,
            Or any other stuff,
        Take warning by the dismal fate
            Of one Lieutenant Luff.
        A sober man he might have been,
            Except in one regard,
        He did not like *soft* water,
            So he took on *drinking hard* !
                                THOMAS HOOD.

[1] In the *Journal to Stella* Swift often mentions the puns he and his friends invent.   The Bishop of Clogher was proud of his *if* puns : *e.g.,* If there was a hackney coach at Mr Pooley's door, what town in Egypt would it be ?   Why, it would be Hecatompolis : ' Hack at Tom Pooley's.'

> Your poems will endure to be well try'd
> I' th' fire like gold, and come forth purify'd ;
> Can only to eternity pretend,
> For they were never writ to any end.
>
> SAMUEL BUTLER.

TOUCHSTONE. I am here with thee and thy goats, as the most capricious poet, honest Ovid, was amongst the Goths.
SHAKESPEARE : *As You Like It.*

ALLITERATION : The use of a sequence of words beginning with the same sound.

> The splendour falls on castle walls
>   And snowy summits old in story :
> The long light shakes across the lakes,
>   And the wild cataract leaps in glory.
> Blow, bugle, blow, set the wild echoes flying,
> Blow, bugle ; answer, echoes, dying, dying, dying.
>
> TENNYSON.

Alliteration was commonly used in Old English poetry. Towards the end of the fourteenth century it was revived for a time.   The most accessible poem is William Langland's *Piers Plowman*.   The following lines are from the *Gest Hystoriale* of the Destruction of Troy (*c.* 1400) :—

> Maistur in mageste, maker of alle,
> endles and on, euer to last,
> now, god, of thi grace graunt me thi helpe
> and wysshe me with wyt this werke for to ende.

Alliteration is often used for humorous effect.

> The raging rocks,
> And shivering shocks,
> Shall break the locks
>   Of prison-gates ;
> And Phibbus' car
> Shall shine from far,
> And make and mar
>   The foolish fates.
>
> SHAKESPEARE : *A Midsummer-Night's Dream.*

ASSONANCE : The use of a sequence of words containing similar vowel sounds. It is often intermingled with alliteration to lessen the monotony of close repetition of exactly the same sound.

> Whereat the Prince full wrath, his strong right hand
> In full avengement heaved up on high,
> And stroke the Pagan with his steely brand
> So sore, that to his saddle-bow thereby
> He bowed low, and so a while did lie :
> And sure had not his massie iron mace
> Betwixt him and his hurt been happily,
> It would have cleft him to the girding place,
> Yet as it was, it did astonish him long space.
>
> SPENSER : Færie Queene, Book IV.

> By the gods,
> You shall digest the venom of your spleen,
> Though it do split you ; for from this day forth
> I'll use you for my mirth, yea, for my laughter,
> When you are waspish.
>
> SHAKESPEARE : Julius Cæsar.

> . . . shall we now
> Contaminate our fingers with base bribes,
> And sell the mighty space of our large honours
> For so much trash as may be grasped thus ?
>
> Ibid.

Notice the effect of the sequence of harsh-sounding words, the indication of Brutus' contempt.

ECHOIC VERSE (sometimes referred to as ONOMATO-PŒIA). Here there is an attempt to show a close connexion between sound and meaning.

> Now doe they rayse gastly lyghtnings, now grislye
>   reboundings
> Of ruffe raffe roaring, men's harts with terror agrysing,
> With peale meale ramping, with thwick thwack
>   sturdelye thundring.
>
> RICHARD STANYHURST :
Translation of Virgil, 1582.

Spenser has a mastery over words : notice the unpleasant sounds he brings into the following picture :—

> At last he came unto a gloomy glade,
> Cover'd with boughes and shrubs from heaven's light,
> Whereas he sitting found in secret shade
> An uncouth, salvage, and uncivile wight,
> Of griesly hew and fowle ill favour'd sight ;
> His face with smoke was tand, and eies were bleard,
> His head and beard with sout were ill bedight,
> His cole-blacke hands did seem to have been seard
> In smythes fire-spitting forge, and nayles like clawes
>   appeard.   *Færie Queene* : Book II.

Coleridge has a different aim in :

> The fair breeze blew, the white foam flew,
>   The furrow followed free :
> We were the first that ever burst
>   Into that silent sea.
>   *Rime of the Ancient Mariner.*

Thus, by the aid of alliteration and assonance, the poet
achieves the effect of making ' the sound an echo to the
sense.' What sound does Tennyson wish to convey in
these lines ?

> Thim's my noätions, Sammy, wheerby I means to stick ;
> But if thou marries a bad un, I'll leäve the land to Dick.—
> Coom oop, proputty, proputty—that's what I 'ears 'im
>   saäy—
> Proputty, proputty, proputty—canter and canter awaäy.

Emerson's poem, *May-Day*, is full of words which echo
the sense of the passage. In *Hiawatha* the names given
to birds and beasts are particularly appropriate. Goldsmith, too, names his characters with similar felicity.

IRONY : A figure of speech in which by the grace of
subtle expression an opposite meaning is conveyed from
the words actually used.

In Jane Austen's *Northanger Abbey*, Henry Tilney
parodies the tales of horror which had a vogue at the end

of the eighteenth century. At times he is delightfully
ironical :

'. . . After a very short search, you will discover a
division in the tapestry so artfully constructed as to defy
the minutest inspection, and on opening it, a door will
immediately appear, which door being only secured by
massy bars and a padlock, you will, after a few efforts,
succeed in opening and, with your lamp in your hand,
will pass through it into a small vaulted room.'

'No, indeed ; I should be too much frightened to do
any such thing.'

'What ! not when Dorothy has given you to understand
that there is a secret subterraneous communication between
your apartment and the chapel of St Anthony, scarcely two
miles off. Could you shrink from so simple an adventure? . . .'

Nobody has any neighbours in China, but in England if
a woman aged ninety or thereabouts goes into hospital and
comes out a corpse she is lucky if she gets into her grave
without an inquest.

W. J. TURNER : *Blow for Balloons.*

DRAMATIC IRONY : This is irony of situation.   Thomas
Hardy makes effective use of it in *Tess of the D'Urbervilles*,
especially where Tess thinks that Angel Clare has read
her confession.   She finds later, to her sorrow, that when
she pushed it under his door she had inadvertently thrust
it out of sight under the carpet.

In *Julius Cæsar* Shakespeare, for dramatic ironical
effect, attributes deafness to Cæsar.

> I rather tell thee what is to be fear'd
> Than what I fear, for always I am Cæsar.
> Come on my right hand, for this ear is deaf,
> And tell me truly what thou think'st of him.

Here the might and the very human weakness of a great
man are shown in immediate sequence.

In his great speech in the Forum Antony passes a shrewd
comment on Brutus' vain attempt to give reasons to the
Roman populace.   The effect of Brutus' words had long

worn off when Antony, now bold enough to use the word
' honourable ' sneeringly, insinuatingly suggests

> They that have done this deed are honourable :
> What private griefs [1] they have, alas ! I know not,
> That made them do it ; they are wise and honourable,
> And will, no doubt, with reasons answer you.[2]

Cassius, whose love for Brutus makes him on several
occasions give way to the latter's opinion and always
disastrously, brings about his own death as the result of
a further tragic mistake.

SARCASM : This is a bitingly obvious discrepancy
between the words used and the meaning intended.

> Justice is open to all, like the Ritz Hotel.

> The atrocious crime of being a young man, which the
> honourable gentleman has with such spirit and decency
> charged upon me, I shall neither attempt to palliate nor
> deny ; but content myself with wishing that I may be one
> of those whose follies may cease with their youth. . . .
> WILLIAM PITT : Speeches.

> Yes ! you will find people ready enough to do the
> Samaritan, without the oil and twopence.

In *She Stoops to Conquer*, young Marlow, in spite of
having been ordered to leave the house by Mr Hardcastle,
is determined to stay. Stung by the latter's subsequent
sarcasm, the young man soon changes his mind.

> HARDCASTLE. . . . Pray, sir (*bantering*), as you take the
> house, what think you of taking the rest of the furniture ?
> There's a pair of silver candlesticks, and there's a fire-screen,
> and here's a pair of brazen-nosed bellows, perhaps you
> may take a fancy to them ?
> MARLOW. Bring me your bill, sir, bring me your bill,
> and let's make no more words about it.

---

[1] *griefs* means grievances.
[2] By this, Antony knows that he has wrought the mob to such a
pitch that they will listen to no reasons.

INNUENDO : Conveying a subtle hint. The word suggests conveying a meaning by nodding. If used sparingly it is an effective device as the listener or reader is caught unawares.

In *Julius Cæsar* when the citizens pour forth their torrent of questions on Cinna the Poet, he replies, ' . . . Then, to answer every man directly and briefly, wisely and truly ; wisely I say, I am a bachelor.'

In Swift's *Gulliver's Travels* where, on the island of Laputa, he acquires the power of calling up spirits from the other world, he is assured that ' they would certainly tell the truth, for lying was a talent of no use in the lower world.'
A few lines later, having evoked the shade of Alexander the Great, Gulliver has a conversation with the monarch in which ' He assured me upon his honour that he was not poisoned, but died of a bad fever by excessive drinking.'

ACRES (who contemplates fighting a duel). . . . What, shall I disgrace my ancestors ?—Think of that, David—think what it would be to disgrace my ancestors !
DAVID. Under favour, the surest way of not disgracing them, is to keep as long as you can out of their company.
SHERIDAN : *The Rivals.*

Innuendo is the pin-prick thrust, irony the rapier-like stroke, and sarcasm the downright bludgeon-blow.

Exercise

Name and explain the figures of speech and stylistic devices in the following :—

1. POLONIUS. I did enact Julius Cæsar : I was killed i' the Capitol ; Brutus killed me.
    HAMLET. It was a brute part of him to kill so capital a calf there.

2. In losing three wickets for eight runs the M.C.C. did not start too well.

3. Even a little spark of native merit can be watered in the
   fire of effort till it grows into a mighty temple.
   STEPHEN LEACOCK : *Humour*.

4. Scholars tell us that Aristophanes was probably the
   wittiest man that ever lived : so witty that it takes
   half a page of notes to explain one of his jokes.
   Ibid.

5.
   > The moan of doves in immemorial elms,
   > And murmuring of innumerable bees.
   TENNYSON : *The Princess*.

6.
   > All my engagements I will construe to thee,
   > All the charactery of my sad brows.
   SHAKESPEARE : *Julius Cæsar*, II, i, 307-8.

7.
   > . . . danger knows full well
   > That Cæsar is more dangerous than he.
   Ibid., II, ii, 44-5.

8.
   > Within my tent his bones to-night shall lie,
   > Most like a soldier, order'd honourably.
   > So call the field to rest ; and let's away,
   > To part the glories of this happy day.
   Ibid. (concluding lines).

9. Reflection is the alchemy which turns knowledge into
   wisdom. JANE PORTER : *Thaddeus of Warsaw*.

10. His book is like a large laughing meadow in early June,
    all diapered with flowers, and sweet with the songs
    of birds, some a mere note or two of merry music,
    some as prolonged and varied, though never so
    passionate, as the complaint of the nightingale.
    ANDREW LANG : *History of English Literature*.
    (Lang is referring to Herrick.)

11. The Government could not make up their minds, nor
    get the Prime Minister to make up his mind. They
    were decided only to be undecided, resolved to be
    irresolute, adamant for drift, solid for fluidity, all-
    powerful but impotent.
    (From a recent speech by
THE RT. HON. MR WINSTON CHURCHILL.)

CHAPTER VIII

INTERPRETATION AND THE TESTING OF COMPREHENSION

IN this chapter the passages have been chosen because they require careful reading to understand their meaning. This is not because of their dullness or obscurity, but because a study of a writer's grappling with his subject is important in helping you to see the value of cohesion and development.

To make progress in literature you must cultivate the patience that seeks sympathetic contact with an author. Some books are lightly read and are as lightly forgotten. They serve to pass away an evening. From other books you gain not only a knowledge of facts but the power to develop them. To do this you have to go out to meet the author, that is, you have to make an effort at comprehension. You have first to interpret his meaning.

Hints

1. You must take notice what use the writer makes of his facts. Be careful not to confuse facts with opinions, especially where both are open to dispute.

2. A theme is built up from a series of statements : examine them to find if there is a logical connexion. Be alert for digressions or for abrupt changes of subject.

3. Remember it is most valuable to write down, as a title to the passage, its central topic. This will help you to preserve a sense of proportion.

4. Give due consideration to any figures of speech that may be introduced, for in all probability they represent an endeavour to drive home a main point.

5. If there is more than one speaker, note who it is that keeps up the main flow of thought.

6. Only after you have read the passage through and have given it a suitable title should you make notes of subsidiary points.

Example

Read the following passage carefully, and then answer the questions on it below.[1]

CYRIL. ' My dear Vivian, don't coop yourself up all day in the library. It is a perfectly lovely afternoon. Let us go and lie on the grass and smoke cigarettes and enjoy Nature.'

VIVIAN. ' Enjoy Nature ! I am glad to say that I have entirely lost that faculty. People tell us that Art makes us love Nature more than we loved her before ; that it reveals her secrets to us. My own experience is that the more we study Art, the less we care for Nature. What Art reveals to us is Nature's lack of design, her curious crudities, her extraordinary monotony, her absolutely unfinished condition. When I look at a landscape I cannot help seeing all its defects. It is fortunate for us, however, that Nature is so imperfect, as otherwise we should have no art at all. Art is our spirited protest, our gallant attempt to teach Nature her proper place.'

CYRIL. ' Well, you need not look at the landscape. You can lie on the grass and smoke and talk.'

VIVIAN. ' But Nature is so uncomfortable. Grass is hard and lumpy and damp, and full of dreadful black insects. Why, even the poorest workman could make you a more comfortable seat than the whole of Nature can. I don't complain. If Nature had been comfortable, mankind would never have invented architecture, and I prefer houses to the open air. In a house . . . everything is subordinated to us,

---

[1] This question was set by the Joint Matriculation Board. The other two parts of it were :—

(b) Turn that part of Vivian's second speech which begins ' But Nature ' and ends ' blooms in the ditch ' into reported speech (e.g., ' Vivian said that . . .').

(c) Divide the sentence in italics into main and dependent clauses, stating the function of each one of the latter.

fashioned for our use and our pleasure . . . Nature is so
indifferent, so unappreciative. *Whenever I am walking in the
park here, I always feel that I am no more to her than the
cattle that browse on the slope, or the burdock that blooms in
the ditch.* Nothing is more evident than that Nature hates
Mind. Thinking is the most unhealthy thing in the world,
and people die of it just as they die of any other disease.
Fortunately, in England at any rate, thought is not catching.
Our splendid physique as a people is entirely due to our
national stupidity. I only hope we shall be able to keep
this great historic bulwark of our happiness for many years
to come ; but I am afraid that we are beginning to be over-
educated.'   OSCAR WILDE.

(*a*) Trace carefully and as far as possible in your own
words the course of this discussion, arranging
your statement of it to show clearly how the last
point in the argument is reached from the first.
(*Use about* 150 *words.*)

Main Steps in the Discussion—Notes

—cannot enjoy Nature
—more we study Art the less we care for Nature
—Art shows Nature's monotony and her crudities
—if Nature were not so imperfect we should have no Art . . .
   (Art is a corrective of Nature)
—Art attempts to teach Nature her place
      (*Nature* uncomfortable and unappreciative)
      (*Art* . . . buildings and furniture made for comfort)
—Nature hates mind (*i.e.,* corrective influence of Art)
—when we think or are reflective Nature punishes us—
   we die of thinking

CHANGE TO . . . the particular case from a general, abstract
      argument
   —people who do not think (like ourselves, the English)
      have a fine physique . . . we owe this to our national
      stupidity
   —gloomy outlook—we are beginning to be over-educated
      —so that we shall soon lose some of our national
      stupidity—and happiness and splendid physique

Notice that these are mere jottings, probably nothing more than underlinings and marginal notes on the question paper. There is, as yet, little attempt to write in one's own words.

From the above notes the following connected summary emerges :—

1. Nature's imperfections shown up by Art.
2. Among these imperfections is her hatred of mind.
3. She punishes those who think (Diseases of thought).
4. We English owe our immunity from such punishment to our national stupidity, which is thus the safe-guard of our fine physique.
5. Future outlook is less bright.   We are beginning to be over-educated.

Connected Summary

Cyril asked Vivian to go out into the garden and enjoy Nature, but Vivian's answer was that he had lost the power of enjoying Nature.   He contradicted the belief that Art drew mankind nearer to Nature, and said that Art made us see Nature's imperfections.   These imperfections were the things which Art was attacking.

Cyril pointed out that Vivian need only sit on the grass and talk, to which the latter replied, continuing his argument about Nature's imperfections, that Nature's resting-places were inferior to those made by an unskilled labourer, and that if Nature had been hospitable there would have been no civilization.   In civilized dwellings everything was our servant, but Nature took no notice of us, which proved that she hated mind.   Thinking, like any other disease, could kill, but an Englishman's stupidity had so far kept him strong and healthy.   However, he concluded that he was afraid we were becoming over-educated.

A Socratic (or Pseudo-Socratic) Inquiry

PEDAGOGUE. What is a luxury ?

CARTER MAJOR. Something that costs a great deal of money.

PED. If a millionaire buys a car for £150, that would be a luxury ?

CARTER. Yes, if he had a car already.

PED. So a luxury is something we do not need ?

CARTER. Yes.

PED. Are you thirsty ?

CARTER. No, thank you, sir.

PED. So that, if I were to give you a glass of water, it would be a luxury ?

CARTER. No, sir, but I should probably drink it and think no more about it.

PED. So that pleasure has to be considered ?

CARTER. I suppose so.

PED. Would you like a piece of bread ?

CARTER. No, thank you. I have a piece of chocolate in my pocket.

PED. You prefer the chocolate ? It is not a necessity for you, is it ?

CARTER. No, you see, sir, I had a good lunch.

PED. Here is a rosy apple.

CARTER. Thank you. (*Begins to munch it.*)

PED. I thought you were not hungry ?

CARTER. Oh, but I love apples.

PED. Would you consider an apple a luxury ?

CARTER. I suppose so : I am not bound to eat it, but think apples are always welcome.

PED. So that a luxury is something desirable ?

CARTER. Yes, that's it.

PED. Do you think a millionaire *desires* a car costing £150 ?

CARTER. He would turn up his nose at it.

PED. Why, I wonder ?

CARTER. It would seem such a paltry affair compared with his magnificent Rolls Royce.

PED. Is his Rolls Royce a luxury ?

CARTER. No, because he can afford to buy it.

PED. Would you like a Rolls Royce ?

CARTER. Is that a serious offer ?

PED. Ahem . . . no. It is purely hypothetical.

CARTER. I'm sorry about that, sir, but need you have doubted my answer ? Such a car is a luxury beyond my wildest dreams.

PED. Is a luxury only a thing that you cannot afford to buy ?

CARTER. Oh, by no means. This flower in my button-hole

cost me sixpence, but I wear it to celebrate Founder's Day. I paid twenty-five shillings for my fountain-pen. I have three cricket bats, and——

PED. Stop. I never heard of such reckless extravagance ! Surely two of the bats are superfluous ?

CARTER. Perhaps so : I could manage with only one. But I prefer a light bat when the wicket is dry and fast, for the ball comes off quickly, and a heavy bat is preferable when the outfield is sodden and I want to put more power into my strokes. The third bat is quite new ; I am keeping it for the wood to become thoroughly seasoned. It is really necessary for me to have three bats.

PED. I feel moved by the pathos of your plea ! I'm quite sorry for the poor fellows who struggle through life with only one bat.

CARTER (*entering into the spirit of this banter*). Or for the poor fellows who shape out a bat from a sugar-box.

PED. Well, from our talk, perhaps you can say what a luxury is ?

CARTER. Oh, sir——

Study the above dialogue carefully, and write out a definition of luxury. When you have finished, look the word up in *The Shorter Oxford English Dictionary*. What have you been able to add ?

Why is it difficult to say whether any specified *thing* is a luxury or not ?

Are there any places where the above dialogue is contradictory ? If so, how are these contradictions reconciled ?

Suggest reasons why people eat chocolates or munch apples when they are not hungry.

Try to compose similar dialogues to arrive at satisfactory definitions of *sport, tyranny, beauty, morality, fair-play, the prime of life, sociability*. In most instances the definition will have to be fairly comprehensive. To define *sociability* as *displaying* a friendly spirit is to ignore occasions when policy would render such a disposition unwise.

If you find it difficult to begin your dialogue, look up the dictionary definitions of the words. For such words as those italicized in the list above, dictionary definitions, limited by considerations of space, must necessarily be inadequate. You can imagine a book three times the size of this still leaving something unsaid on these subjects.

A.

The hardheartedness of fathers is a fine theme for romance writers, a sure and moving topic ; but is there not something untender, to say no more of it, in the hurry which a beloved child is sometimes in to tear herself from the paternal stock, and commit herself to strange graftings ? The case is heightened where the lady, as in the present instance, happens to be an only child. I do not understand these matters experimentally, but I can make a shrewd guess at the wounded pride of a parent upon these occasions. It is no new observation, I believe, that a lover in most cases has no rival so much to be feared as the father. Certainly there is jealousy in unparallel subjects, which is little less heart-rending than the passion which we more strictly christen by that name. Mothers' scruples are more easily got over ; for this reason, I suppose, that the protection transferred to a husband is less a derogation and a loss to their authority than to the paternal. Mothers, besides, have a trembling foresight which paints the inconveniences (impossible to be conceived in the same degree by the other parent) of a life of forlorn celibacy, which the refusal of a tolerable match may entail upon their child. Mothers' instinct is a surer guide here, than the cold reasonings of a father on such a topic. To this instinct may be imputed, and by it alone may be excused, the unbeseeming artifices, by which some wives push on the matrimonial projects of their daughters, which the husband, however approving, shall entertain with comparative indifference. A little shamelessness on this head is pardonable. With this explanation, forwardness becomes a grace, and maternal importunity receives the name of a virtue. CHARLES LAMB, *The Wedding*.

1. Is this argument conducted on cold, matter-of-fact lines, or does Lamb anywhere introduce a note of pathos ?

2. What is it that wounds a father's pride, and why is a mother less affected by her daughter's marriage ?

3. In your own words trace the course of the argument that leads up to the last sentence.

4. Express in your own words the main points in the above passage.

5. What is the difference between instinct and reason ? Why is it that in this instance the former is the surer guide ?

6. In what ways does imagination differ from instinct ?

7. Write a clear, connected summary of the passage; if possible, do not exceed 150 words.

B.

More than I have said, loving countrymen,
The leisure and enforcement of the time
Forbids to dwell upon : yet remember this,
God and our good cause fight upon our side ;
The prayers of holy saints and wronged souls,
Like high-rear'd bulwarks, stand before our faces.
Richard except, those whom we fight against
Had rather have us win than him they follow :
For what is he they follow ? truly, gentlemen,
A bloody tyrant and a homicide ;
One rais'd in blood, and one in blood establish'd ;
One that hath made means to come by what he hath,
And slaughter'd those that were the means to help him ;
A base foul stone, made precious by the foil
Of England's chair, where he is falsely set ;
One that hath ever been God's enemy.
Then, if you fight against God's enemy,
God will in justice ward you as his soldiers ;
If you do sweat to put a tyrant down,
You sleep in peace, the tyrant being slain ;
If you do fight against your country's foes,
Your country's fat shall pay your pains the hire ;
If you do fight in safeguard of your wives,
Your wives shall welcome home the conquerors ;
If you do free your children from the sword,
Your children's children quits it in your age.
Then, in the name of God and all these rights,
Advance your standards, draw your willing swords !
For me, the ransom of my bold attempt
Shall be this cold corpse on the earth's cold face ;

But, if I thrive, the gain of my attempt
The least of you shall share his part thereof.
Sound drums and trumpets boldly and cheerfully ;
God and Saint George !   Richmond and victory !

WILLIAM SHAKESPEARE : King Richard
the Third, Act V, Sc. iii.

1. What is the spirit of this passage ?

2. To which is the chief appeal made, men's reasons or their feelings ?   Quote lines in support of your answer.

3. Summarize the details of this appeal.   Which do you consider the most effective ?

4. This speech is not uttered on the spur of the moment but shows signs of having been carefully prepared. What arguments can you bring in support of or against this opinion ?

5. From the passage quote two metaphors, one transferred epithet, and one instance of effective repetition.   What contribution do these figures of speech make to the the poetic quality of the passage ?

C.

THE MONOPOLY OF WONDER

Few truths receive such publicity as the truth that the world is becoming ever smaller.   Mechanically minded men boast of it and fiction writers bemoan it, but all agree that the days of the traveller's tale are done.   There is now installed in the Savoy Hotel a world directory with millions of names and numbers ; it is already possible to ring up a respectable proportion of the human race, and it will not be long before any man of any colour and any country can be fetched to the other end of the telephone.   The modern Mandeville talks with a miserable lack of imaginative embellishment, knowing that at any moment one of his audience may slip from the room and check his statements.   Even the wild beasts of the heart of Africa enjoy no privacy, are photographed close up, and are watched at their toilet from the air.   And one of the last props of the sense of mystery, the North Pole, has been withdrawn by Dr Stefansson.   The North Pole, it seems, is quite an ordinary place, though on the cold side. It is off the main lines of traffic and there is not much to do there. But it does not deserve its reputation in saga and metaphor as a place to which brave men may penetrate for a few precarious moments. It is not even situated where it ought to be, and its exposure seems richly deserved, for it has imposed upon men for too long.

To travel, to go on sea and ' behold the world so wide ' is becoming less and less a satisfying ideal for the young athirst for incredible things. Foreign countries, from Chinese customs to Bantu ceremonies, are fed into the modern home in story and picture and broadcast so that the ordinary child soon knows pretty clearly what he would see if he took a far journey. Everywhere the travel agencies go before him to make sure that travel shall be without incident. The thinker, the student, the comparer of peoples finds his occupation vastly easier, and wonder of the reflective kind has little to complain of in the world as it is being organized as a side-show to-day. But the more primitive sense of wonder, the pure gape, is no longer gratified. A man cannot grow up like Stevenson's Will of the Mill, with the strange wide world before him, an unopened book. Too many people have been interested, either from altruism or for gain, in bringing to his village enough knowledge to damp the first sense of amazement, and to make sure that wherever he goes he will drop his chin inches less than if they had left him to himself.

From Follow My Leader
(Commentaries from The Times).

1. What is the theme of the first paragraph ? What is the main topic of the second ? What is the connexion between the two ?

2. Summarize this passage in about 150 words, giving due prominence to the chief topics and the link between them.

3. Where does this leader writer make effective use of humour ?

4. Quote some metaphors he uses.

5. What, from this passage, do you learn of the modern child ?

6. What instances of ironical humour can you detect ?

7. What do you understand is meant by ' respectable,' ' imaginative embellishment,' ' precarious,' ' a side-show,' ' altruism ' ?

8. Trace the steps in this argument and comment upon the effectiveness of the illustrations used.

D.

Blessed is he who has found his Work ; let him ask no other blessedness. He has a work, a life-purpose ; he has found it and will follow it ! How as a free-flowing channel, dug and torn by noble force through the sour mud-swamp of one's existence, like an ever-deepening river there it runs and flows ;—draining off the sour festering water gradually from the root of the remotest grass-blade ; making, instead of pestilential swamp, a green fruitful meadow with its clear-flowing stream. How blessed for the meadow itself. Let the stream and *its* value be great or small ! Labour is Life : from the inmost heart of the worker rises his God-given force, the sacred celestial Life-essence breathed into him by Almighty God ; from his inmost heart awakens to all nobleness,—to all knowledge, ' self-knowledge ' and much else, so soon as work fitly begins. Knowledge ? The knowledge that will hold good in working, cleave thou to that ; for Nature herself accredits that, says Yea to that. Properly thou hast no other knowledge but what thou hast got by working : the rest is yet all a hypothesis of knowledge ; a thing to be argued of in schools, a thing floating in the clouds, in endless logic vortices, till we try it and fix it. ' Doubt, of whatever kind, can be ended by action alone.'   THOMAS CARLYLE : *Past and Present.*

1. What is the attitude of the writer towards his subject ?

2. What connexion does Carlyle seek to establish between work and happiness, knowledge and self-knowledge ?

3. Did you find the passage easy or difficult to follow ? Give reasons for your answer.

4. Of what is Carlyle thinking when he speaks of ' the sour mud-swamp of one's existence,' ' the sour festering water,' and ' a pestilential swamp ' ?

5. Discuss the effectiveness of Carlyle's sustained simile.

6. Summarize this passage in about 100 words, making as clear as possible the connexion between the various ideas.

7. ' The shorter the sentence the easier it is to grasp the meaning.'

' Sentences should be varied. Inversions and the casting of sentences into imperative or interrogative forms will relieve monotony.'

Discuss these statement in the light of Carlyle's practice. Does he tend to become monotonous ? Give reasons and quotations in support of your answer.

E.

Books are for various purposes—tracts to teach, almanacs to sell, poetry to make pastry, but this is the rarest sort of book, a book to *read*. As Dr Johnson said, ' Sir, a good book is one you can hold in your hand, and take to the fire.' Now there are extremely few books which can, with any propriety, be so treated. When a great author, as Grote or Gibbon, has devoted a whole life of horrid industry to the composition of a large history, one feels one ought not to touch it with a mere hand—it is not respectful. The idea of slavery hovers over the ' Decline and Fall.' Fancy a stiffly dressed gentleman in a stiff chair, slowly writing that stiff compilation in a stiff hand, it is enough to stiffen you for life. Or is poetry readable ? Of course it is rememberable ; when you have it in the mind, it clings ; if by heart, it haunts. Imagery comes from it ; songs which lull the ear, heroines that waste the time. But this *Biographia* [1] is actually read ; a man is glad to take it up, and slow to lay it down ; it is a book which is truly valuable, for it is truly pleasing ; and which a man who has once had it in his library would miss from his shelves, not only in the common way, by a physical vacuum, but by a mental deprivation. This strange quality it owes to a peculiarity of style. Many people give many theories of literary composition, and Dr Blair, whom we will read, is sometimes said to have exhausted the subject, but, unless he has proved the contrary,

---

[1] Hartley Coleridge's *Lives of the Northern Worthies.*

we believe that the knack in style is to write like a human being. Some think they must be wise, some elaborate, some concise ; Tacitus wrote like a pair of stays ; some startle, as Thomas Carlyle, or a comet, inscribing with his tail. But legibility is given to those who neglect these notions, and are willing to be themselves, to write their own thoughts in their own words, in the simplest words, in the words wherein they were thought.

WALTER BAGEHOT : *Hartley Coleridge.*

1. Which is the key-sentence in this extract ?

2. Express in your own words what the author means by ' a book to *read.*'

3. Make notes showing the construction and development of this paragraph.

4. From your notes, write a précis of the paragraph in about 100 words.

5. Notice Bagehot's use of repetition. Quote examples where he employs it effectively, and where unnecessarily.

6. How far do you consider Bagehot's similes appropriate ? Express their meaning in your own words.

7. What is meant by the following words and phrases as used in this extract :—' propriety,' ' *horrid* industry,' ' a stiff compilation,' ' a mental deprivation ' ?

8. What is Bagehot's opinion of (*a*) poetry, (*b*) almanacs, *as far as you can judge from this passage* ?

F.

It has been observed in all ages, that the advantages of nature or of fortune have contributed very little to the promotion of happiness ; and that those whom the splendour of rank, or the extent of their capacity, have placed upon the summits of human life, have not often given any just occasion to envy in those who look up to them from a lower station : whether it be that apparent superiority incites great designs, and great designs are naturally liable to fatal miscarriages ; or that the general lot of mankind is misery, and the misfortunes of those whose eminence drew upon them an universal attention, have been more carefully recorded, because they were more generally observed, and have in reality been only more conspicuous than those of others, not more frequent, or more severe.

That affluence and power, advantages extrinsic and adventitious, and therefore easily separable from those by whom they are possessed, should very often flatter the mind with expectations of felicity which they cannot give, raises no astonishment ; but it seems rational to hope that intellectual greatness should produce better effects : that minds qualified for great attainments should first endeavour their own benefit ; and that they who are most able to teach others the way to happiness, should with most certainty follow it themselves.

But this expectation, however plausible, has been very frequently disappointed. The heroes of literary as well as civil history have been very often no less remarkable for what they have achieved ; and volumes have been written only to enumerate the miseries of the learned, and relate their unhappy lives and untimely deaths.

Dr Johnson : Life of Savage.

1. What is the chief point in each of these three paragraphs ?

2. Trace the course of Dr Johnson's observations in the first two paragraphs, and show how he diverges in the third.

3. Express more simply ' those whom the splendour of rank, or the extent of their capacity, have placed upon the summits of human life.'

4. Of what kinds of things is Dr Johnson thinking when he refers to extrinsic and adventitious advantages ?

5. This extract is the first three paragraphs of the *Life of Savage*. Assuming Dr Johnson's remarks to be relevant, what can you gather from them about Savage's life ?

6. In what ways does Dr Johnson seek to show that happiness is independent of advantages both of birth and of intellectual attainments ? Trace carefully his statements.

7. What is the writer's attitude towards his subject ? How far has he successfully made out a case for inducing us to believe that 'the general lot of mankind is misery ' ?

G.

. . . I have no opinion of my own wisdom, and little of anybody's else ; but I have an odd system, that what is called *chance* is the instrument of Providence and the secret agent that counteracts what men call wisdom, and preserves order and regularity, and continuation in the whole ; for you must know, madam, that I firmly believe, notwithstanding all our complaints, that almost every person upon earth tastes upon the totality more happiness than misery ; and therefore, if we could correct the world to our fancies, and with the best intentions imaginable, probably we should only produce more misery and confusion. This totally contradicts what I said before, that sensibility or insensibility determines the complexion of our lives ; and yet if the former casts a predominating shade of sadness over the general tenor of our feelings, still that gloom is illumined with delicious flashes. It enjoys the comforts of the compassion it bestows and of the misfortune it relieves ; and the largest dose of the apathy of insensibility can never give any notion of the transport that thrills through the nerves of benevolence when it consoles the anguish of another ; but I am too much a sceptic to pretend to make or reconcile a system and its contradictions. *No* man was ever yet so great as to build that system in which other men could not discover flaws. All our reasoning, therefore, is very imperfect, and this is *my* reason for being so seldom serious and for never disputing. I look upon human reason as I do on the parts of a promising child,—it surprises, may improve or stop short, but is not come to maturity. . . .

HORACE WALPOLE : *Letter to the Countess
of Ossory*, 19th January, 1777.

1. For what reasons does Walpole incline to an optimistic view of life ?

2. What comforts may be enjoyed by melancholy people ?

3. What connexion is there between the first and the last sentences quoted ?

4. Of what was Walpole thinking when he used the words ' *sensibility* ' and ' *complexion* of our lives.'

5. What is Walpole's philosophy of life as far as it is revealed in the above passage ? Express your answer in about 70 words.

H.

OF PREACHING

The excess which is in the defect of Preaching has made the pulpit slighted ; I mean the much bad oratory we find it guilty of. 'Tis a wonder to me how men can preach so little, and so long : so long a time, and so little matter ; as if they thought to please by the inculcation of their vain Tautologies. I see no reason that so high a Princess as Divinity is should be presented to the people in the sordid rags of the tongue ; nor that he which speaks from the *Father of Languages* should deliver his embassage in an ill one. A man can never speak too well while he speaks not too obscure. Long and distended clauses are both tedious to the ear and difficult for their retaining. A Sentence well couched takes both the sense and the understanding. I love not those Cart-rope speeches that are longer than the memory of man can fathom. I see not but that *Divinity*, put into apt significants, might ravish as well as poetry. The weighty lines men find upon the Stage, I am persuaded, have been the lures to draw away the Pulpit's followers. We complain of drowsiness at a Sermon ; when a Play of a doubled length leads us on still with alacrity. But the fault is not all in ourselves. If we saw *Divinity* acted, the gesture and variety would as much invigilate. But it is too high to be personated by Humanity. . . .

A good orator should pierce the ear, allure the eye, and invade the mind of his hearer. And this is Seneca's opinion : fit words are better than fine ones : I like not those that are judiciously made ; but such as be expressively significant, that lead the mind to something beside the naked term. And he that speaks thus must not look to speak thus every day. A *kembed* Oration will cost both sweat and the rubbing of the brain. And *kembed* I wish it, not *frizzled* nor *curled*.

OWEN FELLTHAM : *Resolves*.

1. The book from which this extract is taken was first published in 1623. In view of the context, what is the significance of this date ?

2. What is the subject-matter of the first paragraph and what advice is given about it in the second ?

3. What contrasts does the writer seek to draw ?

4. What, according to Felltham, are the characteristics of bad oratory ?

5. This extract contains a number of metaphors. Select three and comment on their effectiveness.

6. By what means does a successful orator achieve success ?

7. What does the writer mean by a *kembed* oration as distinct from one that is *frizzled* or *curled* ?

8. Explain what is meant by the following words and phrases as used in this context :—' vain Tautologies,' ' the Father of languages,' ' embassage,' ' cart-rope speeches,' ' rubbing of the brain ' ?

9. Express in your own words :—' sordid rags of the tongue ' ; ' a sentence well couched takes both the sense and the understanding ' ; ' apt significants ' ; ' the gesture and variety would . . . much invigilate ' ; ' Divinity . . . is too high to be personated by Humanity ' ; ' words . . . that lead the mind to something beside the naked term.'

10. Write a connected summary of this passage in idiomatic modern English. Do not exceed 150 words. Be careful to show how the main topics are connected and developed.

CHAPTER IX

STYLE

> For my part, I have always thought an easy style more eligible than a pompous diction, lifted up by metaphor, amplified by epithet, and dignified by too frequent insertions of the Latin idiom.
>
> ARTHUR MURPHY (*a friend of* Dr Johnson).

IT is impossible to teach originality, but you can be trained to observe and appreciate. In students' written work the chief fault is vagueness. More perfect observation of sentence and paragraph construction will go far to overcome incoherence of expression.

(1) *Periodic and Loose Sentences*

The shaping even of a single sentence needs thought and care. In the earlier part of this book clarity of thought and conciseness of expression were emphasized : together they can give pleasure to a reader, an important end in itself. You can see how quite a good sentence can be spoilt by the addition of weak tags of after-thought :—

> A library at which the readers pay twopence or threepence a book, or even where they can obtain books free, puts into the hands of people books which they would be unable to buy for themselves unless, of course, they were very rich indeed.

How unnecessary is the last qualifying remark. All that is important has already been said. Such a sentence is like unravelling tangled wool ; you feel that there is no end to it. You speak of its construction as *loose.*

Periodic sentences, where the main fact is suspended

until the end, make for sustained interest and terseness of expression.

A man who owes his position to favour and not to merit may easily earn unequivocal hatred.

(a) PERIODIC	(a) kept in suspense to the end.	
(b) LOOSE	(b) additional ideas.	

It must not be inferred that all periodic sentences are good ones and that, because they happen to be loose, all loose sentences are necessarily bad. Although it is *loose* in construction, there is much to admire in Charles Lamb's observation :—

A child exists not for the very poor as any object of dalliance ; it is only another mouth to be fed, a pair of little hands to be betimes inured to labour.

Popular Fallacies.

Notice that Lamb's afterthoughts enrich and amplify his central idea ; they are not weak tags. He has much to tell us. It is easy to distinguish between the over-flowings of an exuberant intellect and feeble attempts to pad out a few ideas.

LOOSE

It is a modern invention to regard the ocean as a con-fidant, a Laertes that can neither avoid his Hamlets nor bid them hold their peace.

PERIODIC

The ocean as confidant, a Laertes that can neither avoid his Hamlets nor bid them hold their peace, is a modern invention.

W. E. HENLEY :
Views and Reviews.

For Carthage is destroyed, indeed, and forsaken of the sea, yet that one hour of summer is to be unforgotten while man has memory of the story of his past.

ANDREW LANG :
Adventures Among Books.

For, although that one hour of summer is to be unfor-gotten while man has memory of the story of his past, Carthage, forsaken of the sea, is destroyed indeed.

It cannot be claimed that the periodic form of the above sentences is immeasurably preferable to the loose form. Indeed, the forcing of the second sentence into the periodic form has marred the author's meaning.

Often too, in a periodic sentence, the piling up of phrase upon phrase is wearisome to a reader anxious to reach the significant concluding words.

My friend's unfamiliarity with the social arts, his dislike of publicity and his shrinking from the very notion of popularity made him, as if he were as rigid as an obelisk yet as complex as the pattern traced upon it, appear cold and hard.

Here, before you arrive at the main thought, you have to consider five different, though closely related ideas : the significance of his being compared to an obelisk is lost.

A succession of subordinate thoughts conforms better to a loose construction.

My friend's unfamiliarity with the social arts, his dislike of publicity and his shrinking from the very notion of popularity made him appear cold and hard, as if he were as rigid as an obelisk yet as complex as the pattern traced upon it.

Exercise

State whether the sentence is periodic or loose, and, if necessary, recast it, discarding any words you deem superfluous.

1. What the country had lost in its great naval hero—the greatest of our own, and of all former times, was scarcely taken into the account of grief.
   ROBERT SOUTHEY : *Life of Nelson.*

2. The comic scenes in Massinger not only do not harmonize with the tragic, not only interrupt the feeling, but degrade the characters that are to form any part in the action of the piece, so as to render them unfit for any tragic interest.   S. T. COLERIDGE : *Lectures.*

3. If I have not read a book before, it is, to all intents and purposes, new to me, whether it was printed yesterday or three hundred years ago.
   WILLIAM HAZLITT : *On Reading New Books.*

4. Hero was in this manner accused, in this very manner refused, and, upon the grief of this, suddenly died.

WILLIAM SHAKESPEARE : *Much Ado About Nothing.*

5. Football is nothyng but beastely fury and extreme violence, whereof procedeth hurte, and consequently rancour and malice do remayne with thym that be wounded, wherfore it is to be put in perpetuall silence.

SIR THOMAS ELYOT : *The Governour* (1531).

Which of the *loose* sentences above are improved by being recast as periodic sentences ? Why is it that in any page of English prose loose sentences predominate ?

(2) *Emphasis*

Hitherto you will have found that simplicity in writing has been insisted on. Nothing is worse than inflating trivial thoughts in the hope that this will pass for good style. If this is your failing, you must practise restraint and deliberate simplicity. This does not mean childish, namby-pamby stuff ; it means clarity and directness.

Swift's *Journal to Stella* shows that interest can be kept although the style is without adornment.

. . . I am just this minute going to swim. I take Patrick down with me to hold my nightgown, shirt, and slippers and borrow a napkin of my landlady for a cap. So farewell till I come up ; but there's no danger, don't be frightened.— I have been swimming this half-hour and more ; and when I was coming out I dived, to make my head and all through wet, like a cold bath ; but as I dived the napkin fell off and is lost, and I have that to pay for. O faith, the great stones were so sharp, I could hardly set my feet on them as I came out. It was pure and warm. I got to bed, and will now go sleep.

Simplicity, therefore, does not mean monotony. Judicious *emphasis*, an eye for symmetry or *balance*, and an ear for the subtleties of prose *rhythm* will give grace and power to your style.

Study this passage from A. W. Kinglake's *Eothen*. Notice that although he uses simple words there is a richness of expression and certainly no dullness or monotony.

> Wild as that, the nighest woodland of a deserted home in England, but without its sweet sadness, is the sumptuous garden of Damascus. Forest trees, tall and stately enough, if you could see their lofty crests, yet lead a tussling life of it below, with their branches struggling against strong numbers of bushes and wilful shrubs. The shade upon the earth is black as night. High, high above your head, and on every side all down to the ground, the thicket is hemmed in, and choked up by the interlacing boughs that droop with the weight of roses, and load the slow air with their damask breath. There are no other flowers. Here and there, there are patches of ground made clear from the cover, and these are either carelessly planted with some common and useful vegetable, or else are left free to the wayward ways of Nature, and bear rank weeds, moist-looking, and cool to your eyes, and freshening the sense with their earthly and bitter fragrance. There is a lane opened through the thicket, so broad in some places, that you can pass along side by side—in some, so narrow (the shrubs are for ever encroaching) that you ought, if you can, to go on the first, and hold back the bough of the rose tree. And through the sweet wilderness a loud rushing stream flows tumbling along, till it is halted at last in the lowest corner of the garden, and there tossed up in a fountain by the side of the simple alcove. This is all.

1. Notice how emphasis is obtained by putting into *prominent positions* in the sentence effective words and phrases. *Wild as that* . . . is the sumptuous garden of Damascus. *High, high* above your head . . . the thicket is hemmed in.

2. Notice also the effect of *repetition*, not so much of words as of ideas. Why is the word *high* repeated?

What words of kindred meaning almost immediately follow *tall, tussling*, and *strong* ? [1]

Later in the passage, notice the continuity of thought in *hemmed in . . . choked . . . interlacing*; and *moist-looking . . . cool . . . freshening*.

3. Kinglake also uses *antithesis* and *balance* judiciously. He contrasts the stateliness of the trees *above* with their tussling, struggling life *below*.

He uses conjunctions in pairs :—

> These are *either* carelessly planted with some common and useful vegetable, *or* else are left free to the wayward ways of Nature.

By this means he can balance one thought with a second, closely connected thought.

He combines balance and antithesis :—

> There is a lane opened through the thicket, SO BROAD *in some* places, that you can pass along side by side—*in some*, SO NARROW . . . that you ought, if you can, to go on the first . . .

Exercise

Improve the balance or rhythm of the following, either by altering the words or by changing their order :—

1. Some poems are so written that the reader can imagine a picture about which they are written.

2. Canals were used for carrying heavy goods, as the ordinary means of cartage from one town to another was by means of two baskets on a horse's back filled with the goods.

3. In very old times a system of barter was perhaps the first form of exchange ; a man seeing something he would

---

[1] You should, however, be careful to avoid close repetition of sounds, unless you deliberately intend a sound-effect. Kinglake's reference to 'the wayward ways of Nature' is not happily expressed, but it is much less jarring than '*The peasants could stand no more, so that the Peasants' Revolt was the result*'; and '*The sensitiveness of the Press is essential if the Press is to have the public's sympathy.*'

like and that another man had, would try to persuade him to give the thing he liked in exchange for one or some of his goods.

4. The solicitations of sense are always at hand, and a dram to a vacant and solitary person is a speedy and seducing relief. HESTER PIOZZI.

5. Then there was further a practical demonstration of the difficulties of communication.

6. My friends come to visit me because they love to talk politics and an enjoyment of their hospitality leads me to visit them : I am a poor man who cannot provide feasts other than those of the intellect.

7. Giles Blackthorne was always fortunate : as a boy he won two scholarships so that it can be said his success was deserved ; a friend's recommendation led to Blackthorne's rapid promotion in manhood ; he was able to enjoy the leisure of an old age free from want.

8. It would appear that man is a good piece of work, especially in the case of his reason. He appears to have an infinite range in his faculties. In his shapeliness there is much to admire. When he is seen in motion he has many of the assets of an angel. His power of knowing and of apprehending partakes of the nature of a god. He is the most beautiful thing in the world, and certainly no animal can hold a candle to him.

Most of the above examples are from students' written work. Shakespeare gives an improved version of No. 8 in *Hamlet* II, ii.

(3) *Variety*

In the passage from Kinglake you will notice a variety not only in the structure of the sentences but also in their *length*. One sentence you will find has five words and another only three. Can you say what was the writer's intention in introducing them just at those places in his paragraph ?

5 A

At what effect is Carlyle aiming in this extract from
The Hero as Divinity ?

The strong old Norse heart did not go upon theatrical
sublimities ; they had not time to tremble. I like much
their robust simplicity ; their veracity, directness of con-
ception. Thor ' draws down his brows, in a veritable Norse
rage ; grasps his hammer till the *knuckles grow white.*'
Beautiful traits of pity too, an honest pity. Balder ' the
white god ' dies ; the beautiful, benignant ; he is the
Sun-god. They try all Nature for a remedy ; but he is
dead. Frigga, his mother, sends Hermode to seek or see
him ; nine days and nine nights he rides, through gloomy
deep valleys, a labyrinth of gloom ; arrives at the Bridge
with its gold roof : the Keeper says, ' Yes, Balder did pass
here ; but the Kingdom of the Dead is down yonder, far
towards the North.' Hermode rides on ; leaps Hell-gate,
Hela's Gate ; does see Balder, and speak with him : Balder
cannot be delivered. Inexorable ! Hela will not, for Odin
or for any god, give him up. The beautiful and gentle
has to remain there. His Wife had volunteered to go with
him, to die with him. They shall forever remain there.
He sends his ring to Odin ; Nanna his wife sends her
thimble to Frigga, as a remembrance—Ah me !—

Short sentences, although they have the advantage of
being easily within your control, may lead to an appearance of breathless and unwarrantable haste. Often,
however, if you wish to be impressive, to drive a point
home, a short sentence will prove far more effective than
a weighty, pompous one.

Comparisons, similes, and metaphors, unless worn
threadbare by over-use, will give a certain freshness by
their power of *illustration*.

It is a beautiful thing to observe the boundaries which
nature has affixed to the ridiculous. . . . Who ever thinks
of turning into ridicule our great and ardent hope of a
world to come ?

Whenever the man of humour meddles with things, he
is astonished to find that in all the great feelings of their

nature the mass of mankind always think and act aright; that they are ready enough to laugh—but that they are quite as ready to drive away with indignation and contempt the light fool who comes with the feather of wit to crumble the bulwarks of truth, and to beat down the Temples of God! SYDNEY SMITH.

Notice the illustration of the futility of attacking truth, and of the even greater futility of the attack on the Temples of God. What is the propriety of comparing wit with a feather?

Comment on Charles Lamb's saying, 'A pun is not bound by the laws which limit nicer wit. It is a pistol let off at the ear; not a feather to tickle the intellect.'

You must beware of trying to introduce too many metaphors and similes. Ford Madox Ford once remarked that a good style will be found to consist in a constant succession of tiny, unobservable surprises.

Single words play an important part in illustration. Did you appreciate the appropriateness of *damask* in the passage from Kinglake? What is meant by *slow* air? Why does he call the shrubs *wilful*? The word endows them with vigorous life and intention.

(4) *Rhythm*

Prose rhythm is compatible with clarity and simplicity of style. The richer harmonies of poetry are lacking, but prose can impart a feeling of joy in the boldness and vigour of its parallelisms and in the subtlety of its cadences.

When all is done, Human Life is, at the greatest and best, but like a froward child, that must be played with, and humoured a little, to keep it quiet, till it falls asleep, and then the care is over. SIR WILLIAM TEMPLE.

Her eyes are sweet and subtle, wild and sleepy, by turns; oftentimes rising to the clouds, oftentimes challenging the heavens. She wears a diadem round her head. And I knew by childish memories that she could go abroad upon the winds, when she heard the sobbing of the litanies or the thundering of organs, and when she beheld the mustering of summer clouds.   THOMAS DE QUINCEY.

Poetry is not like reasoning, a power to be exerted according to the determination of the will. A man cannot say, ' I will compose poetry.' The greatest poet even cannot say it ; for the mind in creation is as a fading coal, which some invisible influence, like an inconstant wind, awakens to transitory brightness ; this power arises from within, like the colour of a flower which fades and changes as it is developed, and the conscious portions of our natures are unprophetic either of its approach or its departure.

                              PERCY BYSSHE SHELLEY.

Saul and Jonathan were lovely and pleasant in their lives, and in their death they were not divided : they were swifter than eagles, they were stronger than lions.

Ye daughters of Israel, weep over Saul, who clothed you in scarlet, with other delights, who put on ornaments of gold upon your apparel.

How are the mighty fallen in the midst of the battle ! O Jonathan, thou wast slain in thine high places.

                              2 Samuel.

In contrast to the rhythm and beauty of the last passage, read this ' imaginary review ' from *Harvest Home* by E. V. Lucas.

There have been few more exciting careers than that of Joseph, the Egyptian premier. The son of a rich Israelite sheep-farmer, he was early made the recipient of cruelty at the hands of his brothers, whose barbarous treatment culminated in selling him as a slave to foreign traders. Subsequently he was imprisoned on a false charge, liberated by Pharaoh, King of Egypt, in recognition of his extraordinary powers of translating dreams, and constituted Prime Minister of the State. This post he held for some years, fulfilling admirably all his duties, and before his death he had the supreme satisfaction of seeing his father again, and forgiving the malice of his brethren.

Style, you see, is not a matter of dangling long words before a reader's eyes. The passage you have just read is utterly drab and colourless. There is, however, no objection to long words just because they are long ; they must not be handled in a vague, woolly fashion.

(5) *Style and Purpose*

In forming an opinion about a literary passage you must first consider the writer's aim, the effect he wishes to achieve. Then you must think about the spirit of his work : does it harmonize with his aim ? There is, perhaps, not much difference in meaning between

I arise from dreams of thee

and

I say, I had an awfully funny dream about you last night,

but there is as much divergence of spirit as there is of expression.

When, therefore, you are studying a piece of literature, do not first look out for small details of expression, but ask, ' What is the theme that holds the structure together ? ' ' What is the permeating spirit of the whole ? '

How far do you agree with these criticisms as adequate interpretations of the author's purpose ?

> *Ode on a Grecian Urn* (Keats)—The permanence of beauty.
> *Old China* (Charles Lamb)—The thrill of being poor.
> *Markheim* (Robert Louis Stevenson)—Murder will out.
> *Five Birds in a Cage* (Gertrude Jennings)—The instinctive antipathy of people belonging to different social classes.[1]

Exercise

1. What is the central theme of *A Dissertation upon Roast Pig*, *Moll White* (from *The Tatler*), *The Vicar of Wakefield*, and *Jane Eyre* ? This time you will not find it so easy to answer each question in a few words or even in a sentence.

[1] *One* of these shows reasonably good judgment ; *two* an appreciation of the theme, but poor expression ; and *one* a misapprehension.

2. What is the author's purpose in Milton's *Paradise Lost* (Book II), Wordsworth's *Ode on the Intimations of Immortality*, Shelley's *Ode to the West Wind*, Matthew Arnold's *The Strayed Reveller*, Thackeray's *Vanity Fair*, T. E. Lawrence's *The Revolt in the Desert* ?

3. Mention from books you have read, or plays you have seen, instances where the author's subject and his treatment of it appeared to be either wholly at variance or somewhat incongruous.

4. Write down the names of five books you found dull and uninteresting. Why did they seem so to you ?

5. On page 124 you read a short extract from Swift's *Journal to Stella*. The piece printed below is taken from the next day of his journal and treats of a similar theme. Can you distinguish any changes in spirit and in diction ? What reasons can you give for these changes ?

> Then I walked home, and was here by ten, so miserably hot that I was in as perfect a passion as ever I was in my life at the greatest affront or provocation. Then I sat an hour till I was quite dry and cool enough to go swim ; which I did, but with so much vexation, that I think I have given it over ; for I was every moment disturbed by boats, rot them ; and that puppy Patrick, standing ashore, would let them come within a yard or two, and then call sneakingly to them. The only comfort I proposed here in hot weather is gone ; for there is no jesting with those boats after 'tis dark : I had none last night. I dived to dip my head, and held my cap on with both my hands, for fear of losing it.

(6) *Examples of Criticism*

A mistake, which is fortunately becoming rarer, is to think that criticism means searching for faults. Constructive criticism is of great value, especially if you apply some of its lessons to your own written work.

In this chapter you have been asked to consider the structure of sentences ; balance, rhythm, emphasis, variety ; and the writer's aims and achievements. Do not begin to criticize with any preconceived notions of the

author's personality.   It is partly true to say that personality is a sequence of changing moods.

Do not therefore think that you have ' to guess the right
answer ' by saying something which conforms with someone else's opinion.   If you wish to think of personality,
regard it as it comes up to you from the printed page, the
writer's power still to make his presence known after
death.   What was his mood when he wrote the words
you are now reading ?

I

Agreeable to their name, the avowed design of their
institution is mischief ; and upon this foundation all their
rules and orders are framed.   An outrageous ambition of
doing all possible hurt to their fellow-creatures is the great
cement of their assembly, and the only qualification required
in the members.   In order to exert this principle in its full
strength and perfection, they take care to drink themselves
to a pitch, that is, beyond the possibility of attending to
any motions of reason or humanity ; then make a general
sally, and attack all that are so unfortunate as to walk the
streets through which they patrol.   Some are knocked down,
others stabbed, others cut and carbonadoed.   To put the
watch to a total rout, and mortify some of those inoffensive
militia, is reckoned a *coup d'éclat*.   The particular talents by
which these misanthropes are distinguished from one another
consist in the various kinds of barbarities which they execute
upon their prisoners.   Some are celebrated for a happy
dexterity in tipping the lion upon them ; which is performed
by squeezing the nose flat to the face, and boring out the
eyes with their fingers.   Others are called the dancing-
masters, and teach their scholars to cut capers, by running
swords through their legs ; a new invention, whether origin-
ally French I cannot tell. . . .

STEELE : *Spectator*, No. 324.

Notice that the mood is dignified, that the writer has
been moved by a sense of duty and an abhorrence of the
outrageous conduct of these ruffians, or Mohocks, as they
were called.   Nevertheless, something of the humorist

peeps out when he describes ' the particular talents ' displayed. There seems to be just a little too much exuberance of spirit in his description of what they do. A smile steals to the lips, even though you sympathize with the victims.

The subject is treated ironically ; the dignity of the language is made deliberately to contrast with recklessness and licence of conduct. ' In order to exert this principle to its full strength and perfection ' is a criticism that may well be applied to some noble work of art. There is a sting and contempt in these words when you remember that the ' principle ' mentioned is to harm inoffensive people. The ironical mood is sustained by aptly chosen words : *the particular talents ; a happy dexterity ; teach their scholars*.

Although the words are not always simple, the style is clear and forceful. To serve the purpose of his quiet, deadly emphasis, Steele has recourse to inversion. Quote some sentences where inversion is effectively used.

It seems, then, that here Steele is trifling with a theme that is beneath the dignity of his style, but that expression must be given to condemn these outrages.

II

Even now, the emoluments of a professorship are so much smaller than those which ability and industry can obtain in other ways, that it is difficult to find eminent men to fill the chairs. And if there be this difficulty now, when students of all religious persuasions attend the lectures, what is likely to happen when all the members of the Free Church go elsewhere for instruction ? If there be this difficulty when you have all the world to choose professors from, what is likely to happen when your choice is narrowed to less than one-half of Scotland ? As the professorships become poorer, the professors will become less competent. As the professors become less competent, the classes will become thinner. As the classes become thinner, the professorships will again become poorer. The decline will become rapid and headlong. In a short time, the lectures will be delivered to empty rooms ; the grass will grow in the courts ; and men not fit to be village dominies will occupy the chairs of Adam Smith and Dugald Stewart, of Reid and Black, of Playfair and Jamieson.

LORD MACAULAY : *A Speech delivered in
the House of Commons*, 9th July, 1845.

You will notice the frequent use Macaulay makes of repetition and his periodic sentences. *Why should this be typical of a speech* ? Moreover, his sentences are broken up into short clauses of similar patterns. This is to hold the listener's attention.

He is developing an argument from step to step until he reaches a climax.

In style he is persuasive : you feel that he is presenting a strong case in deliberately restrained language, the more effective because of his moderation, until he leads up to the solemn words, ' The decline will become rapid and headlong ' : here he launches forth into the more impassioned style of his concluding sentence.

The language is simple. You may not be familiar with the word ' emoluments,' but a dignified word has to be used of professors' salaries. ' Dominies ' gives the passage an apt Scottish flavour.

III

Here their delicious task the fervent bees,
In swarming millions, tend : around, athwart,
Through the soft air, the busy nations fly,
Cling to the bud, and, with inserted tube,
Suck its pure essence, its ethereal soul ;
And oft, with bolder wing, they soaring dare
The purple heath, or where the wild thyme grows,
And yellow load them with the luscious spoil.

THOMSON : *The Seasons.*

Although the scene is out of doors the treatment of the subject is artificial. The poet appears to be most anxious to select an appropriate epithet for each noun—hardly one escapes. There is little evidence that the poet's spirit leaps in tune with his theme ; it seems more like an academic exercise. In places the language is unnecessarily scientific : *with inserted tube, suck its pure essence.* You should contrast this poem with Burns' *To a Field Mouse.* Thomson's emotions do not appear to be stirred at all ; since, however, the above extract is from a long poem, you cannot expect intensity of feeling throughout.

IV

'Tis true, I might have chosen Piccadilly,
    A place where peccadillos are unknown ;
But I have motives, whether wise or silly,
    For letting that pure sanctuary alone.
Therefore I name not square, street, place, until I
    Find one where nothing naughty can be shown,
A vestal shrine of innocence of heart :
Such are—but I have lost the London Chart.

LORD BYRON : *Don Juan.*

To say that this is not poetry is unnecessarily to limit the scope of poetry. These lines have a vigour, a swiftness of movement, and a verbal felicity that together are powerfully attractive. It is a style full of pleasant surprises ; from the cleverness of his pun, the daring of his rhymes (*Piccadilly . . . until I*), the archness of his ironical references to ' pure sanctuary,' to the solemnity with which he prepares to show us some part of London which is ' a vestal shrine of innocence of heart.' The abrupt breaking off in the last line suggests that no such place can be found, but that it is more respectable to pretend to have lost the map.

The stanza Byron uses, the ottava rima, is a happy choice, for it is of just sufficient scope for these short sallies of wit where he can at will playfully develop a thought or merely trifle with it.

Criticize the following passages from the point of view of style :—

1.   When in the sultry glebe I faint,
        Or on the thirsty mountains pant,
        To fertile vales and dewy meads,
        My weary wandering steps He leads,
        Where peaceful rivers, soft and slow
        Amid the verdant landscape flow.

2. St Agnes' Eve—ah, bitter chill it was !
   The owl, for all his feathers, was a-cold ;
   The hare limp'd trembling through the frozen grass,
   And silent was the flock in woolly fold :
   Numb were the Beadsman's fingers while he told
   His rosary, and while his frosted breath,
   Like pious incense from a censer old,
   Seem'd taking flight for heaven without a death,
   Past the sweet Virgin's picture, while his prayer he saith.

3.   To see a man tread over graves
            I hold it no good mark ;
        'Tis wicked in the sun and moon,
            And bad luck in the dark !

        You see that grave ?   The Lord He gives,
            The Lord, He takes away :
        O Sir ! the child of my old age
            Lies there as cold as clay.

        Except that grave, you scarce see one
            That was not dug by me ;
        I'd rather dance upon 'em all
            Than tread upon these three !

4. Charity ! decent, modest, easy, kind,
    Softens the high, and rears the abject mind ;
    Knows with just reins and gentle hand to guide
    Betwixt vile shame and arbitrary pride.
    Not soon provoked, she easily forgives,
    And much she suffers as she much believes—
    Soft peace she brings wherever she arrives,
    She builds our quiet as she forms our lives ;
    Lays the rough path of peevish nature even,
    And opens in each heart a little heaven.

5. OTHELLO. It is the cause, it is the cause, my soul :
              Let me not name it to you, you chaste stars !
              It is the cause.   Yet I'll not shed her blood,
              Nor scar that whiter skin of hers than snow
              And smooth as monumental alabaster.
              Yet she must die, else she'll betray more men.
              Put out the light, and then put out the light :
              If I quench thee, thou flaming minister,
              I can again thy former light restore,
              Should I repent me : but once put out thy
                 light,
              Thou cunning'st pattern of excelling nature,
              I know not where is that Promethean heat
              That can thy light relume.   When I have
                 pluck'd thy rose,
              I cannot give it vital growth again,
              It must needs wither : I'll smell it on the tree.
                 (*Kissing her.*)
              O balmy breath, that dost almost persuade
              Justice to break her sword !   One more, one
                 more :
              Be thus when thou art dead, and I will kill thee,
              And love thee after : one more, and this the
                 last :
              So sweet was ne'er so fatal.   I must weep,
              But they are cruel tears : this sorrow's
                 heavenly ;
              It strikes where it doth love.   She wakes.

6. Men fear Death as children fear to go in the dark ; and
   as that natural fear in children is increased with tales,
   so is the other.   Certainly, the contemplation of
   Death, as the wages of sin and passage to another
   world, is holy and religious ; but the fear of it, as a
   tribute due unto Nature, is weak. . . . It is as natural
   to die as to be born ; and to a little infant perhaps the
   one is as painful as the other.   He that dies in an
   earnest pursuit is like one that is wounded in hot
   blood, who, for the time, scarce feels the hurt ; and
   therefore a mind fixed and bent upon somewhat that
   is good doth avert the dolours of Death ; but, above

all, believe it, the sweetest canticle is *Nunc dimittis*,
when a man hath obtained worthy ends and expectations. Death hath this also, that it openeth the gate
to good fame, and extinguisheth envy : *Extinctus
amabitur idem.*

7. ' He's got the loveliest head you ever saw, like pictures of
Abraham and Isaac and Jacob all together, with a long
white beard and long white hair that's very thick and
curls over his collar, and a lovely straight nose and
brownish smooth skin on his face. When you see
him sitting down you think goodness me, that's a
real church saint and no mistake. And then he gets
up and you see his legs are tiny, . . . and his beard
looks as if it would be tickling his knees all the time,
and he just looks an old comic. And he's got a little
squeaky voice like a young pig's . . . "
G. D. H. and MARGARET COLE : *Dead Man's Watch.*

8. Why does the sun dart forth its cheerful rays ?
Why do the woods resound with warbling lays ?
Why does the rose her grateful fragrance yield,
And yellow cowslips paint the smiling field ?
Why do the streams with murm'ring music flow,
And why do groves their friendly shade bestow ?
Let sable clouds the cheerful sun deface,
Let mournful silence seize the feather'd race ;
No more, ye roses, grateful fragrance yield,
Droop, droop, ye cowslips, in the blasted field ;
No more, ye streams, with murm'ring music flow,
And let not groves a friendly shade bestow :
With sympathizing grief let nature mourn,
And never know the youthful spring's return :
And shall I never more Alexis see ?
Then what is spring, or grove, or streams to me ?

* 9. Happy those early days, when I
Shined in my angel-infancy !
Before I understood this place
Appointed for my second race,
Or taught my soul to fancy aught
But a white celestial thought :

When yet I had not walk'd above
A mile or two from my first Love,
And looking back—at that short space—
Could see a glimpse of His bright face :
When on some gilded cloud, or flow'r,
My gazing soul would dwell an hour,
And in those weaker glories spy
Some shadows of eternity :
Before I taught my tongue to wound
My conscience with a sinful sound,
Or had the black art to dispense
A several sin to ev'ry sense,
But felt through all this fleshly dress
Bright shoots of everlastingness.

* 10. Our birth is but a sleep and a forgetting ;
The Soul that rises with us, our life's Star,
      Hath had elsewhere its setting
            And cometh from afar ;
      Not in entire forgetfulness,
      And not in utter nakedness,
But trailing clouds of glory do we come
            From God, Who is our home :
Heaven lies about us in our infancy !
Shades of the prison-house begin to close
            Upon the growing Boy,
But he beholds the light, and whence it flows,
            He sees it in his joy ;
The Youth, who daily farther from the east
      Must travel, still is Nature's priest,
            And by the vision splendid
            Is on his way attended ;
At length the Man perceives it die away,
And fade into the light of common day.

11. The reader will here find no regions cursed with
irremediable barrenness, or blest with spontaneous
fecundity ; no perpetual gloom, or unceasing sunshine ;
nor are the nations here described, either devoid of
all sense of humanity, or consummate in all private
and social virtues. Here are no Hottentots without
religious policy or articulate language ; no Chinese

perfectly polite, and completely skilled in all sciences ; he will discover, what will always be discovered by a diligent and impartial inquirer, that wherever human nature is to be found, there is a mixture of vice and virtue, a contest of passion and reason ; and that the Creator doth not appear partial in His distributions, but has balanced, in most countries, their particular inconveniences by particular favours.

12. The fearful day arrived when Sobieski and his grandson were to bid adieu to Villanow, and its peaceful scenes. The well-poised mind of the veteran bade his daughter farewell with a fortitude which imparted some of its strength even to her. But when Thaddeus, ready habited for his journey, entered the room, at the sight of his military accoutrements, she shuddered ; and when, with a glowing countenance, he advanced, smiling through his tears, towards her, she clasped him in her arms, and riveted her lips to that face, the very loveliness of which added to her affliction. She gazed at him, she wept on his neck, she pressed him to her bosom. ' O ! how soon might all that beauty be mingled with the dust ! how soon might that warm heart, which then beat against hers, be pierced by the sword ! be laid on the ground mangled and bleeding, exposed and trampled on ! ' These thoughts thronged upon her soul, and deprived her of sense. She was borne away by her maids, while the palatine compelled Thaddeus to quit the spot.

These passages are not chosen principally for their literary merits. They are intended to stimulate a spirit of criticism. Some of the greatest writers of English are omitted : some are represented by good, and others by inferior work. The omission of most of the authors' names is intentional so that the student will approach each passage without preconception or bias.

Where consecutive passages are marked with an asterisk, the student should compare and contrast them.

REVISION PAPER 2

1. Combine the following sentences in *three* ways, **as** different from each other as possible :—

School magazines are prone to die of inertia. They enjoy an ephemeral existence. Enthusiasm soon wanes. The editorial staff has to write everything.

2. Make a précis of about 100 words, taking care to retain all essential details of the following passage :—

My hold of the colonies is in the close affection which grows from common names, from kindred blood, from similar privileges, and equal protection. These are ties which, though light as air, are as strong as links of iron. Let the Colonists always keep the idea of civil rights associated with your government ;—they will cling and grapple to you ; and no force under heaven will be of power to tear them from their allegiance. But let it be once understood that your government may be one thing, and their privileges another ; that these two things may exist without any mutual relation ;—the cement is gone ; the cohesion is loosened ; and everything hastens to decay and dissolution. As long as you have the wisdom to keep the sovereign authority of this country as the sanctuary of liberty, the sacred temple consecrated to our common faith, wherever the chosen race and sons of England worship freedom, they will turn their faces towards you. The more they multiply, the more friends you will have ; the more ardently they love liberty, the more perfect will be their obedience. Slavery they can have anywhere. It is a weed that grows in every soil. They may have it from Spain, they may have it from Prussia. But, until you have become lost to all feeling of your true interest and your natural dignity, freedom they can have from none but you.   EDMUN

3. Comment upon the following as a successful précis of the passage in question No. 2 :—

Précis of Part of a Speech by Edmund Burke, showing Liberty as the Closest Tie between England and her Colonies

Edmund Burke declared that he was much attached to the colonists, who were powerfully bound to England by ties of race, privilege, and common security. If the Government respected those privileges nothing could undermine the colonists' devotion, but if those rights were withheld, all allegiance would disappear. As long as England was the stronghold of liberty her ever-increasing sons would be loyal : their obedience would increase with their measure of liberty. Slavery could be had from anywhere ; freedom could come only from the Mother Country wisely and graciously alive to a sense of her best interests.

4. Improve the style of the following sentences :—

(*a*) The Turks ransacked Constantinople and scattered the students over Europe.

(*b*) Swimming is a universal sport, enjoyed by the youth of all nations.

(*c*) When Queen Elizabeth came to the throne she offended neither party for she mixed the service so.

(*d*) I have enclosed my reports and character and will let you judge for yourself whether I am fit for the job.

(*e*) Lumber rooms are very interesting, packed with relics and glories of old times, and especially so on rainy days.

(*f*) The cause of the seasons is that as the earth moves round the sun the earth does not move its axis, but lets the sun shine on its face and when it is halfway round the sun it seems to be half light and half dark.

5. The table overleaf represents an analysis of the contents of the seven most important daily papers. So that you may keep an unprejudiced opinion, the actual names are not given. The figures represent in pages the approximate amount of space given to the chief features.

Name	News	Adverts	Editor's Opinions	Pictures	Reviews	Short Story	Sports	Articles	Home and Children	Wireless	Total Pages
Daily Ant . .	6	6	1	1	1	1·75	2·25	0	0·75	0·25	20
Daily Bee . .	3·4	6·5	1·75	1·25	1	0·75	1·5	0·5	0·75	0·6	18
Daily Wasp .	6·5	10	1	1·5	0	0	2·5	1	1	0·5	24
Daily Hornet .	5·5	4	1	2	1·5	0·75	3	1	0·75	0·5	20
Daily Weevil .	6	6·5	2	2	2	1	1	2	1	0·5	24
Daily Spider .	12·75	8	0·5	1	1	0	2·75	1·25	0·25	0·5	28
Daily Moth .	7·25	7·5	0·75	1	1·5	0	2	1	0·5	0·5	22

1. Which of these papers is most worthy of the name NEWSpaper ?

2. Which paper most resembles a magazine which tries to give its readers ' a little of everything ' ?

3. Which paper gives the greatest proportion to advertisement ?

4. Write an essay on the modern newspaper, attacking (or defending) the following tendencies :—

   (*a*) the excessive space devoted to sport,

   (*b*) the obtrusiveness of the editor's opinions,

   (*c*) the introducing of matter that fails to interest you,

   (*d*) the space devoted to matter that, by no stretch of imagination, can be called news. (The advertisements may be necessary in order to sell the newspaper so cheaply.)

6. Comment upon the following parodies, saying which you consider the more successful. In particular deal with these two points : (a) successful imitation of the *spirit* of the original, and (b) effective introduction of some of the original words.

A. (from Shenstone's *Pastoral Ballad*—1743).

> Ye shepherds, give ear to my lay,
>   And take no more heed of my sheep :
> They have nothing to do but to stray ;
>   I have nothing to do but to weep.
> Yet do not my folly reprove ;
>   She was fair, and my passion begun ;
> She smiled, and I could not but love ;
>   She is faithless, and I am undone.

(a) Parody of *A* (from *Leaves and Fruit*, by Sir Edmund Gosse).

> I sits with me feet in a brook
>   And if anyone axes me why,
> I hits 'em a crack with my crook,
>   For 'tis sentiment kills me, says I.

B. Read W. E. Henley's well-known poem, *Invictus* (No. 842 in *The Oxford Book of English Verse*).

(b) Parody of *B.*

> Out of the mud which covers me,
>   Black as my hat from head to sole,
> I thank the friendly referee
>   For our unconquerable goal
>
> In the fell clutch of quarter backs
>   I have not funked nor sworn aloud,
> Under rough batterings or hacks
>   My head is bloody, but unbowed.
>
> It matters not how good their back,
>   How straight the drop towards the pole,
> I am the captain of the pack ;
>   I am the keeper of the goal.

7. Give the names and explain the aptness of the figures of speech in the following :—

(a)   Her voice was like the whisper of the wood
        In prime of even, when the stars are few.

ALFORD.

(b)   Her habitual state of querulous serenity.

JANE AUSTEN.

(c) An iron plate, covered with crackling wood, sustained a ponderous black cauldron, the rich steam of which gratefully affected the olfactory organs of the highway-men.   HARRISON AINSWORTH.

(d)   O conspiracy !
        Sham'st thou to show thy dangerous brow by night,
        When evils are most free ?   SHAKESPEARE.

(e) To grow bigger every moment in your own conceit, and the world to lessen ; to deify yourself at the expense of your species ; to judge the world—this is the acme and supreme point of your mystery—these the true PLEASURES OF SULKINESS.   CHARLES LAMB.

(f)   See how the world its veterans rewards
        A youth of frolics, an old age of cards ;
        Fair to no purpose, artful to no end,
        Young without lovers, old without a friend ;
        A fop their passion, but their prize a sot,
        Alive ridiculous, and dead forgot !   POPE.

(g) This world in that great earthquake languished,
    For in a common bath of tears it bled.

JOHN DONNE (referring to the
death of Queen Elizabeth).

(h) Meanwhile, by aid of virtue and blank verse, Amanda converts the passion of Mr Worthy into profound admiration and esteem.

ANDREW LANG (in a criticism
of Vanbrugh's play, *The Relapse*).

(i) Now dawn broke, like sudden good news ; the sea caught fire from the sky and became diamond drops and emerald gulfs ; and every stem and frond and rock in the island quivered and leaped into life. It was as if a great orchestra had swept into some superb opening movement.   J. B. PRIESTLEY : *Faraway*.

8. Read the following passages carefully and then point out their differences in style. Comment especially upon their diction.

' At length my father resolved to initiate me in commerce ; and, opening one of his subterranean treasuries, counted out ten thousand pieces of gold. " This, young man," said he, " is the stock with which you must negotiate. I began with less than a fifth part, and you see how diligence and parsimony have increased it. This is your own, to waste or improve. If you squander it by negligence or caprice, you must wait for my death before you will be rich ; if in four years you double your stock, we will thenceforward let subordination cease, and live together as friends and partners, for he shall be always equal with me who is equally skilled in the art of growing rich."

' We laid out our money upon camels, concealed in bales of cheap goods, and travelled to the shore of the Red Sea. When I cast my eye on the expanse of waters, my heart bounded like that of a prisoner escaped. I felt an inextinguishable curiosity kindle in my mind, and resolved to snatch this opportunity of seeing the manners of other nations, and of learning sciences unknown in Abyssinia.

' I remembered that my father had obliged me to the improvement of my stock, not by a promise, which I ought not to violate, but by a penalty, which I was at liberty to incur ; and therefore determined to gratify my predominant desire, and, by drinking at the fountain of knowledge, to quench the thirst of curiosity.'   DR JOHNSON : *Rasselas*.

I cannot say that after this, for five years, any extraordinary thing happened to me, but I lived on in the same course, in the same posture and place, just as before. The chief things I was employed in, besides my yearly labour of planting my barley and rice and curing my raisins, of both which I always kept up just enough to have sufficient stock of one year's provisions beforehand—I say, besides this yearly labour and my daily labour of going out with my gun,

I had one labour to make me a canoe, which at last I finished ; so that, by the digging a canal to it of six feet wide and four feet deep, I brought it into the creek, almost half a mile. As for the first, which was so vastly big, as I made it without considering beforehand, as I ought to do, how I should be able to launch it, so never being able to bring it to the water, or bring the water to it, I was obliged to let it lie where it was, as a memorandum to teach me to be wiser next time. Indeed, the next time, though I could not get a tree proper for it, at any less distance than as I have said, near half a mile, yet, as I saw that it was practicable at last, I never gave it over ; and though I was near two years about it, yet I never grudged my labour, in hopes of having a boat to go off to sea at last.

DANIEL DEFOE : *Robinson Crusoe.*

9. Comment upon the style of the following passage from *Rookwood*, by Harrison Ainsworth. Consider especially how far the diction is suitable to the subject-matter.

' Peace,' cried Luke ; ' you blight everything—even this smiling landscape you would turn to gloom. Does not this morn awaken a happier train of thoughts within your mind ? With me it makes amends for want of sleep, effaces resentment, and banishes every black misgiving. 'Tis a joyous thing, thus to scour the country at earliest dawn ; to catch all the spirit and freshness of the morning ; to be abroad before the lazy world is half awake ; to make the most of brief existence ; and to have spent a day of keen enjoyment, almost before the day begins with some. I like to anticipate the rising of the glorious luminary ; to watch every line of light changing, as at this moment, from shuddering grey to blushing rose ! See how the heavens are dyed ! Who would exchange yon gorgeous spectacle,' continued he, pointing towards the east, and again urging his horse to full speed down the hill, endangering the sexton's seat, and threatening to impale him upon the crupper of the saddle—' who would exchange that sight, and the exhilarating feeling of this fresh morn, for a couch of eiderdown, and a headache in reversion ? '

(The passage is taken from Book III, Chapter I. The two men are on horseback : they are riding the same horse.)

CHAPTER X

PARAPHRASING

To paraphrase is to express in one's own words the substance and sense of a passage. Unlike the précis, it takes into consideration not only all the turns of thought but also the spirit of the passage.

It is thus important first to read the extract through in order to grasp its matter and to appreciate its style. Certain phrases which seem to be obscure should be underlined for further consideration. These must be understood before you begin to write : the whole passage must make clear sense or your interpretation of it will not be sense.

The purport of figures of speech, especially of metaphors, must be understood. It is usually preferable to employ non-metaphorical language, for you must note first, that you are required to express yourself in your own words, not to cling weakly to another's diction ; second, that you do not normally express yourself in metaphors ; third, that attempts to replace metaphors by other metaphors are almost certain to lead to mixed or to badly-sustained metaphors. Do not set the ship of state to climb the ladder of victory or to chew the cud of bitter reflection.

Paraphrase is a valuable exercise in that it brings you immediately into contact with the writer's craft.[1] Turns of thought must be understood and rendered again in a language and a manner worthy of the original.

[1] In studying a writer's expression you will be faced with problems of proportion, sentence construction, and punctuation : paraphrasing helps to show how these contribute to the writer's purpose.

Paraphrase

Thy soul was like a star, and dwelt apart ;
Thou hadst a voice whose sound was like the sea :

WORDSWORTH : *London*, 1802.

A STUDENT'S ATTEMPT

Your soul is unlike others and your voice is distinctly
hoarse.

Comment

This is a woeful effort. The student has utterly failed
to appreciate the spirit in which Wordsworth wrote, the
praise of Milton's majesty of soul and grandeur of utterance.
Here Milton is made to sink to the level of a coal-heaver.
There has been no attempt at a sympathetic understanding
of the lines. *Distinctly* is surely a contradiction of the idea
contained in *hoarse*.

ANOTHER STUDENT'S ATTEMPT

Majestically thy soul held its sway alone : sonorous and
deep flowed the melody of thy verse.

Comment

At once you feel that a responding chord has been struck :
there is a kinship of spirit with the original. The words
majestically, *sonorous*, and *melody* are happily chosen.

Choice of words is of paramount importance. When
you are told to write in your own words it does not mean
that you are free to use any words you like so long as
you avoid those of the original. The word is not the
unit ; you must think out complete sentences as you
write. Merely to change words is not a high form of
art ; it is akin to a jig-saw puzzle.

To render *Hence, loathèd Melancholy* and *Good my
complexion !* ' Bye-bye, Blues ' and ' Strike me pink ! '
is not a literary achievement.

To sum up : you must be careful (1) to reproduce the
spirit of the passage, (2) to omit none of its ideas, and
(3) to exceed the length of the original if necessary. A
proverb or an epigram is already expressed as pithily as
possible.

Example

Poets are the unacknowledged legislators of the world.
Here you must concentrate on *legislators*. In what sense
are poets law-makers ?

Which of these do you consider the best paraphrase ?

(*a*) Poets do the thinking : the world, in general, steals their
thoughts and the poets are forgotten.

(*b*) Poets reveal universal truths which all follow though
they may contemn those who have opened their eyes.

(*c*) Although few realize it, this world is ruled by the truths
revealed by its poets.

(*d*) Poets express universal truths which, without stopping
to question by whose authority, all follow.

Exercises

1. Explain the meaning of the following proverbial expressions :—

(*a*) Virtue dwells not in the tongue, but in the heart.

(*b*) The married man must turn his staff into a stake.

(*c*) Nature passes nurture.

(*d*) Burn not your house to fright away the mice.

(*e*) To throw the helve after the hatchet.

(*f*) Fame is a magnifying glass.

2. Use the following phrases in sentences which show their
appropriate use, then express the same thoughts in your own
words :—

(*a*) a bone of contention ; to make bones about ; to have a
bone to pick with someone.

(*b*) to breed bad blood ; to run in the blood ; in cold blood.

(*c*) to bring to book ; to be in a person's bad books ; to
speak like a book.

(*d*) to set by the ears ; to draw the long bow ; to break a
lance with.

(*e*) to call in question ; to change front ; to chop and
change.

(*f*) to show the cold shoulder ; to have an inferiority complex ; to have cognizance of.

(*g*) to be in clover ; to call over the coals ; to show the
cloven hoof.

6

3. Express in your own words the meaning of the following epigrams :—

(a) Every age, like every human body, has its own dis-
    temper.   EMERSON.

(b) Freedom consists in the recognition of one's limitations.

(c) This long defeat of doing nothing well.
                                        JOHN MASEFIELD.

(d) Measure not dispatch by the times of sitting, but by the
    advancement of the business.   BACON.

(e) A vow is a horrible thing ; it is a snare for sin.
                                        DR JOHNSON.

(f) The road of excess leads to the palace of wisdom.
                                        WILLIAM BLAKE.

(g) Censure is the tax a man pays to the public for being
    eminent.   JONATHAN SWIFT.

4. Interpret the following passages :—

(a) Kings are like stars—they rise and set—they have
    The worship of the world, but no repose.
                                        SHELLEY.

(b) Suit the action to the word, the word to the action, with
    this special observance, that you o'erstep not the
    modesty of nature.   SHAKESPEARE.

(c) Do not, as some ungracious pastors do,
    Show me the steep and thorny way to Heaven,
    Whilst, like a puff'd and reckless libertine,
    Himself the primrose path of dalliance treads,
    And recks not his own rede.   SHAKESPEARE.

(d) Waller was smooth ; but Dryden taught to join
    The varying verse, the full resounding line,
    The long majestic march, and energy divine.
                                        POPE.

(e)   I have seen
    A curious child, who dwelt upon a tract
    Of inland ground, applying to his ear
    The convolutions of a smooth-lipped shell ;
    To which, in silence hushed, his very soul

Listened intensely ; and his countenance soon
Brightened with joy ; for from within were heard
Murmurings, whereby the monitor expressed
Mysterious unions with its native sea.

WORDSWORTH.

Paraphrasing Verse

Although it is important to remember to preserve the spirit of every passage to be paraphrased, once a poet's thoughts are recast in prose the poetry is gone. The wealth of poetry cannot be appreciated at one reading ; to understand its meaning is but a step in the process. Nevertheless it is a step worth taking.

Many hold that to paraphrase poetry is desecration. Poetry has form, melody, and a richness of word-associations ; a paraphrase will cope vainly with these. It can, however, aim at interpreting most of the ideas and some of the spirit of the original.

When you have finished writing, look over what you have written just to see if it reads as a piece of sensible English prose.

Example

Hope humbly then ; with trembling pinions soar ;
Wait the great teacher Death ; and God adore.
What future bliss, He gives not thee to know,
But gives that hope to be thy blessing now.
Hope springs eternal in the human breast :
Man never Is, but always To be blest :
The soul, uneasy and confined from home,
Rests and expatiates in a life to come.

FIRST ATTEMPT

Hope humbly ; but let your thoughts tremblingly aspire to heaven. Worship God as you await death with patience. In this world Hope is a token of a greater bliss which you may not now enjoy.

Let Hope ever rise within you : the great blessing is in futurity ; it is eternal, not something that lives only in the present. The soul, restless through being absent from its true home, waits patiently, aspiring only to the life to come.

Comments

No attempt has been made to interpret the idea contained in *teacher*.

Let Hope ever rise within you. The poet states this as a fact, not as an exhortation.

It is eternal, not something that lives only in the present is a feeble repetition.

Absent is not so forceful as the *confined* of the original. The soul is imprisoned by the body and thus is shut out of its natural home.

REVISED ATTEMPT

Hope humbly ; but let your thoughts tremblingly aspire to Heaven. Love and worship God as you await death with patience, for after death there is much to be revealed. In this world Hope is a blest token of a greater bliss which God does not intend now to be yours. Hope ever rises from within : God's blessing is not merely transient but eternal. The soul, restless through being shut out from its true home, waits patiently, aspiring only to the life to come.

Exercises

Give in your own words the meaning of the following passages :—

1. As yet amid this elemental war,
   That scatters desolation from afar,
   Nor toil, nor hazard, nor distress appear
   To sink the seamen with unmanly fear.
   Though their firm hearts no pageant honour boast,
   They scorn the wretch that trembles at his post ;
   Who from the face of danger strives to turn,
   Indignant from the social hour they spurn.
   Though now full oft they felt the raging tide,
   In proud rebellion climb the vessel's side,
   No future ills unknown their souls appal ;
   They know no danger, or they scorn it all !
   But even the generous spirits of the brave,
   Subdued by toil, a friendly respite crave ;
   A short repose alone their thoughts implore,
   Their harassed powers by slumber to restore.

   WILLIAM FALCONER : *The Shipwreck.*

Be careful with the line *Indignant from the social hour they spurn.* What does it mean ?

2. All nobilitie
(But pride, that schisme of incivilitie)
She had, and it became her ! she was fit
T' have known no envy, but by suffring it !
She had a mind as calme, as she was faire ;
Not tost or troubled with light Lady-aire :
But kept an even gate, as some streight tree
Mov'd by the wind, so comely moved she.
And by the awfull manage of her Eye
She swaied all bus'nesse in the Familie.
To one she said, Doe this, he did it ; So
To another, Move : he went ; to a third, Go,
He run, and all did strive with diligence
T' obey, and serve her sweet Commandements.
She was in one, a many parts of life ;
A tender *Mother*, a discreeter *Wife*,
A solemne *Mistresse*, and so good a *Friend*,
So charitable, to religious end
In all her petite actions, so devote
As her whole life was now become one note
Of Pietie, and private holinesse.

BEN JONSON.

3. Four seasons fill the measure of the year ;
There are four seasons in the mind of man :
He has his lusty Spring, when fancy clear
Takes in all beauty with an easy span :
He has his Summer, when luxuriously
Spring's honied cud of youthful thought he loves
To ruminate, and by such dreaming high
Is nearest unto heaven : quiet coves
His soul has in its Autumn, when his wings
He furleth close ; contented so to look
On mists in idleness—to let fair things
Pass by unheeded as a threshold brook.
He has his Winter too of pale misfeature,
Or else he would forgo his mortal nature.

JOHN KEATS : *The Human Seasons.*

4. My dearest friend ! would I had died for thee !
Life and this world, henceforth, will tedious be ;
Nor shall I know hereafter what to do,
If once my grief prove tedious too.
Silent and sad I walk about all day,
As sullen ghosts stalk speechless by
Where their hid treasures lie :
Alas ! my treasure's gone, why do I stay ?

ABRAHAM COWLEY : *On the Death of
Mr William Harvey.*

5.   How beautiful is night !
A dewy freshness fills the silent air ;
No mist obscures, nor cloud, nor speck, nor stain,
Breaks the serene of heaven :
In full-orbed glory, yonder moon divine
Rolls through the dark-blue depths.
Beneath her steady ray
The desert-circle spreads,
Like the round ocean, girdled with the sky.
How beautiful is night !

ROBERT SOUTHEY : *Thalaba the Destroyer.*

6.   Yes ! let the rich deride, the proud disdain,
These simple blessings of the lowly train ;
To me more dear, congenial to my heart,
Our native charm, than all the gloss of art ;
Spontaneous joys, where Nature has its play,
The soul adopts, and owns the first-born sway ;
Lightly they frolic o'er the vacant mind,
Unenvied, unmolested, unconfined :
But the long pomp, the midnight masquerade,
With all the freaks of wanton wealth array'd,
In these, ere triflers half their wish obtain,
The toiling pleasure sickens into pain ;
And, e'en while fashion's brightest arts decoy,
The heart distrusting asks, if this be joy.

OLIVER GOLDSMITH : *The Deserted Village.*

Paraphrasing Prose Passages

Here, although archaic words and turns of expression present some difficulty, more trouble is found in coping with the punctuation and the arrangement of these passages. Turn to Smollett and notice how heavily over-punctuated his novels appear.

You must read the passage right through. Make sure you understand its purport. If, as most probably will be the case, the periods are turgid or involved, deliberately aim at a direct and forceful expression, just as if you were making a précis. You will often find passages rich and sonorous, packed with Biblical phraseology, and you will wonder how you can possibly improve on them. It is not your task to try to improve an author's prose style : you have to get at his meaning and then develop your own power of expression.

When you have finished, read your work as a piece of modern English. Does it survive the test ?

Exercises

Reproduce the substance of the following passages, taking care to express yourself in idiomatic modern English :—

1. I must therefore desire you, in the first place, to be very slow in changing the modest behaviour of a virgin : it is usual in young wives, before they have been many weeks married, to assume a bold, forward look, and manner of talking, as if they intended to signify in all companies that they were no longer girls, and consequently that their whole demeanour, before they got a husband, was but a countenance and constraint upon their nature : whereas, I suppose, if the votes of wise men were gathered, a very great majority would be in favour of those ladies who, after they were entered into that state, rather chose to double their portion of modesty and reservedness.

JONATHAN SWIFT : *A Letter to a Very Young Lady on Her Marriage.*

2. From hence returning to Paris shortly after, I found
   myself welcome to all those ministers of state there,
   and noblemen, who either envied the greatness or
   loved not the insolencies of Monsieur de Luynes ; by
   whom also I was told, that the said Luynes had intended to send a brother of his into England with an
   embassy, the effect whereof should be chiefly to
   complain against me, and to obtain that I should be
   repealed ; and that he intended to relate the passages
   betwixt us at Saint-Jean-d'Angély, in a much different
   manner from that I reported, and that he would charge
   me with giving the first offence.   After thanks for this
   advertisement, I told them my relation of the business
   betwixt us, in the manner I delivered, was true, and
   that I would justify it with my sword ; at which they
   being nothing scandalized, wished me good fortune.

   LORD HERBERT OF CHERBURY : *Autobiography*.

3. The cat . . . in youth is swift, pliant, and merry, and
   leapeth and rusheth on everything that is before him ;
   and is led by a straw, and playeth therewith ; and is a
   right heavy beast in age and full sleepy, and lieth
   slyly in wait for mice : and is aware where they be
   more by smell than by sight, and hunteth and rusheth
   on them in privy places ; and when he taketh a mouse,
   he playeth therewith, and eateth him after the play.
   In time of love is hard fighting for wives, and one
   scratcheth and rendeth the other grievously with biting
   and with claws.   And he maketh a ruthful noise and
   ghastful, when one proffereth to fight with another ;
   and hardly is hurt when he is thrown down off an high
   place.   And when he hath a fair skin, he is as it were
   proud thereof, and goeth fast about ; and when his
   skin is burnt, then he bideth at home, and is oft for
   his fair skin taken of the skinner, and slain and flayed.

   BARTHOLOMEW ANGLICUS : *De Proprietatibus Rerum*
   (*c.* 1240).
   Translated by John Trevisa
   (1398, modernized 1582).

4. And those of the first age were Chaucer and Gower, both
   of them as I suppose Knights.   After whom followed

John Lydgate, the monk of Bury, and that nameless
who wrote the Satire called *Piers Plowman*. Next him
followed Harding the Chronicler, then in King Henry
the Eighth's times Skelton (I wot not for what great
worthness), surnamed the Poet Laureate. In the
latter end of the same king's reign sprang up a new
company of courtly makers, of whom Sir Thomas
Wyat the elder and Henry Earl of Surrey were the two
chieftains, who having travelled into Italy, and there
tasted the sweet and stately measures and style of the
Italian Poesy as novices newly crept out of the schools
of Dante, Ariosto and Petrarch, they greatly polished
our rude and homely manner of vulgar Poesy, from
that it had been before, and for that cause may justly
be said the first reformers of our English metre and style.
In the same time or not long after was the Lord Nicholas
Vaux, a man of much facility in vulgar makings.

GEORGE PUTTENHAM : *Of Poets and Poesy.*

5. *March* 6.—Up betimes, and . . . to Sir W. Coventry's
chamber ; where the first word he said to me was,
' Good-morrow, Mr Pepys, that must be Speaker of
the Parliament-house ' : and did protest I had got
honour for ever in Parliament. He said that his
brother, that sat by him, admires me ; and that another
gentleman said that I could not get less than £1,000
a year if I would put on a gown and plead at the
Chancery-bar ; but, what pleased me most, he tells
me that the Solicitor-General did protest that he
thought I spoke the best of any man in England. . . .
I to the Duke of York's lodgings . . . and, as soon
as he saw me, he told me, with great satisfaction that I
had converted a great many yesterday, and did, with
great praise of me, go on the discourse with me. And,
by and by, overtaking the King, the King and Duke of
York come to me both ; and he said, ' Mr Pepys, I
am very glad of your success yesterday ' ; and fell to
talk of my well speaking, and many of the Lords there.
My Lord Barkeley did cry me up for what they had
heard of it ; and others, Parliament men there, about
the King, did say that they never heard such a speech

in their lives delivered in that manner.   Progers, of the
Bedchamber, swore to me . . . that he did tell the King
that he thought I might teach the Solicitor-General.

SAMUEL PEPYS : *Diary* (*March* 1668).

6. If we consider how much men can suffer if they list, and
how much they do suffer for greater and little causes,
and that no causes are greater than the proper causes of
patience in sickness (that is necessity and religion),
we cannot, without huge shame to our nature, to our
persons, and to our manners, complain of this tax
and impost of nature.   This experience added something to the old philosophy.[1]   When the gladiators
were exposed naked to each other's short swords, and
were to cut each other's souls away in portions of
flesh, as if their forms had been as divisible as the life
of worms, they did not sigh or groan—it was a shame
to decline the blow but according to the just measures
of art.   The women that see the wound shriek out ;
and he that receives it holds his peace.   He did not
only stand bravely, but would also fall so ; and when
he was down, scorned to shrink his head when the
insolent conqueror came to lift it from his shoulders ;
and yet this man, in his first design, only aimed at
liberty, and the reputation of a good fencer.

JEREMY TAYLOR : *Holy Dying*.

7. Many persons of admirable abilities (if they have been
wisely managed and profitably employed) have spent
their whole time and diligence in commentating upon
Aristotle's philosophy, who could never go beyond
him because their design was only to follow, not
grasp, or lay hold on or so much as touch Nature,
because they caught only at the shadow of her in their
own brains.   And therefore we see, that for above a
thousand years together, nothing almost of ornament
or advantage was added to the uses of human society,
except only guns and printing ; whereas, since the
industry of men has ventured to go abroad, out of
books and out of themselves, and to work among God's

[1] Stoicism.

creatures instead of playing among their own, every age has abounded with excellent inventions and every year perhaps might do so, if a considerable number of select persons were set apart, and well directed and plentifully provided for the search of them. But our universities having been founded in those former times that I complain of, it is no wonder if they be defective in their constitution as to this way of learning which was not then thought on.

For the supplying of which defect it is humbly proposed to his sacred Majesty, his most honourable parliament and privy council, and to all such of his subjects as are willing and able to contribute anything towards the advancement of real and useful learning, that by their authority, encouragement, patronage, and bounty a philosophical college may be erected after this ensuing, or some such like model.

(Here follows a detailed description of the proposed college.)

ABRAHAM COWLEY : *A Proposition for the Advancement of Experimental Philosophy*.

8. A letter from Sir John Hawkins to Lord William Cecil :—

MY VERY GOOD LORD,—It may please your Honour to be advertised that Fitzwilliam is returned from Spain, where his message was acceptably received, both by the King himself, the Duke of Feria, and others of the Privy Council. His dispatch and answer were with great expedition and great countenance and favour of the King. The Articles are sent to the Ambassador with orders also for the money to be paid to me by him, for the enterprise to proceed with all diligence. The pretence is that my powers should join with the Duke of Alva's powers, which he doth secretly provide in Flanders, as well as with powers which will come with the Duke of Medina Celi out of Spain, and to invade this realm and set up the Queen of Scots. They have practised with us for the burning of Her Majesty's ships. Therefore there should be some good care had of them, but not as it may appear that anything is discovered. The

King has sent a ruby of good price to the Queen of Scots, with letters also which in my judgment were good to be delivered.   The letters be of no importance, but his message by word is to comfort her, and say that he hath now none other care but to place her in her own.   It were good also that Fitzwilliam may have access to the Queen of Scots to render thanks for the delivery of the prisoners who are now at liberty. It will be a very good colour for your Lordship to confer with him more largely.

I have sent your Lordship the copy of my pardon from the King of Spain in the order and manner I have it, with my great titles and honours from the King, from which God deliver me.   Their practices be very mischievous, and they be never idle ; but God, I hope, will confound them and turn their devices on their own necks.

Your Lordship's most faithfully to my power,

JOHN HAWKINS.

9. If the imitation of Nature be the business of a poet, I know no author who can justly be compared with ours, especially in the description of the passions. And to prove this, I shall need no other judges than the generality of his readers : for, all passions being inborn with us, we are almost equally judges when we are concerned in the representation of them.   Now I will appeal to any man, who has read this poet, whether he finds not the natural emotion of the same passion in himself which the poet describes in his feigned persons ?   His thoughts, which are the pictures and results of those passions, are generally such as naturally arise from those disorderly motions of our spirits.   Yet, not to speak too partially on his behalf, I will confess that the copiousness of his wit was such that he often writ too pointedly for his subject, and made his persons speak more eloquently than the violence of their passion would admit : so that he is frequently witty out of season ; leaving the imitation of Nature, and the cooler dictates of his judgment, for the false applause of Fancy.

JOHN DRYDEN : *Ovid and the Art of Translation.*

CHAPTER XI

PUNCTUATION

THE purpose of punctuation is to help clarity of expression. If your thoughts were expressed always in short sentences the chief objection would be, not the monotony of sound and sense, but the difficulty for your listener to distinguish important remarks from matters of trivial interest. Merely parenthetical matter, such as asides or qualifications of statements just made, will thus be given unnecessary prominence instead of being properly subordinated.

Punctuation is valuable in showing the relationships between words and ideas. It maintains the unity of the sentence and of the paragraph. You have already worked some exercises in sentence-joining where you were told that your efforts made for greater continuity of a short passage. In the extracts given in Chapter IX, see how modern writers achieve power and grace of expression by the grouping, sequence, and subordination of thought. Punctuation is their powerful aid.

You will find that the older writers loved to sprinkle commas and semicolons without considering whether any useful purpose was being served.

In the meantime, loss of blood, vexation, and want of food contributed, with the noisome stench of the place, to throw me into a swoon ; out of which I was recovered by a tweak of the nose, administered by the tar who stood over us, who at the same time regaled me with a draught of flip, and comforted me with the hopes of being put on board the *Thunder* next day, where I should be freed of my handcuffs, and cured of my wounds by the doctor. I no sooner heard him name the *Thunder*, than I asked if he had belonged to that ship long ? and he giving me to understand he had belonged to her five years, I inquired if he knew Lieutenant Bowling ? ' Know Lieutenant Bowling,' said he,—' odds my life ! and that I do ! and a good seaman he is, as ever stepp'd upon forecastle,—and a brave fellow as ever crack'd biscuit ; none of your Guinea pigs,—nor your fresh-water, wishy-washy, fair-weather fowls. Many a taut gale of wind have honest Tom Bowling and I weathered together. Here's his health with all my heart, wherever he is, aloft or alow—in heaven or in hell—all's one for that—he needs not be ashamed to show himself.' I was so much affected with this eulogium, that I could not refrain from telling him that I was Lieutenant Bowling's kinsman ; in consequence of which connection he expressed an inclination to serve me, and, when he was relieved, brought some cold boiled beef in a platter, and biscuit, on which we supped plentifully, and afterwards drank another can of flip together.

TOBIAS SMOLLETT : *Roderick Random.*

If you rewrite this passage, giving it modern paragraphing and punctuation, you will find that the writer is inconsistent, especially in his treatment of parentheses. Which parentheses, for instance, does he leave without punctuation ? How does he indicate the others ? In the last sentence which commas could advantageously be omitted ? If you read much of Smollett you will find that his sentences are usually long and rambling and that he uses semicolons as convenient resting-places, spread out at intervals to give the reader time to pause. Even to-day there are many who have this incorrect, ' resting-place ' notion of punctuation ; to them the far more important aspects are lost.

Nowadays it is considered a misconception to think that whenever you make a pause in reading it is necessary to insert at least a comma. Punctuation has become more logical : there should be a reason for each stop used. Since writers' styles differ it is not possible to give hard-and-fast rules. You would soon tire of reading several pages of clipped, staccato sentences, consisting of half-a-dozen words followed by a full stop. These broken pieces are not all of equal importance ; their relation-ships and degrees of dependence emerge if the passage is properly punctuated, and if helpful link-words are given.

Compare these passages :—

(*a*) The money was paid. It was not enough. The Company had financial embarrassments. The late events in the south of India had increased these financial embarrassments. Hastings was determined to plunder Cheyte Sing. For that end he determined to fasten a quarrel on him. Cheyte Sing was now required to keep a body of cavalry for the service of the British government. He objected and evaded. Hastings wanted him to do this. . . .

(*b*) The money was paid. But this was not enough. The late events in the south of India had increased the financial embarrassments of the Company. Hastings was determined to plunder Cheyte Sing, and, for that end, to fasten a quarrel on him. Accordingly, the Rajah was now required to keep a body of cavalry for the service of the British government. He objected and evaded. This was exactly what the Governor-General wanted.

LORD MACAULAY : Warren Hastings.

Notice how link-words were used in passage (*b*), the one which Macaulay actually wrote. Now write this passage as a single sentence. You will probably use some semicolons : you will be unable to dispense with commas.

Punctuation thus has a structural value in composition. It is not profitable to assign degrees of importance for punctuation marks : often you will find authors using semicolons where the change in construction is so abrupt that you would expect a colon at least.

' Let's look out of the window,' said Pa ; he had three favourite pastimes, and this was one of them.

STELLA GIBBONS : Miss Linsey and Pa.

More often still you will find closely-related clauses separated only by commas.

> The children of Radford Street were shut in school, Pa was at his cinema, Mrs Fell was out, and only the hidden Mr Fell moved now and again across the floor of the room overhead, among the sweet, piping, ejaculatory noises behind the shut door.   STELLA GIBBONS : *ibid.*

Here the statements are closely related in sequence ; compare them with the sequence of adjectives at the end of the passage. What would be the effect of putting semi-colons after *school, cinema,* and *out* ?

COMMAS are used to separate words, phrases, and, as you have seen above, clauses appearing in a series.

> Tom had won his School colours for football, cricket, swimming, and athletics. (*The use of the last comma is optional.*)

> Such a rogue is cool, irrepressible, persistent, and wholly obnoxious.

> Happily, noisily, excitedly, the children boarded the excursion steamer.

> There are those upon whom we feel an immediate and daily dependence in health and in sickness, in infancy and in old age.

> What we have said of the word ' self-interest ' applies to all the synonyms and circumlocutions which are employed to convey the same meaning ; pain and pleasure, happiness and misery, objects of desire, and so forth.
>   LORD MACAULAY.

In the above passage many writers would prefer a colon to the semicolon as an introduction to the words which amplify ' self-interest.'

COMMAS are also used to enclose parentheses, though this work is often done by dashes or brackets.

> It would seem, merely from the appearance of this document, that it is a clumsy forgery.

> If a philosopher were always to state facts in the following form—' There is a shower : but whatever is, is ; therefore,

there is a shower,'—his reasoning would be perfectly sound ; but we do not apprehend that it would materially enlarge the circle of human knowledge.   LORD MACAULAY.

Mr Hathaway, the then steward (for this happened a little before my time), with that patient sagacity which tempered all his conduct, determined to investigate the matter, before he proceeded to sentence.

Parenthetical relative clauses should also be enclosed : here the comma is to be preferred to the bracket or the dash.

These Chinese pirates, *who for years plundered at will*, have all been captured.

If the relative clause is *not* parenthetical, *i.e.*, if it merely defines, there is no need to enclose it between commas.

Those who saw the Chinese Exhibition were amazed at the Sung vases.

All boys who have bought dinner tickets can exchange them for a basket of strawberries.

(*Who have bought dinner tickets* does not give us a wealth of additional information about the boys.)

Words that stand in the same grammatical relationship to each other, that is, words which are in *apposition*, are indicated by commas.   The same indication often applies to parallel phrases and clauses.

Tom, the doctor's son, carefully took out the book's appendix.

His father, his uncle, and his two cousins searched vainly for the missing pages.

His father stamped with rage, gritted his teeth, threatened all kinds of punishments, but finally saw the humour of the situation.

COMMAS also indicate subordinate clauses.   Clause analysis becomes easier if punctuation is studied.

As you will see, Tom was imitating his father.

Although we have lived in this district for five years, we have very few friends.

Since you are so pressing, I will take another cup of tea.

Tom was very late that morning, for he had stayed up overnight to finish his book.

The SEMICOLON is used to subordinate ideas closely related to, or dependent on, a main topic.[1]

Not only may judges be made peers ; but all the peers are necessarily judges.   MACAULAY.

Cows awake on the meadows ; sheep break their fast on dewy hillsides, and change to a new lair among the ferns ; and houseless men, who have lain down with the fowls, open their dim eyes and behold the beauty of the night.

In a narrative passage semicolons speed up the movement.

She put on her spectacles because they made her look older, and thus gave her confidence ; took them off again because she despised herself for requiring such a prop ; put them on once more because she usually wore them at this hour while digesting the *Daily Herald* ; stood in front of the gas-mask ; then sat on the sofa ; stood by the window . . .   STELLA GIBBONS.

At what effect is the writer aiming ?

The semicolon is often a convenient way of dispensing with a conjunction. Too often in students' essays a long sequence of thoughts is strung together with ands, buts, and the almost ubiquitous *so*.

The semicolon is often used in place of a comma to give the reader a little extra time to assimilate a remark.

Ideas have changed ; invention has followed invention. Soldiers were monumental objects then. A divinity still hedged kings here and there ; and war was considered a glorious thing.   THOMAS HARDY.

What would be the effect of removing the second semicolon ?

[1] Explanatory matter is usually enclosed in a square bracket. It also denotes words conjecturally supplied by the editor of a text.

Napoleon said that without him [Rousseau] the French Revolution would not have occurred.

The COLON is considered by many modern writers to be useful for doing odd jobs. Others assign to it special tasks, such as introducing statements amplifying a preceding sentence ; separating the parts of antitheses ; or introducing lists of words or quotations.

The landscape in which the cottage stood was most seductive : a bland line of undulations too indefinite to be called hills ran behind it, scattered with tufty sturdy oak trees, whence came the occasional soft, rounded call of a ring-dove. STELLA GIBBONS.

Therefore, the better the government, the greater is the inequality of conditions : and the greater the inequality of conditions, the stronger are the motives which impel the populace to spoliation. LORD MACAULAY.

This is the crowning passage : ' Fiercest heat-giver of all timber is green oak, from him none may escape unhurt ; by partiality for him the head is set on aching, and by his acrid embers the eye is made sore. . . .' W. B. YEATS.

All really happened exactly as I have described it : the story is told in letters and documents of the authenticity of which there is not the smallest doubt. J. A. FROUDE.

A FULL STOP or PERIOD [1] terminates the expression of a thought. It is, of course, usually linked in thought to a preceding or subsequent sentence, but the writer has decided to make a break for the reader to assimilate the ideas. The sentence need not contain a verb ; its omission sometimes conduces to an effect, perhaps a shrewd thrust :—

And Mrs Fell was in the kitchen as usual, smelling the place out with those Epicure bathsalts which told you on

---

[1] At this stage it is assumed that the student is familiar with the use of the full stop for abbreviations and with the use of capital letters. It is also assumed that no comment is necessary on the question mark or the exclamation mark, and the fact that they are not invariably followed by a capital letter.

the packet to enjoy a luxury which the Greeks might envy.
Twopence a cube.   STELLA GIBBONS.

The DASH, when not used in a parenthesis, is often
used singly to denote a sudden break in the sentence or
a change in construction.   Charles Lamb uses it most
effectively.

I like to meet a sweep—understand me—not a grown
sweeper—old chimney-sweepers are by no means attractive
—but one of those tender novices, blooming through their
first nigritude, the maternal washings not quite effaced
from the cheek—such as come forth with the dawn, or
somewhat earlier, with their little professional notes sound-
ing like the *peep peep* of a young sparrow ; or liker to the
matin lark should I pronounce them in their aerial ascents
not seldom anticipating the sunrise ?

The Praise of Chimney-Sweepers.

INVERTED COMMAS, or QUOTATION MARKS, denote a
speaker's actual words.   In quoting from an author you
should use quotation marks only when you are giving
the exact words ; you should not use them if you are
merely giving the gist of a passage.   A quotation within a
quotation is often printed with double instead of single
inverted commas.   This practice is not universal ; you
should therefore aim only at being consistent.

Study the examples :—

' Why, I hope not,' returned Mr Swiveller, ' but the
average number of letters it takes to soften her is six, and
this time we have got as far as eight without any effect at
all.   I'll write another to-morrow morning.   I mean to blot
it a good deal and shake some water over it out of the pepper-
castor, to make it look penitent.   " I'm in such a state of
mind that I hardly know what I write "—blot—" if you
could see me at this minute shedding tears for my past
misconduct "—pepper-castor—" my hand trembles when I
think "—blot again—if that don't produce the effect, it's
all over.'

CHARLES DICKENS : *The Old Curiosity Shop.*

HOTSPUR.   You say true.
          Why, what a candy deal of courtesy
          This fawning greyhound then did proffer me !
          Look, ' when his infant fortune came to age,'
          And ' gentle Harry Percy,' and ' kind cousin.'
          O ! the devil take such cozeners.
                    SHAKESPEARE : 1 *Henry IV*, I, iii.

Titles of literary works, unless italicized, are printed with inverted commas.

The apostrophe is used to denote possession. You are doubtless familiar with the rule, but be careful with plural words ending in —*n*.

> The boy's bat.   The boys' department.   Men's overcoats.
> Children's admission tickets.

Notice also the following examples :—

> Cassius' last speech ; Keats's odes ; for goodness' sake ;
> for old acquaintance' sake.

The apostrophe is also used to indicate the omission of letters, when, in spoken rather than in written English, words are contracted. It is better to write *I should* and not *I'd*.

The HYPHEN joins two or more words which are re-garded as one. This temporary union sometimes becomes permanent. *Nowadays* is always written as one word ; it used to be *now-a-days*.

You will find a present-day tendency to hyphen words that are used as compound adjectives, but otherwise to write them without the hyphen.

> Scouts prefer an *out-of-door* life : they have great fun out of doors.

The hyphen also serves to link parts of a word separated for reasons of space. You should see that such words are beheaded rather than curtailed ; *e.g.*, dis-concerted and not disconcert-ed ; you must divide them into pro-nounceable syllables ; *e.g.*, il-lustrations or illustra-tions but not illustratio-ns.

H. W. Fowler's *Dictionary of Modern English Usage* will entertain you for a whole evening on this subject alone.

Subtleties and Shades [1]

In speaking you can tell by intonation whether a question is being asked. In writing, punctuation helps to interpret the speaker's intention.

> You have joined the army ?
> You have joined the army !
> Don't look round every time the door opens and join in the singing.
> Don't look round every time the door opens, and join in the singing.

What is the difference in meaning of the above sentences? Punctuation is full of subtlety.

> I called for Tom this evening but found that he was out.

This is a plain, straightforward statement. There is no expression of disappointment; in fact no emotion is expressed.

What shades of meaning are suggested by the following ?

> I called for Tom this evening, but found that he was out.
> I called for Tom this evening ; but found that he was out.
> I called for Tom this evening. But found that he was out.
>
> (The last is *not* wrong. It is foolish to make an inviolable rule; 'You must not begin a sentence with a conjunction,' or, ' You must not end a sentence with a preposition.')

Dots, dashes, and asterisks are all called in to assist emotional expression. Sterne's *Tristram Shandy* and, in modern times, the novels of Mr H. G. Wells illustrate this aspect of punctuation.

*   *   *   *   *   *   *

Here, these are not emotional asterisks ! In speaking of

---

[1] Among the subtleties may be included the use of inverted commas for ironical purposes. We should be unlikely to patronize the furniture shop which displayed as an advertisement, ' genuine ' antiques.

There is no necessity to use several exclamation marks together; it is a device best left to trading circulars and circus posters.

punctuation you should beware of hard and fast rules. There are fashions in punctuation, so that you should study the work of modern writers.[1] In particular, you should notice how their sentences are linked. Take some of their paragraphs ; write out each remark as a separate simple sentence ; close the book, and see how effectively you can rebuild.

Exercises

1. Punctuate the following, each in two ways, and explain the difference :—

(a) West said the sailor climbing the rigging was incapable.
(b) While struggling for words the chairman said to do your best is impossible to read much is the secret.
(c) In answer to your letter I got up too late to come to work.
(d) I cannot agree with you and I prefer to see things in their true light retorted Mrs Smith.

2. Punctuate the following sentences :—

(a) A lecture on silk worms-it is a waste of time.
(b) The manager is usually a kind fellow it isnt his fault.
(c) The manager is a kind fellow therefore it is not his fault.
(d) If this statement is true there is nothing to be explained.
(e) However we are going home to-morrow.
(f) However we are to get home I dont know.
(g) You fortunate ones however have a car.
(h) The weather looks very overcast still the children have had several fine days.
(i) The frozen snow greatly impeded the explorers also the motor sledges had broken down.
(k) Every facility will be offered so that your holiday will be free from care.
(l) Experienced guides will meet you at the station so dont let the language difficulty worry you.

3. Punctuate the following and insert the necessary capitals :—

(a) What talkest thou to me of the hangman if I hang Ill make a fat pair of gallows for if I hang old sir john hangs with me and thou knowest hes no starveling

[1] What is the effect of omitting the comma in this sentence ?

(*b*) May the present moment said dick sticking his fork into a large carbuncular potato be the worst of our lives I like this plan of sending em with the peel on theres a charm in drawing a potato from its native element if I may so express it to which the rich and powerful are strangers ah man wants but little here below nor wants that little long how true that is after dinner

(*c*) Is it possible that institutions may be established which without the help of earthquake of famine of pestilence or of the foreign sword may undo the work of so many ages of wisdom and glory and gradually sweep away taste literature science commerce manufactures everything but the rude arts necessary to the support of human life

3. Criticize the punctuation of the following, and, if necessary, rewrite them with improved punctuation :—

(*a*) There was once a poorly paid scholar in Germany who was in love with a rich miller's daughter named Gretchen, but her father did not approve of him having other plans.

(*b*) A chance had fallen to him which might never return ; not for the vain distinction of carrying prizes into English ports, not for the ray of honour which would fall on him if he could carry off the sacred banner itself and hang it in the Abbey at Westminster, but a chance so to handle the Armada that it should never be seen again in English waters, and deal such a blow on Philip that the Spanish Empire should reel with it.
J. A. FROUDE.

(*c*) If she be rich, then she is fair, fine, absolute and perfect, then they burn like fire, they love her dearly, like pig and pie, and are ready to hang themselves if they may not have her.   ROBERT BURTON.

(*d*) The world, in short, may cry out at a bankrupt who appears at a ball ; at an author who laughs at the public which pronounces him a dunce ; at a general who smiles at the reproach of the vulgar, or the lady who keeps her good humour in spite of scandal ; but such is the wisest behaviour they can possibly assume ; it is certainly a better way to oppose calamity by dissipation, than to take up the arms of reason or resolution to oppose it : by the first method we forget our miseries, by the last we only conceal them from others ; by struggling with misfortunes we are sure to receive some wounds in the conflict. The only method to come off victorious is by running away.

OLIVER GOLDSMITH.

(e) This critic refers to Mr Shaw's play *Joan of Arc*, she surely means *St Joan*.

(f) Any woman who says she was born in 1871 can be relied upon to be speaking the truth.

4. Write in the form of verse :—

(a) There was a faith healer of Deal who said although pain isn't real if I sit on a pin and puncture my skin I don't like what I fancy I feel.

(b) O happy peasant O unhappy bard his the mere tinsel hers the rich reward he prais'd perhaps for ages yet to come she never heard of half a mile from home he lost in errors his vain heart prefers she safe in the simplicity of hers. WILLIAM COWPER : *Truth*.

(c) Say that she rail why then I'll tell her plain she sings as sweetly as a nightingale say that she frown I'll say she looks as clear as morning roses newly wash'd with dew say she be mute and will not speak a word then I'll commend her volubility and say she uttereth piercing eloquence if she do bid me pack I'll give her thanks as though she bid me stay by her a week if she deny to wed I'll crave the day when I shall ask the banns and when be married but here she comes and now Petruchio speak.

LETTER WRITING

It is the fashion nowadays to treat letter writing as a nuisance ; indeed, some would declare it an unnecessary nuisance as there are so many other forms of communication. There are still occasions when letters give pleasure to friends,[1] and in business it is often essential to write

[1] A short letter to a distant friend, is, in my opinion, an insult like that of a slight bow or a cursory salutation ;—a proof of unwillingness to do much, even where there is a necessity of doing something.

DR JOHNSON : *Letter to Mr Joseph Baretti*.

to make detailed inquiries or to confirm an arrangement or appointment made.

(1) *Private Letters*

In letters to friends there is often a desire to throw off the shackles of convention, to give no heed to expression or paragraphing, and to contemn punctuation as unworthy of consideration. In cultivating a racy style for the occasion you lapse into slang, so much so, that if your friend is not thoroughly up-to-date in his knowledge of the latest catch-phrases, you are incoherent.

To speak badly is not a rich and rare form of humour. There is even less excuse for writing incorrectly, since a letter is a more permanent record of expression. Examiners heavily penalize bad English, so that if you are asked to write a letter and you produce something that requires copious footnotes to be understood, you are assured of failure. So also, unless friendship is very strong it may not stand the stress of being subjected to an intermittent bombardment of illiteracy.

The austerity of an examination room curbs levity; the result is that the letters written are often unduly staid, serious, and dull. The reader feels that the writers have given up all hope of ever being happy in this world : perhaps this is the natural reaction from the careless scrawls hastily posted off as tokens of friendship.

The address and date must be given, not omitted or squeezed in at the top as an afterthought. The conclusion should clearly show something of a friendly warmth—aim at a compromise between aloof frigidity and Wodehousean inconsequence.[1]

Above all, the letter should be paragraphed as carefully as if you were writing an essay.

In the opening paragraph it is a good plan to make a

[1] This is not a pedant's attack on Mr Wodehouse's delightful fooling. Grown-ups ape the speech of his characters ; adolescents sometimes regard it as the consummation of epistolary style.

few friendly inquiries and to give some personal details. After that you can plunge into the main theme. There is no need to introduce the word I into every sentence ; thoughts and reflections can just as easily be expressed in the third person, unless, of course, you wish to be in an intimate or playful mood.

In 1739 the poet Thomas Gray and his friend Horace Walpole were on a tour of the Continent. Here are two letters written to the same friend Richard West. Fashions have changed : you will notice that the letters are not paragraphed.

PARIS, *May* 22, 1739.

After the little particulars aforesaid I should have proceeded to a journal of our transactions for this week past, should have carried you post from hence to Versailles, hurried you through the gardens to Trianon, back again to Paris, so away to Chantilly. But the fatigue is perhaps more than you can bear, and moreover I think I have reason to stomach your last piece of gravity. Supposing you were in your soberest mood, I am sorry you should think me capable of ever being so *dissipé* so *evaporé*, as not to be in a condition of relishing anything you could say to me. And now, if you have a mind to make your peace with me, arouse ye from your megrims and your melancholies, and (for exercise is good for you) throw away your night-cap, call for your jack-boots, and set out with me, last Saturday evening, for Versailles—and so at eight o'clock, passing through a road speckled with vines and villas and hares and partridges, we arrive at the great avenue, flanked on either hand with a double row of trees about half a mile long, and with the palace itself to terminate the view ; facing which, on each side of you is placed a semi-circle of very handsome buildings, which form the stables. These we will not enter into, because you know we are no jockeys. Well ! and is this the great front of Versailles ? What a huge heap of littleness ! it is composed, as it were, of three courts, all open to the eye at once, and gradually diminishing till you come to the royal apartments, which on this side present but half a dozen windows and a balcony. This last is all that can be called a front, for the rest is only great wings. The hue of all this mass is black, dirty red, and yellow ; the first proceeding from stone changed by age ; the second from a mixture of brick ; and the last, from a profusion of tarnished gilding. You cannot see a more disagreeable *tout-ensemble* ; and, to finish the matter, it is all stuck over in many places with small busts of a tawny hue between every two windows. We pass through this to go into the garden, and here the case is indeed altered ; nothing can be vaster and more magnificent than the back front ; before it a very spacious terrace spreads itself, adorned with two large basons ; these are bordered and lined (as most of the others) with white marble, with handsome statues of bronze reclined on their edges. From hence you descend a huge flight of steps into a semi-circle formed by woods that are cut all around into niches, which are filled with beautiful copies of all the famous antique statues in white marble. Just in the midst is the bason of Latona ; she and her children are standing on the top of a rock in the middle, on the sides of which are the peasants, some half, some totally changed into frogs, all which throw water at her in great plenty. From this place runs on the great alley, which brings you into a complete round, where is the bason of Apollo, the biggest in the gardens. He is rising in his car out of the water, surrounded by nymphs and tritons, all in bronze, and finely executed, and these, as they play, raise a perfect storm about him ; beyond this is the great canal, a prodigious long piece of water that terminates the whole. All this you have at one *coup d'œil* in entering the garden, which is truly great. I cannot say as much of the general taste of the place ; everything you behold savours too much of art ; all is forced, all is constrained about you ; statues and vases sowed everywhere without distinction ; sugar-loaves and minced pies of yew ; scrawl work of box, and little squirting *jets-d'eau*, besides a great sameness in the walks, cannot help striking one at first sight, not to mention the silliest of laby-rinths, and all Æsop's fables in water ; since these were designed *in usum Delphini* only. Here then we walk by moon-light, and hear the ladies and the nightingales sing. Next morning, being Whitsunday, make ready to go to the installa-tion of nine Knights du Saint Esprit, Cambis is one : high mass celebrated with music, great crowd, much incense, king, queen, dauphin, mesdames, cardinals, and court : knights arrayed by his majesty ; reverences before the altar, not bows but curtsies ; stiff hams ; much tittering among the ladies ;

trumpets, kettledrums, and fifes. My dear West, I am vastly
delighted with Trianon, all of us with Chantilly ; if you would
know why, you must have patience, for I can hold my pen no
longer, except to tell you that I saw ' Britannicus ' last night ;
all the characters, particularly Agrippina and Nero, done to
perfection ; to-morrow " Phædra and Hippolitus." We are
making you a little bundle of *petites pièces* ; there is nothing in
them, but they are acting at present ; there are too Crebillon's
' Letters,' and ' Amusemens sur le langage des Bêtes,' said to
be of one Bougeant, a Jesuit ; they are both esteemed, and
lately come out. This day se'nnight we go to Rheims.

This letter may be somewhat breathless, but it is full
of interesting impressions and descriptions. It is infinitely
more satisfying than a casual post-card :—' Saw Versailles
today—fountains playing—interesting investiture ceremony—went to the Opéra—hope all are well—please
send another five pounds. Will write again soon. Love.
Tom.'

To Richard West, Esq.

FROM A HAMLET AMONG THE MOUNTAINS
OF SAVOY.
28*th Sept.*, 1739.

Precipices, mountains, torrents, wolves, rumblings, Salvator
Rosa—the pomp of our park and the meekness of our palace !
Here we are, the lonely lords of glorious, desolate prospects. I
have kept a sort of resolution which I made of not writing to
you as long as I stayed in France ; I am now a quarter of an
hour out of it, and write to you. Mind, 'tis three months since
we heard from you. I begin this letter among the clouds ;
where I shall finish, my neighbour, Heaven, probably knows :
'tis an odd wish in a mortal letter to hope not to finish it on
this side the atmosphere. You will have a billet tumble to
you from the stars when you least think of it ; and that I
should write it too ! Lord, how potent that sounds ! But
I am to undergo many transmigrations before I come to
' yours ever.' Yesterday I was a shepherd of Dauphiné ;
today an Alpine savage ; tomorrow a Carthusian monk ; and
Friday a Swiss Calvinist. I have one quality which I find
remains with me in all worlds and in all ethers ; I brought it
with me from your world, and am admired for it in this,—'tis

my esteem for you.   This is a common thought among you, and you will laugh at it ; but it is new here,—as new to remember one's friends in the world one has left, as for you to remember those you have lost.   (From *Horace Walpole*.)

Here there is a delicate air of mockery, a spirit of friendly banter. Although not so detailed a letter as Gray's, it was probably not the less welcome. You should read some of the ' divine chit-chat ' of Cowper, and as much as you can of the correspondence of Shelley, Keats, and Charles Lamb.

(2) *Commercial Correspondence*

A business letter should be courteous and concise.

Commercial English is the same language as ordinary English, though some business men try to smarten up their English by using clichés and ugly abbreviations. For some years there has been a reaction against business jargon.   It may seem more courteous to say, ' Your esteemed favour is before us,' but it is wasting the reader's time when all you mean is ' We have read your letter,' and even this is an unnecessary remark.   ' Your letter to hand ' is neither good English nor courtesy.

Since it is often necessary to refer to a particular letter from a number that have passed between correspondents it is preferable to make references to a given date clearly —15th June—and not the 15th *prox.*, which, as business correspondence is filed, may lead to lost time in turning back to the date of the letter to translate *prox.*, especially, as Mr Herbert assures us, that some are by no means clear about *prox.*, *ult.*, *inst.*, and the baby of this obnoxious brood, *idem !* You should take to heart the exercise on page 70 of A. P. Herbert's *What a Word !*

Mr Herbert asks pointedly whether it is courteous to bombard people with ' rubber-stamp phrases which stink of insincerity ' ? It is amusing to be told by the manager of a huge hotel that he is ' looking forward to your visit ' when you are staying for only one night *four months hence*. You are, however, inclined to extend the visit.

Typical Business Letters

A.

EDS/F

THE ——— MUTUAL BENEFIT SOCIETY,
LONG LANE, W.C.6.
1st August, 1937.

E. H. JONES, Esq.,
541 Hatton Gardens, E.C.

DEAR SIR,
I am instructed by the Finance Committee
to direct your attention to the fact that our records show that
your subscription of five guineas for the year 1937 is still
outstanding, and to ask you to forward this amount as soon as
possible.

We understand the difficulties of our members, and we are
anxious to co-operate with them in every possible way, hence
we shall be glad to hear from you.

Possibly your subscription has been paid since we received
information from the Treasurer of your Branch, in which
case I need scarcely ask you to excuse this communication. I
shall be glad, however, if you will let me know if you have paid
your subscription so that we may immediately correct our
records.

Yours faithfully,
EDMUND D. SINCLAIR,
Secretary.

Notice the courtesy of this letter and its suggesting
that the subscription may already have been paid. Are
there any sentences in which you can detect the note of
insincerity ?

B.

RM/D

THE REMOV-DIRT CO., LTD,
353 VILLIERS ST., W.C.2.
1st March, 1937.

H. ELVES, Esq.,
582 Revel Drive, Edmonton, N. 9.

DEAR SIR,
In reply to your letter of 26th February, we
regret the delay in returning the suit you sent to be cleaned.

You will recall that it was collected in accordance with our recent advertising scheme whereby our normal charges were specially reduced by 50 %. You will appreciate that this exceptional offer led to a tremendous rush of business.

The young man who called on you gave your address as Reevers Drive, Beckenham, instead of Revel Drive, Edmonton. The suit was cleaned promptly and was sent to our Beckenham Branch.

We quite understand your anxiety ; we, however, wish to make it clear that this is an isolated case and that in a large business like ours we are continually employing new agents who, at times, fail to reach our high standard of efficiency.

Yours faithfully,

RODNEY MARCHANT,
Assistant Manager.

Notice that in these two letters the position held by the writer is indicated.

Exercises

1. Write a reply to the following invitation : use the third person.

ST GABRIEL'S HOSPITAL, EDEN HILL, N.W.26
NEW CHILDREN'S WARD
In memory of the late Rt. Rev. Hugh Briancourt

The Administrator
requests the pleasure of the company of
....

on the occasion of the
LAYING OF THE FOUNDATION STONE
at 3.30 *p.m., Thursday, June* 15*th,* 19—

Garden Party, 4 P.M. to 6 P.M.

R.S.V.P. to Administrator,
St Gabriel's Hospital,
Eden Hill, N.W.26.

---

2. Write some of the following letters, taking care to arrange your material in paragraphs, and to show something of a friendly spirit.

(a) To a friend whom you have not seen for two years, telling him of a visit your hockey club is paying to the town in which he lives.

(b) To a friend who is on holiday in Paris.

(c) To a cantankerous uncle who suggests coming to spend a fortnight with you. Be tactful.

(d) To a friend who is contemptuous of Rovers (or Rangers).

(e) To a chance acquaintance whom you met on a railway journey and from whom you borrowed a book which you are returning.

3. Write a reply to Specimen Letter A.

4. Write what in all probability was Mr Elves' letter to the cleaners. (Specimen Letter B.)

5. Write to the Editor of the School Magazine asking why he overlooked your article and printed others of, in your opinion, inferior merit.

6. Write the Editor's firm but patient reply.

7. You are the Secretary of a Cricket club which rents a ground from the local Council. On arriving one evening for net practice, not only do you find no nets up, but also there are two clubs playing on your wicket. Write a letter of inquiry or protest to the appropriate department.

8. The captain of one of the teams writes his account of what happened on the evening in question.

9. The Council reply to your letter.

10. The Vicar of St Jude's has permitted your Rangers' Company to hold a sports meeting in his field. Make your letter something more than an expression of thanks.

11. Apply to the Headmaster of your school for a testimonial as you are seeking the post of junior assistant chemist to a scent factory. You have recently been dismissed from your first post on account of unpunctuality.

12. A firm has supplied you with goods under a profit-sharing scheme whereby, if you become a regular customer,

7

you will receive a cash bonus. The agent has told you that you will receive from the firm a signed guarantee within forty-eight hours. This guarantee, however, has not been forthcoming within the stipulated time.

Write to the firm in question, Messrs Hollowson & Pickthank, Manton Square, E.C.4, inquiring about the delay and asking for details of the scheme. You should give full particulars about what has happened.

Sign your letter with a fictitious name.

London Chamber of Commerce.

13. Write to a foreigner who, when you were staying in France, gave you French lessons which have since proved of the greatest value.

14. Write to the Editor of your local newspaper in reply to a letter condemning carol-singing.

15. Apply to the skipper of a North Sea trawler asking his permission to accompany the ship on its next Iceland voyage. You will have to overcome his scruples about your being immune from sea-sickness and his superstitions about the bad luck that may ensue from his taking a passenger.

16. Write to the firm which has supplied you with a lawn-mower or a sewing-machine which fails to give satisfaction. Give full details.

17. Write the firm's reply to your letter. They are anxious to give you satisfaction but at the same time are conscious of the excellent quality of their goods.

18. Apply for the following post :—

> A SALESMAN required for sales work in London area. Must be energetic and have first-class references. Previous experience unnecessary but must have youth, personality, and unfailing optimism. Wages £2 a week together with liberal commission on sales. Box 10756, *Evening Herald.*

CHAPTER XII

ESSAY WRITING

. . . he remembers that she once set him to write an essay on the poet Gray which he did in very lofty terms, dismissing Gray as without genius, no true poet but a mere academic literary man. He sent her his essay full of confidence, thinking that he had done what no English critic had hitherto achieved—finally demolished Gray and destroyed his reputation. When he next went to her she began on his essay and with cold and scornful deliberation pulled it to pieces, criticizing unfavourably sentence after sentence and exposing to his shocked mind the cheapness of his style, the triteness of his ideas, the borrowed criticism and the ridiculously lofty tone of his precious effort.

W. J. Turner : *Blow for Balloons.*

(1) *Beginning to Write*

It is clear that before you can write on a variety of subjects you must be equipped with ideas. That is one reason why the reading of essays is included in your literature syllabus. You will see how an unpromising subject can be made into an interesting essay by a greater writer's power of linking and developing his thoughts. With him there is *a sense of structure.* You should, after having read an essay, notice how the paragraphs are constructed and how each contributes to the advancement of the central theme.

Whether you are reading fiction or non-fiction you should try to get at the very heart and spirit of the book. If the book is yours, mark passages of special interest and make marginal comments on happy turns of expression. This is not impudent presumption ; it shows that you are alert, that your mind is active and not dulled into quiescence.

Reading is but one form of mental activity. Ideas come from lectures and debates heard on the wireless and from talks with school-fellows. Discussion is a good way of testing the value of your ideas. Even if you find no one to agree with you, you are learning the lesson of swiftly coming to the point. Discussion helps you to acquire a directness of thought and expression which is so valuable in essay writing. Just as wavering, hesitant speech will soon make your audience melt away, so will an uncertain or pompous opening to an essay give the impression that you are going to be tedious and boring.

Reading, acquiring ideas, and learning to present them orally are but means to the essay writer's end. *He must write*. Too many shun the task of writing essays because of the work involved. A literary style does not proceed from reading alone. Much more is gained from practice in writing and from the will to delete feeble or inapt expressions.

In earlier chapters you have had practice in expressing yourself clearly. Simplicity of expression, as you will have seen from Chapter I, means neither childishness nor vagueness.

Your subject must also be clearly planned. To that end you must see that it has unity and that not too much is made of introductory or subordinate ideas. Many a candidate in School Certificate and even in severely competitive examinations courts failure by trying to rush down all his ideas into one long, rambling paragraph. If your failing is to spend too much time on an introduction to your subject, cure yourself by boldly taking your chief point into your first sentence.

Surprisingly often an opening paragraph is weak, for you have not yet got into your stride ; you are groping for words. You find that your second paragraph will make a far better opening to your essay. When this is so, strike out that first paragraph.

Do not fall into the habit of writing a long sequence of

short, scrappy paragraphs. The effect is like offering the reader meagre pinches of birdseed instead of a substantial meal. The length of the paragraph is unimportant so long as it is sustained by unity and interest. Little scraps of writing do not make for unity.

(2) *Essay Subjects*

If you are given a choice of subjects, before deciding on which you will write, think of the possibilities of some of the apparently unattractive ones. Do not necessarily write on an 'easy' subject. Probably the majority of candidates will choose that subject, so that there will be less chance of your distinguishing yourself; the ideas which occur to you will almost certainly have occurred to hosts of others. Consider, then, at least one other subject for a few moments, preferably one which has some 'body' in it, a subject which may provoke and develop a discussion. You need have no fear of being so provocative as to give offence. Your work is valued chiefly for its English. Fertility of thought is usually followed by richness of expression. Too many people if asked to write about *The Lumber Room* will try to weave a romance about it, filling their essays with unconvincing sentiment. Not many will roundly condemn the foolish passion for hoarding old rubbish. Some of the dullest essays are written on deceptively easy subjects : *My Future Career* seldom leads to a meritorious essay. Try setting down some ideas on this subject.

Now that you have finished you will probably agree how thin these ideas are. Everything is cut and dried : you will leave school in a year or two, have a short period of training, and then enter a profession. Why not adopt the attitude of a rebel against your own smug little community and, with your tongue in your cheek, show how utterly unfitted you are for the career planned for you, and confess that your real ambition is to be a steeple-jack ;

or a private detective, for fiction shows that detectives are born ready-made, no detail is ever given of their having been trained ; or just to do house-work. An essay is a writer's opinions on a subject ; he need not agree with all he writes. If sincerity leads you into writing dull essays, try to be provocative instead.

(3) *Setting to Work*

If you are going to write a narrative or a short biography, providing you have the necessary knowledge, your task is comparatively simple. The events will follow in chronological order, but you should be careful to make a preliminary plan in which the right proportion is allotted to the most important events. Do not neglect description : a description of the chief character gives value and interest to biographical study. You should also leave time for a concluding paragraph in which you will estimate the importance of the life's work of your central character.[1]

Exercise

Write an essay on one of the following subjects :—

(*a*) My first voyage.
(*b*) The story of Stonehenge.
(*c*) Launching a famous ship.
(*d*) The gipsy's curse.
(*e*) A play or a film that has impressed me.
(*f*) How Wolfe took Quebec.
(*g*) The career of Robert Clive.
(*h*) Sir Christopher Wren.

In a descriptive essay, such as *A Busy Station*, give some clear details, not a blurred confusion of noise and bustle. Make as vivid as you can brief impressions of

---

[1] Whatever the subject, read the question carefully to grasp its purport. Several candidates when asked to write about a local celebrity wrote a description of a local *celebration*. Others wrote about four or five celebrities.

two or three different groups of people rather than write out strings of words.

> There they were, the holiday makers, all ready for the seaside : fathers, mothers, big boys, babes in arms, nurses, soldiers, old men, strapping young fellows, cyclists : the station echoed with the shouts of porters, the cries of lost children, the poppings of corks, the wails of babies, the grumbles of late arrivals, the hissing of steam . . .

This is far too vague. It shows little observation or imagination ; you could write this kind of stuff by the hour. Why not, for a contrast, write one paragraph about a quiet spot in the midst of all this bustle ? Must *everybody* be excited with the thought of going to the seaside ? Are they all thinking exactly alike ? Are they all dressed alike ? You see, there is plenty of scope for clear detail. Do not make the mistake of trying to describe everything at once.

Exercise

Write an essay on one of the following subjects :—

(*a*) A place of great beauty.
(*b*) The trees in the city.
(*c*) Nature awaking.
(*d*) A visit to an art gallery.
(*e*) Castles in the air.
(*f*) The path of a great storm.
(*g*) A petrol station.
(*h*) Harvesting.
(*i*) The return of the fishing fleet.

Surprisingly good essays are written when a topic is being explained or described, especially if it has been the subject of a recent wireless talk. For this kind of matter you should be careful to put down as many ideas as you can and then shape them into an outline of your essay before you begin to write. Do not try to reproduce the talk or lecture word for word. As your essay advances, from time to time you should show, but not too obtrusively, how you react to the subject under discussion. In mentioning your opinions you do not have to prove that they are right, so that you need not hammer at them as if you have mistaken mere reiteration for forceful expression.

Exercise

An elderly friend of yours has had a talk with you. His ideas may be summarized thus :—

A Play performed in a Theatre

(a) is too long, the last act having been stuck on to pad the thing out till 10.50 at the earliest.

(b) is too dear, for unless I am prepared to pay twelve shillings and sixpence, plus sixpence for my hat and coat, plus sixpence for programme, plus an exorbitant charge for drinks, I have to mew myself up in seats from which I can scarcely see and hear, and which send me home with dented knees and other physical inflictions.

(c) means that nine times out of ten I am bored,

(d) but on the tenth occasion not even a seventh heaven is adequate to my ecstasy.

A Film performed in a Cinema :

(a) if I don't like it I know there will be a second feature or at least a Silly Symphony and a News Gazette :

(b) it is cheap and comfortable, and I can see and hear perfectly from any seat in the house :

(c) nine times out of ten I enjoy myself hugely :

(d) even so, I have forgotten all about the film and who played in it before I have turned the corner of the street.

Write a defence of the theatre and show that it has a vitality that will enable it to survive in spite of the encroachments of its newer rival.

Spend several minutes in thinking about this essay subject and in jotting down any ideas it suggests together with your feelings about them.

Arrange these thoughts under headings. *Do not start with the headings* and try to force ideas to conform with them One heading may cover three or four paragraphs. See that the ideas from which these paragraphs are to spring have a close connexion in thought.

Write your opening sentence. Let it be an attractive one; a good plan is to mention the title of the essay in this opening remark. Be relevant : do not leave your reader in doubt which subject you have chosen.

See that there is a development from the opening paragraph. Paragraphs do not just happen; they are the stepping-stones of your thoughts. If, when you have written about twenty lines you find yourself with only a very few ideas left, do not indulge in feeble repetition for it is now obvious you have chosen the wrong subject. It is far better to begin another subject than to become lost in deeper and deeper obscurity.

Leading articles from such papers as *The Times* or *The Manchester Guardian* are useful in showing ways of developing a subject in only a small space. If, for instance, you are asked to write on *Old Roads and New* and you are inclined to write a scathing condemnation of the ugliness of modern arterial roads, a reading of *The Times* leader on this subject [1] will show that there is a grandeur in the bold curves and undulations of these wide and efficient modern roads and that lovely colours may be thrown up from their surfaces. It is a lesson not to think of the picturesque as the only form of beauty.

If the subject is *The Merry Springtime*, you need not write the usual kind of essay which speaks of dancing round the maypole and of fields carpeted with flowers and of Nature rousing herself from her winter's sleep ; you may, of course, write a good essay even though the ideas are commonplace, but novelty of thought will attract more attention. It is, fortunately, impossible to teach originality.

[1] See *Third Leaders from* The Time‾, p. 74.

7 A

The following leader appeared recently in *The Times* :—

The Merry Springtime

The MINISTER OF AGRICULTURE, if anyone, ought to have the secret of making things grow. But it would seem that even he has at times to defer to the mysterious and apparently irrational agencies which regulate, or refrain from regulating, the changes of our weather. In describing recently the fight for life of the crocuses in his London window-boxes, the Minister remarked sorrowfully that they were ' wearying for the sun to come through.' A spring-like day or two seemed to be the immediate answer to the implicit prayer. The parks were heartened to open their own crocus display of purple and gold in a setting of vivid green, and their lunch-time population promptly manifolded itself in sympathy. Then back came the grey skies and the cold winds, until even the plain, blunt man could sympathize with the sensitive singer who ' dream'd that Spring would be no more.' We know in our hearts that the dream is only a nightmare. The lengthening of the day at either end, however chilly, contradicts the morbid fancy. But the long denial of sun and warmth breeds an unreasoning disposition to take a gloomy view of things, and all the statistics of the weather experts and all the reminders of experience cannot wholly exorcise it.

In winter, or in a cold spring, it needs a real effort of the imagination to conceive of an England in which men and women shed all the clothes they decently can, or even more, and go about bathed in perspiration and gasping for fresh air. In a heat-wave great-coats and mufflers and the biting east wind which finds the joints even in that armour seem just as distant and unreal. With human perversity, we have only to be in the one extreme to desire the other ardently. But there is much merit in the alternation. Continuous cold may be the bugbear at the moment, but continuous heat can be just as wearisome and just as trying. It does not need a patriarchal memory to recall summers in which the glare and the heat went on and on, until a grey sky and pouring rain came as a boon and a blessing to a parched people and a thirsty land. We may be thankful for our weather contrasts without forfeiting our birthright to grumble about them. It is not a very far-fetched idea that to them we owe a great deal of our national characteristic of refusing to get into a fuss about things before they happen, and, when happen they do, of dealing with them in a bluff, practical way which may not owe much to logic or theory but yet disposes of the difficulty with fair success. It is a useful quality in more than meteorological emergencies. In far more important things even the wisest and most clear-sighted of men cannot tell what is waiting for him round the next corner. In such a world there is much value in being compelled to develop and exercise a faculty of improvisation and in being trained to keep an equal mind under severe and sudden changes of condition. Whatever else we may say about the vagaries of our weather, we have at least to thank them for countless opportunities for such painful practice.

Notice the length of the second paragraph. Has it unity ? What is its chief topic ? Do not confuse the observations at the end of this passage with ' sermonizing.' In their place sermons are praiseworthy, but in your essays you should avoid trying to disguise that you have nothing to say by spreading a moral cloak over your writing. In other words, do not lecture or moralize at any great length.

Consider these two essays written during a recent examination. Which do you prefer ? Give reasons for your choice.

Electricity

Electricity made by dynamos through the continuous rush of water, has been, and still is, a great help to all people, for it is so convenient and there is less fear of there being an explosion.

Modern homes are all fitted with electricity because of its convenience and capabilities.

Electric lights are fitted in all rooms. A room is very soon cosy and warm after an afternoon's outing when using an electric fire. Ironing is a simple matter when using an electric iron for there is no time wasted as the iron is heating all the time.

Electricity is used for a means of execution in America by means of the electric chair.   It is a more sudden death than that of hanging as used in England.

In Tynemouth and many other places electricity is used to drive trains.

Electricity is used to drive engines as in the water-works at Bishop Auckland.

Even in fish-shops electricity is used to blaze the fires to fry the fish and chips.

Electric ovens are most useful and clean for the heat may be regulated and there is no fear of smoky dishes or pans as there is no flame.

An electric light may be taken into a gas-filled room with no fear of there being an explosion.

Electricity used in heating, lighting, driving engines and execution is most convenient, useful, and clean.

Chivalry

There were three grades in the order of chivalry—page, esquire, and knight.

The education of the page was conducted with the greatest care.   He was confined to the charge of a noble lady who inspired him with high deference to womanhood and taught him to appreciate the glories of the profession of arms.

When he was old enough he was presented to a priest before the altar who consecrated his sword and entrusted his future to some worthy knight.   He was forthwith attached to the personal service of his master, who instructed him in knightly exercises.   As his esquire, the former page now bore the knight's shield and accompanied him into battle and in all his wanderings.

Having acquitted himself well in war and peace, the esquire was at last deemed worthy of admission to the Order of Knighthood.   His admission was a sacred ceremony.   The day before his installation was spent in prayer and fasting and in the evening his armour was laid on the altar of some holy church.   All night long the future knight watched his armour on the altar, and on the morrow he knelt before the Sovereign Knight, who was to receive him, and took a solemn obligation to be ever ready to sacrifice himself in the defence of the honour and mysteries of Chivalry.

The installing knight gave the novice the accolade with his own sword, then raising him to his feet, took his sword from the altar and girded it to his side. The new knight was then clothed with the various pieces of his armour, and as he was invested, the emblematic sense of each piece was explained to him. He was told that his sword was the arm of mercy and was directed to conquer his enemies by mercy rather than force of arms. Its blade, he was reminded, was two-edged to enable him to maintain not only Chivalry but Justice, and he was instructed to contend only for the support of these Two Chief Pillars of the Temple of Honour.

His lance was the symbol of Truth because Truth, like the lance, is straight and to the point.

His coat of mail represented a fortress erected against vice, and just as a castle was surrounded by defensive works, so the knight's body was enveloped in his armour to defend him against Treason, Disloyalty, Pride and all other evil passions.

The spur was given to the knight symbolically to urge him on to deeds of honour and virtue. His shield was an emblem to remind him that the Knight of Chivalry was placed as a buckler between prince and people to preserve peace.

After his reception, the new champion of Chivalry paraded with great pomp before the populace and the stately ceremonial ended with a banquet followed by the bestowal of alms on the poor.

The public ceremonies were followed by a secret initiation in which the knight was introduced into a system of mysteries and placed in possession of the means of recognizing his brethren of the Order of Chivalry wherever he might meet them, whether by night or by day.

The motto of chivalry is also the motto of wisdom : to serve all and love but one.

Exercises

1. Write suitable opening sentences to an essay on

(*a*) This enlightened age.
(*b*) Slum clearance.
(*c*) Penny wise, pound foolish.
(*d*) Arterial roads.
(*e*) Wit and humour.

2. Write an opening paragraph for an essay on

(*a*) The month of May.
(*b*) On making mistakes.
(*c*) A visit of condolence.
(*d*) The pleasures and pains of business life.
(*e*) Luxuries and necessities.

3. Write the concluding paragraph to each one of the above essays. A wag once advised budding essayists to conclude by reproducing the opening paragraph, prefixing the words ' Thus it may be seen that . . . '

4. Develop each of the following topics by writing three paragraphs along the lines indicated :—

(*a*) The care of public health.	Illustration.
(*b*) The beauty of little things.	Contrast.
(*c*) A man in a huff.	Cause.
(*d*) Looking for lodgings.	Chronological.
(*e*) Civilization is an intermittent phenomenon.	Proof.
(*f*) How a lawn-mower works.	Explanation.

5. Subjects for Essays. Where you can, illustrate your ideas from your own observation or experience.

(i) Precautions I should take before buying a second-hand car.
(ii) How our town could be improved.
(iii) A day's outing ruined by the weather.
(iv) This modern cult of ugliness.
(v) A Red-letter day.
(vi) Machines of to-morrow.
(vii) In the kitchen.
(viii) Having to make a speech.

(ix) Careers for women.

(x) Dawn.

(xi) Church bells.

(xii) How to spend one's leisure.

(xiii) William Cowper. (Read Lord David Cecil's *The Stricken Deer*.)

(xiv) Nature's imperfections.

(xv) A mediæval castle.

(xvi) Soft words with nothing in them make a song.

(xvii) The village policeman.

(xviii) Modern smugglers.

(xix) Our daily newspaper.

(xx) Safety on the roads.

(xxi) Sea chanties.

(xxii) A dirty errand boy.

(xxiii) A walk in the country this month.

(xxiv) Inopportune laughter.

(xxv) A rogue in disguise.

(xxvi) For farmers only.

(xxvii) Why keep pets ?

(xxviii) The future of airways.

(xxix) The uses and abuses of advertising.

(xxx) The last moments of an exciting match.

(xxxi) A wasp with a sense of humour.

(xxxii) A humorous character whether in real life or in fiction.

(xxxiii) Comfort in the modern home.

(xxxiv) The function of the theatre.

(xxxv) The problem of over-production.

(xxxvi) It was the function of the nineteenth century to liberate : the function of the twentieth century is to control.

Three books you will find useful for further study are *Follow My Leader* (leaders from *The Times*), with an introduction by Sir John Squire ; *The Good New Days* by Marjorie and C. H. B. Quennell : and *The Reading and Writing of English* by E. G. Biaggini.

CHAPTER XIII

SYNTAX

> Your English style still continues in its purity and vigour.
> With vigour your genius will supply it : but its purity must
> be continued by close attention.
> DR JOHNSON (*Letter to Mr Joseph Baretti*).

THIS chapter is not an exhaustive treatise on minute and
arguable details. It draws the student's attention to such
errors of grammar and construction as are made in essays,
especially those written during examinations.

A. *Revision of Functional Grammar*

WORDS USED AS DIFFERENT PARTS OF SPEECH

NEEDS

(*a*) The farmer's place is important as he satisfies one of our
chief *needs*. (*Noun* : A Noun is the name by which a
thing is known.)

(*b*) Such a problem as this *needs* a little knowledge of algebra.
(*Verb* : A Verb is a word used to express what actions
are being done, or to say what state things are in.)

(*c*) To succeed, John *needs* must strive hard. (*Adverb* : An
Adverb is a word used with a verb to describe *how*,
when, *where*, *why*, or *how many times* the action expressed
by the verb is done. Adverbs are used with the other
parts of speech, except for nouns and pronouns.[1])

ALL

(*a*) From this schedule it appears that *all* is not hopeless.
(*Pronoun* : A Pronoun is a word used to refer to some
person or thing without mentioning the name.)

[1] For a fuller treatment of the kinds of adverbs, see p. 232.

(b) *All* the books in this box are to be sold for twopence each. (*Adjective* : An Adjective is a word used with a noun to describe more fully what is named by the noun.)

—Compose sentences in which *all* is used as a noun and as an adverb.

EXCEPT

(a) It was decided to *except* the rebel leader from the list of prisoners pardoned. (*Verb*.)

(b) All the rebels were pardoned *except* their leader. (*Preposition* : A Preposition is a word placed before a noun or pronoun to show some relation between the person or thing for which the noun or pronoun stands, and some thing or action indicated by another word.)

—To day it is an archaism to use *except* as a conjunction. We do, however, use *except that* as a conjunction.

THAT

The tide was rising so rapidly *that* escape was impossible. (*Conjunction* : A Conjunction is a word used to link the names of things or ideas. These ideas may be *co-ordinated*, *i.e.*, as separate statements of equivalent importance : It is raining $\frac{\text{and}}{\text{but}}$ I am going out ; or one or more ideas may be *subordinated* to a main idea. Whenever I want to go out it is always raining so that I have to be bothered with an umbrella as well as an attaché case and my shopping basket.)

Exercise

1. Pick out the conjunctions in the last sentence above and say what kind of work they do.

2. Define an Interjection. Give examples of interjections which express surprise, dismay, satisfaction, and contempt.

3. State the part of speech of the words italicized :—

(a) *Like* will to like. We *like* apricots. Please treat me *like* one of your family. The sisters were of a *like* disposition, so that you could not help *liking* them.

(*b*) The wrestler was *as* strong *as* a steel girder.   Grumbling *as* he went, the butler left the room.   Here you are, late *as* usual !   I appeal to you *as* my only sympathetic friend.   These poor creatures are but men *as* we are.

(*c*) I expect the baker has finished his *round* by now.   Well, *to round* off the discussion, let Mr Jones give his views.   Over and over again, *round* the ring, *round* and *round*, the elephants lumbered heavily.

(*d*) Well, we have *only* fourpence as the result of three hours' *singing*.   Thompson is *only* careless, *not* lazy.   The inspector would have *passed* me when I took my *driving* test *only* I twice flashed *past* the red lights.

4. Write sentences illustrating the different grammatical uses of the words in the following list.

(a. adjective ;   adv. adverb ;   n. noun ;   v. verb ;   prep. preposition ;   pron. pronoun ;   conj. conjunction.)

advance, n. v.	little, n. a. adv. pron.
any, a. adv. pro.	more, a. adv. pron.
as, adv. pron. conj.	near, a. v. adv. prep.
back, n. v. adv.	only, a. adv. conj.
before, adv. prep. conj.	short, n. a. adv.
bell, n. v.	since, adv. prep. conj.
better, n. a. adv. v.	that, a. pron. conj.
catch, n. a. v.	through, a. prep. adv.
club, n. v. a.	to, adv. prep.
compound, n. v. a.	what, pron. a. interjection.
either, a. adv. conj.	when, n. adv. conj. compound relative [1]
enough, a. pron. adv.	
equal, n. v. a.	where, adv. conj. compound relative [1]
express, n. a. v.	
forward, n. a. v. adv.	which, a. pron.
last, n. a. v. adv.	yet, adv. conj.

[1] For this use, consult *The Shorter Oxford English Dictionary*. When you do *that* and *what*, do not be satisfied with only *one* of the pronominal uses.

B. *Forms of the Verb Infinite*

1. The Infinitive

The Infinitive, as its name implies, is under no restrictions imposed by agreement with a subject. In the examples *I reach, he reaches, they reach*, the verb is inflected in order to accord with the number and person of its subject. The Infinitive *to reach* is always uninflected. There are, of course, past and future forms of the Infinitive, *to have fetched*, and *to be about to fetch*, and there are the Passive Voice forms, *to be fetched*, etc.

Although a part of a verb, the infinitive may exercise other functions : it can be used as a *noun*, as an *adjective*, and as an *adverb*.

As A NOUN, it can be the subject, object, or complement of a sentence.

> *To steal* is a punishable offence.   (Subject.)
> *To steam* the fish for five minutes was an easy task.
> *To be brought* home on a stretcher will be an unhappy ending to my hopes of success as a boxer.

> The referee decided *to abandon* the match.   (Object.)
> Barnsley hope *to be drawn* at home in the next round.
> John's friends watched him *go* to the cupboard.

> Another trick was *to tie* the door knockers of houses next door to each other.   (Complement.)
> To be happy is also *to be* wise.
> The new secretary's chief concern will be *to feather* his nest.

As AN ADJECTIVE, it is used with a noun or pronoun.

> These are idle words and not *to be remembered*.
> There was no water *to drink*.   (Cp. ' drinking water.')
> At last they found a house *to let*.
> I want the tie and handkerchief *to match*.

> We shall want someone *to let* us in.
> You ask for money ?   There is none *to come* to you.

As AN ADVERB, it is generally used (*a*) with a verb or (*b*) with an adjective.

(*a*) The car has come *to take* you away. (*Purpose.*)
   To hear him tell these droll stories, you would almost die of laughing. (*Condition.*)
   My aunt's deafness was such as *to make* her very irritable. (*Result.*)

(*b*) I do not understand this problem; it is too difficult *to follow*. It is not suitable *to set* in an examination.
   This cloth is too cheap *to be worth* buying. The witness was reluctant *to say* anything about his father.

In which of these twenty-two examples of the uses of the infinitive do you find a verb function in addition to that of a noun, adjective, or adverb?

2. The Gerund

The Gerund performs two functions; it is partly a noun, and partly a verb. Although it is identical in form with the active present participle, the latter has a different function since it is partly a verb and partly an adjective, or often only part of a continuous tense: *e.g.*, The vicar saw them as they were *coming* from church.

Compare

   Selling matches is not my life's ambition. (Gerund.)

with

   My friends saw Brown (as he was) *selling* handkerchiefs. (Present participle.)

The gerund can be the subject, object, or complement of a sentence.

   Stealing[1] is a punishable offence. (Subject.)
   Steaming the fish for five minutes is an easy task.
   To be singing in the streets at two o'clock in the morning may not prove his passion for music.
   The frequent *ringing* of the town crier's bell annoyed the visitors.

[1] Those who distinguish the Gerund from the Verbal Noun use the latter term when the *-ing* word has the function of a noun only.

Each nation considered *decreasing* its armaments. (Object.)

A good batsman will avoid *flicking* at a rising ball.

What is the grammatical function of *rising* in the above sentence ?

My friend's delight was *painting* portraits.   (Complement.)

Another feat was *balancing* a feather on the tip of his nose.

Compare the last two examples with ' Either he was *painting* portraits or *balancing* feathers.' What is the grammatical function of the words italicized ?

The Gerund can also be used as the object of a preposition.

The poachers, on *seeing* the gamekeeper, took to their heels.

Before *leaving* the theatre we stood up for the National Anthem.

No one was more careful in *driving* a car.

Father has forgotten about *winding* the clock.

Can you remember your recipe for *making* mince-pies ?

Exercise

Comment upon the functions of the words italicized.

1. We have no substitute *to replace* Kingaby.
2. Surely Thompson is fit *to replace* him ?
3. *Making* puns with the Bishop of Clogher gave Swift much joy.
4. The explorers were sad *to see* the end of all their hopes.
5. *Paying* a shilling, I went into the football ground.
6. By *paying* a further shilling I was admitted to the grandstand.
7. The home team was *playing* a new half-back.
8. By *joining* our Christmas club you will be assured of one of your family's *becoming* the richer by ten shillings.
9. Is this water fit *to drink* ?   I should not call it water *to drink*.
10. *Seeing* is *believing*.   *To deny* is often more easy than *to prove*.   Some things are impossible *to prove*, and you know how difficult I find *proving* things.

C. *The Absolute Construction*[1]

Consider these examples :—

> *The weather being dull*, few spectators were present at the opening of the Test Match.
> *All preparations having been completed*, the guests began to arrive in large numbers.

The italicized phrases are Absolute constructions. They are really adverb phrases.[2]

These absolute phrases can be expanded into adverb clauses.

The weather being dull $= \begin{cases} \text{As} \\ \text{Because the weather was dull} \ldots \\ \text{Since} \\ \text{While} \end{cases}$

The apparent neatness and conciseness of the absolute construction often leads to its over-use. In newspapers the writers of biographical particulars are fond of this method of slipping in an additional fact : ' His father dying at the age of thirty-five, Mr —— proceeded to South Africa where he soon won recognition as an engineer of considerable promise.' As you will see later, this construction may give rise to that common error, the unattached participle ; moreover, good critics regard the nominative absolute as inelegant.

You must not regard the subject of a finite verb as part of the absolute construction.

> The boy, having been warned of the dangers of the weir,[3] never ventured on that stretch of the river again.

---

[1] This is sometimes alluded to as the *Nominative Absolute*. As this chapter is concerned chiefly with grammar as a means of understanding details of expression, little mention is made of case.

[2] A *clause* is a group of words expressing a thought and *containing a finite verb*. A phrase is a group of words that does *not* contain a finite verb.

[3] Those who use the term *nominative absolute* will rightly point out that this parenthetical phrase contains no nominative.

It is clear that *having been warned of the dangers of the river* is an *adjective* phrase telling us more about boy, whereas an absolute construction, as its name suggests, stands apart from the structure of the rest of the sentence.

Exercise

In the following sentences quote examples of the absolute construction, and, in each instance, express the same thought by an adverb clause. Comment upon and correct any sentences that contain grammatical errors.

1. The slums having been cleared away, a new block of flats was erected.

2. Julius Cæsar lying dead, the conspirators felt that their task was nobly done.

3. On entering Bremerhaven the gigantic liner was soon berthed.

4. I returned home early, but, having chilblains on my fingers, my mother said I need not help with the washing-up.

5. There we were, both hanging precariously in mid-air, glaring into each other's eyes.

6. Clinging to one of the girders, it gave way beneath me.

7. Clinging to one of the girders, I felt it give way beneath me.

8. Seeing an open door, the baby crawled out into the garden.

9. Father coming downstairs, the baby, hearing his footsteps, made her way into some bushes.

10. The troopship having put in at Southampton, crowds of relatives who had gone to Plymouth were bitterly disappointed.

11. Having left Southampton, the captain agreed to take the ship into Plymouth for three hours only.

12. Before buying a violin the instrument should be thoroughly tested.

D. *Some Special Verbs*

Can, *dare*, *must*, *need*, and *ought* are Principal verbs, not auxiliaries, like *shall*, *will*, *may*, *might*. *To have* and *to be* are also frequently used as auxiliaries. *Shall* and *will* help to form the future tenses : *may* and *might* help to form the subjunctive mood : *to have*, as an auxiliary, helps to form the perfect tenses : *to be*, as an auxiliary, helps to form the continuous tenses with the present participle, and passive voice with the past participle.[1]

Where *shall* and *will* express determination or the imposing of one's will upon another person, they are also Principal verbs.

> I *will* take every care that my sons *shall* learn the lesson of tidiness.

Must and *ought* are defective verbs as they have no separate form for the past tense. The final *t* is a trace of the past tense in an Old English weak verb. This original past tense now does duty for the present. You can distinguish which tense is being used by noticing the tense of the infinitive that follows :—

> I must *go* to sleep. I must *have gone* to sleep.

Exercise

Comment upon the grammar of the words in italics.

1. Are you quite sure I *shall* be fit *to play* to-morrow ?
2. You *shall* not *stir* from this room and I need not *tell* you why.
3. There is some further evidence *to sift*.
4. I durst not *tell* him he had brought nothing further to light.
5. The cowboys could not *help* themselves ; they did not know where to *go*.

---

[1] It is assumed that, at this stage, the student is familiar with the terms *tense*, *mood*, and *voice*. They are referred to in *An English Highway*, Stage I. (Longmans, Green).

6. I *will hear* these men *give* their opinions.

7. *Craning* her neck, Gladys *could see* over the balustrade.

8. I said that I *might come*, not that I *would come*.

9 I *have* three letters *to post*. I *have* been *all* the evening *writing* them.

10. *Nine o'clock having struck*, the men ought *to have been* still deeply *engrossed* in the lecture, but they *all* seemed *bored*.

E. *Practice in Grammar and English Usage*

1. Subject and Verb

(*a*) Finite verbs must agree with their subjects in number and person. Consider these examples :—

1. A red and yellow jug *hangs* on the dresser. (*One jug.*)

2. A red and a yellow jug *hang* on the dresser. (*Two jugs.*)

3. Bursts of joy *greet* me. (*Bursts* is the subject.)

4. A stream of happy children *comes* along the High Street.

5. Liver and bacon *is* a dish I detest.

6. Pain and suffering *is* not always the result of neglect.

7. ' Fishers of Men ' *was* published last July.

8. Having lost eight matches in succession our eleven *is* disheartened.

9. In absolute silence the eleven *are* stowing away their bats.

10. Measles *has* broken out again.

Where brackets follow the above sentences the meaning should be sufficiently clear. Why are the verbs in sentences Nos. 4 to 8 all singular in number ? In No. 9, the members of the collective group, the eleven, are regarded as separate units. You would not, for instance, say ' The team is putting on its blazers.'

(*b*) 1. For the first time there is shown in the school feelings of devotion to the house captains.—WRONG.

2. What pleases me are men trying to take work on the land.—WRONG.

These two sentences illustrate errors which occur when the normal order is reversed. The first is the result of sheer carelessness ; the intervention of words between subject and verb is a poor excuse. The second shows the error of making the verb agree in number with the *complement* and not with the subject.

(*c*) The difficulty of deciding whether, with alternative subjects, the verb is to be singular or plural, or whether it is to be first, second, or third person, is overcome (1) by making the verb conform to the last subject named, or better (2) by avoiding such awkward constructions. Although it is grammatically correct, do not say, ' Neither the father nor the children are to leave us ' : nor, ' Either Tom or you are mistaken.' Say, ' We do not wish either the father or the children to leave us ' : and, ' Either Tom is mistaken, or you are.'

2. Tenses of Verbs (*see Appendix*)

(*a*) Frequently, when a past tense is used, it is incorrectly followed by the perfect infinitive. Thus : ' I meant to have brought my book ' implies that at the time the speaker was conscious of his intention he regarded the action of ' having brought the book ' as already a completed thing. If so, the sentence is correct. Most likely, however, he simply wished to convey the idea that he had forgotten to bring the book. ' I meant to bring my book ' therefore expresses his meaning. The perfect infinitive may be used to denote past time : The necklace appears *to have been stolen*, or some unfulfilled obligation : My friend ought *to have overlooked* my slight error.

(*b*) There is no difficulty in dealing with the *sequence* of the tenses of verbs if you are mindful of the time when the various acts took place.

1. Tom *came* here in order that his absence *may* be excused.—WRONG.

2. I *knew* that you *have replaced* the stolen clock.—WRONG.

Why is the first example obviously wrong ? In the second example the correct tense is either the simple past *replaced*, or, if you wish to draw attention to the fact that the clock had been replaced before you came to know about it, then you must use the *past* perfect, *had replaced* and not the *present* perfect.

Notice that all these sentences are correct :—

This is a book *which*
- *I should read.*
- *I shall read.*
- *I am reading.*
- *I was reading.*
- *I have been reading.*
- *I should have been reading.*
- *I have read.*
- *I had read.*

All the clauses italicized are *adjectival* : they tell you more about the *book* and are not dependent in any way upon the verb *is*. In *describing* the book I can use any tense I choose without any reference to the verb in the main part of the sentence, always provided that the result makes sense. What kind of clause is ' *in order that his absence may be excused,*' and what kind of a clause is ' *you have replaced the stolen clock* ' in the examples on p. 208 ? Can you say why you must be careful about the sequence of tenses in those kinds of subordinate clauses ?

(*c*) In letter writing you often meet with the incorrect use of tenses, especially the use of the future instead of the present. ' I shall have much pleasure in accepting your invitation ' is incorrect, as you are writing your acceptance *now*, and presumably you ' have much pleasure ' now.

(*d*) In changing from one construction to another, be careful not to destroy a sense of balance in the sentence. It is correct to write

> To err is human, but robbing the poor and oppressing the weak cannot be lightly forgiven.

It is incorrect to write

> It is more difficult *to keep* account of one's stock than *selling* the goods to customers. (*To sell.*)

The sentence gains in effect when these constructions are made parallel.

3. Pronouns

(*a*) A pronoun must agree with its antecedent in number and person.

> Mr Abelson poured all the diamonds into a heap which *was* to be sorted the next day.
> All the diamonds which *were* to be sorted were carefully locked away.

Explain why the above sentences are correct.

> It is I who *am* to blame.
> No. It is we who have deserted you who *are* culpable.
> Have you heard the rumour that *is* being circulated ?

Explain why the above sentences are correct.

(*b*) It is not always easy to see whether a relative pronoun in a parenthetical clause is to be regarded as a subject or as an object.

1. It was some years since Tom and I had seen this planter *whom* we found *to be* happy and prosperous.

2. It was some years since Tom and I had seen the planter *whom* we found was happy and prosperous.—Wrong.

3. We saw some other planters *whom* we left with reluctance.

The first sentence illustrates the Accusative and Infinitive construction. *Whom* is the object of the verb *found*.

The second sentence is wrong, possibly through confusing its construction with the accusative and infinitive construction. Instead of the infinitive *to be*, you now have the finite form *was*. The subject of this verb should therefore be *who* and not *whom*. In this sentence the object of *found* is the noun clause *who was happy and prosperous*.

The third sentence is correct. *Whom* is the object of *left*.

Which of the sentences Nos. 1 to 3 contains a parenthesis ? Quote the parenthetical words.

(*c*) A frequent source of error is the separation of a pronoun from its antecedent, the person or thing to which it refers. As you have already seen on p. 40, care is needed when you are turning a passage into reported speech.

(*d*) *Which* and *that* when used as relative pronouns are not to be regarded as interchangeable. You cannot, for instance, replace *which* by *that* in the sentence, ' The ground on which our eleven lost by eight goals.'

Elsewhere, however, it is the practice of modern writers not to distinguish the limiting or restrictive use of a *that* clause from the explanatory use of a *which* clause. H. W. Fowler's *Dictionary of Modern English Usage* discusses this topic at great length. It is said to have hastened the death of a famous journalist, who prided himself on his infallibility in the use of *that* and *which*, after he found he had written, ' The convicts opened the gate which led to freedom.' As the second clause defines the gate they opened, but does not give us any additional information about the gate, *that* should have been used. Had he written, ' The convicts opened the gate, which was fifteen feet high and heavily studded with octagonal nails ' his life would have been spared.

Fill in the gaps in the following sentences with *which* or *that*. In which of the sentences can you omit the relative pronoun altogether ?

1. This is not the book   I ordered.
2. To present prizes is an occasion   gives me great pleasure.
3. The guide has lost the path   leads back to Saltzburg.
4. Bridge is the game in   my aunt indulges.
5. I want a catalogue   illustrates wild flowers.

6. The half-back kicked into touch,   was not what his opponents expected.

7. The half-back kicked into touch ;   was not what his opponents expected.

8. To drink soup noisily is not a thing   a young lady should do.

(*e*) *And who, and whose, and whom,* and *and which* must be preceded by a clause in which you have used the same relative pronoun.

1. The philanthropist liked people of good character *and who* were happy. (Omit *and*, but it is better to recast the sentence.)

2. George Cotter, whose skill with the bat *and whose* ability to bowl are widely known, is to play for Gloucestershire.

3. This is a problem which I tried to do last year, *but which* I had to leave.

Comment upon Nos. 2 and 3 and state if they are correct, and even if correct, how they can be better expressed.

(*f*) When you are analysing sentences you should notice that *what*, when used as a relative pronoun is equivalent to *that which*.

> Tell him what he is to do.
> Tell him that which he is to do. (The antecedent of *which* is *that*.)

(*g*) Consistency in the use of pronouns is important. This is one of the commonest sources of error in students' essays.

1. When we reach Heidelberg, as you know, one is anxious to visit the castle.

2. If one is to see the most interesting part of the building he must be sure to find a guide for whose services you have to pay so little that one can easily afford it.

3. From the top of Ben Nevis one can see a magnificent view if one has chosen a fine day and one is not too exhausted by one's climb up the mountain.

What do you learn from No. 3 ? Notice that it is wrong to say ' *One* must always do *his* best.'

(*h*) *Someone, everyone*, and *anyone* are always singular in number. In referring to these pronouns it is correct to use *he, his, him* (or *she, her*, if the persons referred to are women).

(*i*) *No one, nobody, nothing, many a one, either, neither*, are all singular in number and must be used with the singular forms of verbs and be referred to by pronouns in the singular. When the subject of a sentence *each* is also singular. *None* can be either singular or plural according to the context. H. W. Fowler states that the plural use is the commoner. *All* is usually plural, except where it means *everything*. *E.g.*, To prayers ! all is lost.

(*k*) *Either* and *neither* refer to two things or two groups of things only.

> *Neither* boy answers the question. (Refers to two boys.)
> None of the boys can answer. (Refers to several boys.)
> Neither her hats nor her shoes fit me. (Two groups of things.)
> This plan will not be acceptable to *either* country. (Refers to two countries.)
> The plan will not be acceptable to any country. (Indefinite, but refers to more than two.)
> To *either* of you I will give three wishes. (Two people.)
> I will grant no boon to any of you. (A number of people.)
> To each of you I will give a silver spoon. (This may refer to two or more people.)

4. Adjectives

(*a*) In comparing groups of people or of things a common error is to forget to keep them distinct and to *in*clude when you wish to *ex*clude.

> Britain has made a more rapid recovery than *any* country in Europe. (*Any other country.*)

Britain (the first group) should be compared with the rest of Europe (the second group). To compare Britain with the whole of Europe is to include it in both groups, and so to compare it with itself. The same mistake occurs if you say *I prefer Sussex to any part of the south coast.*

Here again you have not isolated Sussex to compare it with the rest of the south coast, for Sussex is included in both parts of your comparison.

(*b*) Adjectives like *unique* and *peerless* in which a superlative quality is already expressed can have no degrees of comparison like *strong*, *stronger*, *strongest*. It is therefore incorrect to speak of a rather unique tower or a most peerless lady. To live in a unique Tudor house is an attraction offered by a builder of thousands of them.

5. Adverbs

(*a*) Do not regard all words ending in -*ly* as necessarily adverbs. You must always think of the function a word performs. In the phrases *an only child*, *a sickly smile*, and in the sentences *I feel poorly*, *This gift is costly*, the -*ly* words are all adjectives. In the last two examples they are used predicatively.

You must be prepared to find adjectives used instead of adverbs. Sit *closer* together. Hold your tickets *tight*. You make your downstrokes too *thin*. Such sentences are correct.

(*b*) *Only* is frequently misplaced in sentences. The tendency is to introduce *only* too early : a writer, conscious of an intention to qualify or restrict what he is saying, gives *only* a more prominent place than is warranted by the syntax.

> I only meant to give the beggar a penny.—WRONG.
> I meant to give the beggar only a penny.
> If I had only done what I wanted.—WRONG.
> If I had done only what I wanted.
> In conclusion, the lecturer said that he only wanted his audience to remember three things.—WRONG.
> In conclusion, the lecturer said that he wanted his audience to remember only three things. (Or *three things only*.)

In the following sentence introduce *only* into as many places as you can, consistent with sense, and say (i) whether you have used it as an adjective or as an adverb, and (ii) what alteration in meaning the sentence has undergone.

> On Thursday my friend practised the piano for twenty minutes.

(*c*) Since neither *hardly* nor *scarcely* implies a comparison, the correct conjunction to follow is *when* and not *than*. The incorrect use of hardly (or scarcely) . . . than is probably due to analogy with the construction *no sooner . . . than*, where a comparison is implied.

(*d*) The split infinitive is often the subject of profitless controversy. In *M.E.U.* pp. 558 to 561, Fowler gives much space to this topic. He begins by showing how happy are those who know nothing and care less about its alleged difficulties. Since there are many people who are sensitive on this point, even though their knowledge of English usage is less than Fowler's, it is best never to split an infinitive. Instances of unnecessarily splitting the infinitive by interposing a long parenthesis are to be condemned as a breach of the normal order of words.

Equally ugly and unnecessary are :—

> My friends hope to, as soon as they are settled in their new house, have me as one of their first guests.
> I ought to, if I get up in time, catch the 8.15 train.

With the passive form of the infinitive an adverb intervening before the past participle does not split the infinitive. 'This old man appears to be seriously hurt,' and 'Timid people are wont to be easily alarmed by rumours' are correct. Few would write 'to easily be alarmed' or 'to seriously be hurt.' These are incorrect.

6. Prepositions

(*a*) Prepositions contribute largely to the correct idiomatic use of expressions. What do these expressions mean :—

> to buy *in* ; to buy *off* ; to buy *out* ; to buy *up* ?

> The referee tells the boxers to break *away* ; the reluctant witness breaks *down* and cries ; a strong-willed man

8

breaks *down* resistance ; a burglar breaks *into* a house ; a spendthrift may break *into* his savings ; a woman is said to look as thin as if she were about to break *in* two ; an intruder will make us break *off* our discussion ; influenza breaks *out in* Wales ; a tramp breaks *in out* of the cold, or *in out of* a spirit of mischief ; the tennis champion breaks *through* his opponent's service ; the latter's health is said to have broken *up* ; we break *up* bread for the thrushes ; school will break *up* in three weeks.

Which of the above italicized words are used as adverbs and which as prepositions ?

(*b*) It is clear that you should know which prepositions to use. Study the following examples :—

1. The travellers expressed their appreciation *of*, and their confidence *in*, this most able guide.

2. Matters were at a deadlock ; the dictator was unable to insist *on* obedience to his decrees, nor was he able to refrain *from* his policy of government by threats.

3. In consideration and out of regard for your devotion to duty, the committee has awarded a pension.—WRONG.

4. The sardines are packed with great care and olive oil.—WRONG.

5. Do not pay any heed, or allow yourselves to be distracted, by such unmannerly interruptions.—WRONG.

Correct the last three and say why they were wrong.

(*c*) *Between* should refer to two things. If you are speaking of more than two things you must use *among*. A common error is to use *between* with one thing only as in the expression ' between each.'

Divide this basket of apples *between* the five boys. (*Among*.)
I want to see four paces between each boy.—WRONG.
I want to see four paces between each boy *and his neighbour*.
There was a full page illustration between each chapter.—WRONG.
Between the chapters there was a full page illustration.

(*d*) Fortunately there is no hard and fast rule about ending a sentence with a preposition. By noticing the practice of standard modern authors you will acquire an ear sufficiently sensitive to discriminate between the ugly and oft-quoted, 'What did you choose such a book to be read *to out of for* ? ' and the unnecessarily prim, ' For what have you come ? ' Notice that 'Why have you come ? ' differs in meaning from ' What have you come for ? '

7. Conjunctions

(*a*) *While* is occasionally misused as an adverbial conjunction when no regard is paid to its referring to time.

> The headmaster made a speech while the Mayor gave the prizes.

(*b*) The confusion in use between *like* and *as* arises from mixing two constructions. *Like* is not to be used as a conjunction.

1. This man is not a skilful architect *like* Paul Burton. (Preposition.)
2. This man is not a skilful architect, *as* Paul Burton is. (Conjunction.)
3. I can't help loving you like I do.—Wrong.
4. This man is not a skilful architect like Paul Burton is.— Wrong.

The first sentence is correct. The second is grammatically correct, but it may be better expressed by concluding ' as is Paul Burton.' A better sentence is, ' Unlike Paul Burton, this man is not a skilful architect.' The third sentence is crooners' English. The fourth confuses the constructions of Nos. 1 and 2.

(*c*) *Use of Pairs of Conjunctions.*—Both . . . and : Neither . . . nor : Either . . . or : Not only . . . but (also). Each of the pair should be followed by the same part of speech or by the same kind of construction.

1. Either screws or nails will do.
2. Your parents were both pleased with, and proud of, your success.

3. Instead of frowning, the old man was seen to be in a frolicsome mood; not only was he laughing and jesting but trying to devise some absurd practical joke.

4. Neither cycling nor playing cricket with a hard ball is allowed in this open space.

5. There is little choice now; you can either make restitution or pay the penalty.

6. The new regulations were better both for the nurses and the patients.—WRONG.

7. It is a long time since we had either an invitation to a dance or even to afternoon tea.—WRONG.

8. 'I regret to inform your lordship,' said the footman, 'that the Honourable Bertie has been rude both to the butler and me.'—WRONG.

In the last three examples the second of each pair is followed by a different part of speech from that which follows the first. No word put between the pairs of conjunctions can be regarded as common to both expressions. In No. 6, *for* is intended to be used both with *nurses* and *patients*. The sentence should therefore read: The new regulations were better both *for* the nurses and *for* the patients; or, The new regulations were better *for* both nurses and patients. Which do you consider to be the better correction? Why?

Correct sentences Nos. 7 and 8, and explain where they were wrong.

(*d*) It is customary to omit *and* except before the last of a list of words in series. Often *and* is omitted even here.

The fire spread rapidly until grain, tobacco, rubber, tea, all were consumed.

The omission of conjunctions often has the effect of speeding up the action of a story.

Tom climbed the ladder, tried the window, found it unfastened. He looked round cautiously. No one in sight! Swiftly he pushed open the window, stepped inside, closed it. What was next to be done?

(e) The incorrect omission of conjunctions is often found when comparisons are being made.

> This book is as good, if not better than any I have previously read. (*As* must be inserted after *good*.)

Express this as two separate statements joined by *and*. Which words are common to both sentences ? Is the second *as* common to both ?

8. Interjections

Do not imitate country fairs and circuses by using a string of exclamation marks. One is sufficient at a time. Do not be carried away by a dramatic moment and say, ' You villain ! ' she *hissed*.

9. Participles and Gerunds

(a) The unattached or unrelated or pendent participle is the source of amusing errors, but those who laugh loudest are often caught making the same mistake. You may not write, ' After walking for a quarter of an hour the sun rose.' A modern novelist has, ' Getting his ship to Barbados, his face started to swell.' Thus practised writers are often as slipshod as careless schoolboys. Always think carefully when you commence a sentence with a participle. Notice also the hints given on pp. 28 and 204.

Make sure that your participle is in close proximity to its correct noun or pronoun. If this does not offer a way out of your difficulty, delete the participle and use a finite verb.

> *Scoring* his third goal the ball shot from his foot like a rocket.
> When he scored his third goal, the ball shot from his foot like a rocket. (Is the comparison appropriate ?)

(b) The Gerund must be attached to some noun or pronoun. If this is not done correctly, the gerund will tend to attach itself to the subject of the finite verb. The mistake is similar to that of the unattached participle.

> In bowling Davidson his leg stump was broken.—WRONG.
> When Davidson was bowled his leg stump was broken.

(*c*) Consider these examples :—

1. Why do you object to me coming home after midnight ? —WRONG.
2. Why do you object to my *coming* home after midnight ?
3. I could not understand my father enduring the man's insults.—WRONG.
4. I could not understand my father's *enduring* the man's insults.
5. My *studying* Greek has left little time for music.
6. Upon my *entering* the room all stood up gravely.

Notice that the gerunds are preceded by *possessive* adjectives. In Nos. 2 and 6 the gerund is the object of a preposition : in No. 3 it is the object of the infinitive **understand** : in No. 5 the subject of *has left* is the gerund phrase ' *My studying Greek* ' and not *Greek*, for *Greek* is clearly the object of *studying*.

In Nos. 1 and 3 neither meaning nor syntax will bear examination. In No. 1 there is no objection to *me* as a person : in No. 3 it is not true that I could not understand my father ; it was his unwonted endurance or enduring of insult that I could not understand.

The Rule of Proximity

1. The smallest inhabited island in the British Empire is the one upon which stands the Eddystone Lighthouse, followed closely by the Wolf Rock. (The past participle *followed* should be brought into closer proximity with *island*, but the sentence is so badly constructed that *followed* will still be out of place. The whole sentence must be recast.)

2. The men arrived at the road which was going to be mended, with their foreman. (The comma does not save this from being ludicrous. The phrase *with their foreman* must be brought into closer proximity with *men*.)

The men, together with their foreman . . .

3. A Cavalier wears leggings or big boots that reach over his knees to which are fixed a pair of spurs. (*Which* is too far from its correct antecedent *boots*. Merely to move *which* will result in the same kind of error.)

To his leggings or big boots that reach over his knees a Cavalier fixes a pair of spurs.

4. In 1553, Sir Hugh Willoughby fitted out an expedition in search of a north-east passage to India of which Chancellor was appointed pilot general. (*Which* should be brought nearer to its antecedent *expedition*.)

5. The skin, too, is even more important, being an organ with a three-fold function, than these members. (The modern novelist who wrote this sentence has made a most ugly parenthesis. Put *being* immediately after the noun it qualifies, *skin*, and bring *than* nearer to the comparative *more*.)

6. Next in the film you see Jim Hawkins in the kitchen taking a cake out of the oven accompanied by a little girl. (Comment is unnecessary, except to assert the genuiness of this specimen.)

Exercises

Where a word or a sentence is italicized in the following exercise there is no previous reference to it. It illustrates a point that candidates for examinations of School Certificate standard should know from experience. If you are in any doubt you should consult *The Shorter Oxford English Dictionary* or H. W. Fowler's *Dictionary of Modern English Usage*.

Most of the examples are from candidates' work in examinations up to School Certificate standard. A few of the errors are so bad as to be classed as ' howlers.'

Correct or justify the syntax of the following sentences, and give your reasons for any changes you make :—

1. The skaters became entangled so that they *laid* on the ice to disengage their skates.

2. He would either have employed dishonest means or not at all.

3. A ship's log consists of a small propeller trailing astern on the end of a rope and which turns an instrument like a car's speedometer.

4. While furling the sails a pair of pliers was lost overboard.

5. I did not like to risk the sail blowing away.

6. I do not think a square sail would be satisfactory when single-handed.

7. The author who puts pen to paper in order to gain profit deserves no more success than the ruthless escapades of a Chicago gunman.

8. Dr Primrose and his family only liked people with a good character and who were happy.

9. To send a registered parcel I should take it to the post office where the *former* would be weighed.

10. Very little intelligence has been exercised in the use of the present pedestrian crossings which is a complete failure.

11. The government of Louis XIV., on the contrary, exhibited alacrity for all sorts of innovations, and showed itself favourable to the progress of letters, arts, wealth, in short of civilization. This was the veritable cause of its preponderance in Europe, which rose to such a pitch, that it became the type of a government not only to sovereigns, but also to nations, during the seventeenth century.

    SIR EDWARD CREASY : *Fifteen Decisive Battles
    of the World.*

12. *I have read less books this year than I have ever before, but I have had less time.*

13. If for any reason this chocolate should reach you out of condition, please return it with the wrapper to the address below, when we *will* be pleased to exchange for a fresh block and refund postage.

14. These neon signs can and are imitated by the use of translucent glass.

15. Fireworks are dangerous to young children because they are filled with explosives.

16. At length harvests were safely gathered and confidence restored. (See the article on *ellipsis* in *Modern English Usage*.)

17. Whilst on a voyage the crew demanded fresh meat to prevent scurvy obtainable only on the mainland.

18. The girl was only dancing a week before her tragic illness.

19. Why not make terms with your brother such as you having the football for a week and him the next ?

20. This department has broken all records for each year they have been open.

21. Marlow mistakes Miss Hardcastle who is wearing a country girl's clothes for her father's sake as the barmaid.

22. Go slow : no hospital in this town.

23. If a novelist's intention cannot be put into a phrase it is no subject for a novel.

24. I would never allow posters to be put in the country unless it were exceptionally delightful to see.

25. A very dainty lady stepped from the limousine with a fresh, brilliant complexion.

26. Lumber rooms are very interesting, packed with relics and glories of old times and especially so on rainy days.

27. The restive horse kicked his groom so much that he could not wash it down.

28. These notes would have been even better if they were properly written.

29. Hardly had the bell sounded than the children trooped out.

8 A

30. At my age I greatly prefer riding than walking.

31. Here is a book which I have read. I am lending it to you so that you might also enjoy it.

32. Branson is one of the best players that has ever played for Milstone.

33. If you *shall* send me your address I *will* be seeing you on Friday.

34. None are too poor to do him service and everyone ought to do their best to help him.

35. George and *myself* decided on walking either to Harrow or to ride to Kenton and walk from there.

36. My father is a plumber and he explains many things to me at home which occurs in sanitary engineering.

37. You must first mix the rubber with the different powders given you, and then when soft and plastic you put it into an oven.

38. Captain Absolute explained it was a sword for to fight his rival with.

39. I have four sisters neither of which are any good at net-ball.

40. My old clothes together with my sisters are kept in that trunk. Their's were always neat and tidy, but it's obvious that even my best suit had more than it's fair wear and tear.

41. The miser found a piece of tattered cloth that moths had made their home.

42. Once, while trying to decide in what part of the Alps to take a holiday—Savoy, Switzerland, or the Tyrol—a letter was forwarded to me by my father.

43. I asked Tom who he thought was going to win.

44. The bear sniffed suspiciously at the hunter who he thought was only pretending to be dead.

Suggest other ways of correcting the last sentence but one on p. 216 (c).

CHAPTER XIV

CLAUSE ANALYSIS

SENTENCES may be classified as Simple, Double (or Multiple), or Complex.

Simple

A Simple sentence contains one finite verb. If you find a passage expressing a series of thoughts each in a separate sentence and with no sentence in any way dependent on another, you have a sequence of Simple sentences.

> A new housing estate was being built. The district had for many years been undeveloped. Some of the houses had remarkably long gardens. I saw the builder. I asked him the price of a house. He told me. The prices ranged from £800 to £1,200.

A Simple sentence may have more than one *subject*. In such instances, when you are analysing do not supply another finite verb and turn the Simple sentence into a Double sentence.

> My friend and her sister took part in the procession. (*Double subject. Simple sentence.*)

Often you will find a *Double object*.

> My uncle gave me a book of stamps and five rare specimens. (*Simple sentence.*)

Double

A Double sentence (or a Multiple sentence) expresses two (or more) ideas. They are stated separately, but are joined by co-ordinating conjunctions. The sentence previous to this one is a Double sentence and so is the one you are now reading. Here are some further examples :—

> The district had for many years been undeveloped but a new housing estate was being built. I saw the builder and I asked him the price of a house.
>
> I can accompany you myself or I will ask my brother to do so.
>
> The young man was now famous both for the plays he had written and for the pictures he had exhibited.

Complex

A Complex sentence contains one main idea (Main clause) and one or more ideas dependent upon it. Some of these dependent ideas may also be dependent upon other dependent ideas. It is not, however, profitable to talk of sub-dependent and sub-sub-dependent clauses.

> When they came yesterday the decorators, who were dressed in smart white overalls, brought a ladder with which to reach the second-floor windows which were eighteen feet from the ground.

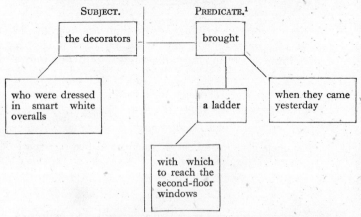

---

[1] The continued use and acceptance of this graphic method of analysis bears witness to the ingenuity of its authors, Messrs E. M. Palser and R. T. Lewis in their *New Outline Grammar of Function*.

Here you see the Main clause. *The decorators brought a ladder ;* two Adjective clauses—*who were dressed in white overalls* (Qualifying DECORATORS) and *with which to reach the second-floor windows* (Qualifying *ladder*, as *which* refers to *ladder*) ; and an Adverb clause of Time *when they came yesterday* (Qualifying [1] *brought*).

If to this sentence you add *which were eighteen feet from the ground*, you will have an additional Adjective clause, qualifying *windows*.

Notice that you often find sentences which are partly Double and partly Complex.

> The bewildered inventor thrust his fingers through the bars and drew out fragments of metal which resembled silver.
>
> The greedy child picked up baby's apple which had fallen on the ground and took a large mouthful.

Exercise

1. What is the difference between a phrase and a clause ?

2. What is the difference between a clause and a sentence ?

3. In the following sentences state which words, phrases, and clauses have an adjectival function. Which words do they qualify ?

(i) In each of the three films which were shown last night there was much flourishing of revolvers.

(ii) Few can resist the temptation of crawling underneath the flap of a tent at a circus which happens to visit their town.

(iii) The last book you brought from the library I read only a fortnight ago.

(iv) Here are some lines written by Pope in the Spenserian stanza. (*Comment on this sentence.*)

(v) Those who select the teams to represent England must feel elated at the way in which the new-comers have shown themselves worthy of the confidence put in them.

[1] Some prefer the term *Modifying* when speaking of Adverbial functions.

4. Expand the following sentences by adding suitable adjective phrases :—

   (i) The gardener paused to mop his brow.
  (ii) Buy your note-paper and envelopes from an established firm.
 (iii) Would those onlookers like to join in our game ?
 (iv) At last the housemaid had finished tidying the room.
  (v) From the statistics, the new methods are producing results.

5. Describe with an adjective clause each noun in the above sentences.

6. Expand the sentences in question No. 4 by adding adverb phrases or adverb clauses.   Underline the *clauses* only.

7. Which phrases here do the work of nouns ?   State whether the phrases are the Subject, Object, or Complement of the sentence.

   (i) Catching the last train home means arriving late at the office.
  (ii) To appear a simpleton seems to be one way to succeed.
 (iii) John's intention is to be a master mariner.
 (iv) The old man's delight in painting meant much to his daughter too.

8. In the following sentences state the finite verbs.   Then say which is the Main clause and whether the subordinate clause is Noun, Adjective, or Adverb in function.

   (i) When Tom hailed his friend the latter stopped his car.
  (ii) It always comes on to rain if we plan a picnic.
 (iii) Mr Freestone is working hard in the garden while his wife is cooking the dinner.
 (iv) That neither of you saw the gypsies is obvious.
  (v) The career I have mapped out for myself may be fraught with danger.
 (vi) That you take delight in cricket is obvious to all who know you.
 (vii) That is the shelter where Gladys lost her purse.
(viii) ' Keep away from the bull,' roared the farmer to the Scouts who could not help smiling at this unnecessary advice.

(ix) The child asked the aviator whether the seaplane could attain a speed of 400 miles an hour.

(x) Why you call so frequently at the office is beyond my comprehension.

You must not regard all dependent clauses beginning with *who* or *which* as adjectival and all those beginning with an adverb as necessarily adverbial. See if you can compose sentences using ' Where the procession begins ' as a noun subordinate, an adjective subordinate, and an adverb subordinate clause.

Dependent Clauses : Summary

Noun Clauses

> *That your work is improving* shows *how hard you must have worked.*

The Noun clauses are in italics : *shows* is the Main verb. What is the Subject and what the Object of this sentence ?

> Tell the gamekeeper *when you saw the men, where they were,* and *what they were doing.*

Notice that here you have four finite verbs (*tell, saw, were,* and *were doing*). Why is each of the three subordinate clauses a Noun clause ?

> The reason for choosing Tom as captain is *that he has the most experience.* (*Noun clause as Complement.*)

> From *what we hear* there is no evidence against the prisoner. (*Noun clause as Object of a preposition.*)

> The company issued a warning *that passengers were to cross the line by the sub-way.* (*Noun clause in apposition to a noun.*)

> His statement amounts to this, *that John is waiting for news.* (*Noun clause in apposition to a pronoun.* this.)

> *Anticipatory Subject* (or ' Formal Subject ') *and Object.*

> It is true *that these flower-girls have seen better days.*

> (The italicized Noun clause is the subject of *is.* *It* does not stand for any known thing : it is used impersonally

as a mere conventional opening to the sentence. In a similar way *there* is also used as a conventional way of opening a sentence, but in these instances *there* is not a noun and so must not be spoken of as an anticipatory subject.[1])

The English tourists found that it was easy to change their travellers' cheques. (Here *it* anticipates the Object. What is the Object of this sentence ?)

Noun clauses may also be classified as :—

(a) Dependent Statements

That my son is a weakling is no fault of mine.
The detective discovered *that the jewels had been replaced*.

(b) Dependent Questions

The principal actor asked who that strange little girl was.
(' Who is this strange little girl ? ' is the direct question.)

(c) Dependent Desires

Would *it were the last day of term*.

(d) Dependent Exclamations

Look *what a difference a little organization means*.
Now see *what a plight we are in*.

Adjective Clauses

It was one of my friends *who suggested a holiday at Chepstow*.
Where have you put the cover *which was taken off the type-writer* ?
Those are the flowers *that you asked us to bring*.
Can you tell me the date *when Columbus set sail* ?
The bathers were told to keep away from the spot *where the cliffs were crumbling*.

---

[1] ' There ' *can* be used as a Noun but only in examples such as, Tom wrote the word ' there ' on the board.

When *there* is merely a formal opening word, the fact should be stated. Do not call it an Adverb of place as no notion of place is intended.

You should certainly pay heed to the rowing instructor *from whom much may be learned.*

Last year my friends called at Baden-Baden, *at which spa they took the waters.*

Against Sussex, Middlesex had in the field the same side *as they had had against Yorkshire.*

Avoidance of Confusion—Noun and Adjective Clauses

A. Occasionally you will be asked to analyse sentences in which there is a parenthetical clause.

1. The old man's breathing, the doctors noticed, became more regular.
2. Above the hill I noticed that a cloud was rising. (No parenthesis here. *Main clause*—I noticed : *Noun subordinate clause, Object of* ' noticed '—that a cloud was rising above the hill.)

As far as meaning goes, in the first example *the doctors noticed* is merely a parenthesis, an intrusion, as it were, into a statement. It does not therefore seem correct to call this interruption a Main clause and the more important part of the sentence *The old man's breathing became more regular* only a Noun subordinate clause. It is preferable to treat such examples as parentheses introduced into Simple sentences. In analysing you will not often meet this little problem. It has, at times, proved baffling to candidates not expecting it.

B. A far more common source of error is a failure to distinguish an Adjective clause from a Noun clause in apposition.

This is a statement *that none can refute.* (Adjective clause, *describes* statement.)

The railway company issued a statement *that they accepted no responsibility.* (This does not *describe* the statement ; it is the statement itself. The clause in italics is therefore a Noun clause in apposition to ' statement.')

Apposition means ' standing in the same grammatical relationship.'

Jones, *the hope of his side*, was out first ball.
Sir John Squire has brought out a new book, *a monumental addition to English criticism.*
My cousin's laziness is *a difficult proposition.*

but

My cousin's laziness presents a difficult proposition. Here *a difficult proposition* is the OBJECT of ' presents ' whereas *laziness* is the SUBJECT. No longer, therefore, are they in apposition.
I have a feeling *that I cannot describe.* (Adj. clause: it is an attempt to describe the feeling.)
I have a feeling *that I am going to suffocate.* (Noun clause in apposition to *feeling*: it *is* the feeling.)

Adverb Clauses

In clause analysis you are expected to state what kind each adverbial clause is. There are nine kinds :—

(*a*) TIME.
    When the ambassadors have accomplished their mission, they will return.

(*b*) PLACE.
    Fools rush in *where angels fear to tread.*

(*c*) CAUSE.
    As the boy had only just begun his apprenticeship, he did not expect high wages.
    Because he was ambitious, I slew him.

(*d*) PURPOSE.
    The secretary carefully arranged the papers *so that they could be found at a moment's notice.*
    The old lady was afraid to take a deck chair *lest a heavy shower should compel her to leave it.*
    I shouted *that the coastguard might hear me.*

(*e*) MANNER.
    As ye sow, so shall ye also reap.
    You will never bowl a googly unless you hold the ball *as I am doing.*

(*f*) COMPARISON OR DEGREE.

His eyes were green *as leeks* (*are*).[1]

Fewer men strove harder *than Captain Scott* (*strove*).[1]

(*g*) RESULT.

Some men are so indifferent *that they will not even answer important letters.* (Do not confuse this with Comparison.)

Mrs Adams was such a long time in changing her dress *that her husband fell fast asleep on the settee.*

(*h*) CONDITION.

Unless the treatment begins at once there is little hope of a quick restoration to health.

The bully will at once begin to calm down *if you face him resolutely.*

(*i*) CONCESSION.

Although this capital has been invested wisely there are even better investments to be made.

There is still something to be said for a green and yellow tie *though at first sight it seems vivid.*

Exercise

1. Write four sentences, in the first of which is a Noun clause as the subject; in the second, a Noun clause as the object; in the third, a Noun clause as the complement; and in the fourth, a Noun clause in apposition to the object.

2. Compose a sentence with a Noun clause as the object of a preposition.

3. Write a paragraph containing at least one example of each of the following: (i) a Noun clause as the object of a verb; (ii) an Adjective clause qualifying a pronoun; (iii) an Adverb clause of concession.

4. Combine the following simple sentences so as to form *one* complex sentence :—

Richard Longstaff was a clever inventor. Three weeks after his first invention scholars had begun to take interest in his motor-harvester. His motor-harvester was destined to revolutionize agriculture.

State what kind of subordinate clauses you have used.

[1] In analysing *elliptical* sentences you must supply the missing words.

Clause Analysis : An Example Worked in Detail

Although the results of this investigation may be uncertain, all scientists know that progress has been made which has amply justified the cost the committee has borne since Dr Spenlow first began these researches.

London Chamber of Commerce, Certificate.

	CLAUSE	KIND	FUNCTION
1	Although the results of this investigation may be uncertain	Adverbial sub-ordinate of Con-cession to 2	Qualifying *know*
2	all scientists know	Main clause to 1 and 3	Makes a statement
3	that progress has been made	Noun sub-ordinate to 2 (Main to 4)	Object of the verb *know*
4	which has amply justified the cost	Adjective sub-ordinate to 3 (Main to 5)	Qualifying *pro-gress*
5	the committee has borne	Adjective sub-ordinate to 4 (Main to 6)	Qualifying *cost*
6	since Dr Spenlow first began these researches	Adverbial sub-ordinate of Time to 5	Qualifying *has borne*

Notes : The first step was to underline the Finite verbs. There are six of these and there are no elliptical constructions, so that there will be six clauses.

These clauses are interwoven into a pattern ; there is a Main clause, but some of the subordinate clauses depend, not upon this Main clause but upon another subordinate clause. Thus the 3rd clause is Noun subordinate to 2, but it is a main clause to 4. The 4th clause is an Adjective subordinate to 3, but it is also main to 5, and 5 is main to 6. Some teachers would insist on these additional points appearing in the table.

It is advisable to number your clauses *and to refer to these numbers in your analysis*, especially if you are dealing with a lengthy passage.

The FUNCTION column should be filled in accurately. It is there that you show you have a reason for classifying the clause as Main, Noun, Adjective, or Adverbial. If two clauses are co-ordinate the fact is to be stated in this column.

Notice that verbs may consist of more than one word. Sometimes an adverb qualifies not the verb alone but several words in a clause.

> Her father's irritable outbursts are so mingled with equally warm expressions of generosity that a new acquaintance is bewildered.

The Adverbial subordinate of Result clause, *that a new acquaintance is bewildered*, qualifies *are so mingled*, not merely the verb *are*.

Exercises

A. Analyse the following passages into clauses, stating clearly the nature of each clause :—

1. My friend was sorry to hear of our loss but hoped that we should once again begin to make profits now that trade was improving.

2. At length the beadle called my name with a voice that made me tremble as much as the sound of the Last Trumpet would have done.

3. Suppose you were called to a patient who had broken his arm by a fall, what would you do ?

4. A bluff country fellow, disposed to be merry at my expense, told me that I looked little better than a scarecrow and that when he first saw me talking to the village policeman I resembled Jim Dowkin, a disreputable fellow of whom they were glad to be rid.

5. Those who say that scientists make serious mistakes should remember that, although they are cautious in making decisions, they are quite prepared to admit their work should be carefully checked and confirmed before any new theory is advanced.

6. In order to give no grounds for a suspicion of favouritism the manager decided that there should be no praise lest the worker commended should be regarded with jealousy and distrust, yet the manager warned the men that the effect would be harmful as it would discourage effort.

7. ' It's no use trying here,' they would say, ' you are blamed if anything goes wrong, but you'll never have a word of praise, no matter how hard you try.'

B. (a) Analyse the following passage into clauses, stating clearly the nature of each and its relationship to the rest of the sentence in which it stands, and (b) state fully and in precise grammatical terms the functions of the words and phrases in italics.

1. *However* satisfactory the report may seem to the directors, the fact is that the firm must continue its policy *of stringent economy* wherever this is consistent with *good feeling*, for we, *a firm of high repute*, must not neglect our duty to *those* who occupy posts of lesser responsibility but whose service is *so* valuable that it can *be* said *to be* indispensable.

2. Perhaps you will disagree with my statement, *but what* I think is that the people who do not give earnest thought *to the problem* of imperial preference are *unworthy* to have a voice *in the government* of their country.

3.   For want of cash he soon had pawn'd
                 One half *that* he possess'd,
             And *drinking* show'd *him* duplicates
                 Beforehand of the rest !
             So now his Creditors resolved
                 To seize on his assets,—
             For why—they found *that* his half-pay
                 Did not half pay his debts.

                                         Thomas Hood.

4. But each contented with his humble sphere,
 Moves unambitious through the circling year ;
 Nor e'er forgets the fortune of his race,
 Nor pines *tc quit*, or strives to change his place.
 Ah ! who has seen the *mailed* lobster *rise*,
 Clap her broad wings, and soaring claim the skies ?
 When did the owl, *descending* from her bow'r
 Crop, 'midst the fleecy flocks, the tender flow'r ;
 Or the young heifer *plunge*, with pliant limb,
 In the *salt* wave, and fish-like strive to swim.

From the *Anti-Jacobin*.[1]

C. Construct sentences in which the main and dependent clauses appear in the order indicated.

1. Main clause ; noun clause as object ; adjective clause.

2. Adverb clause of concession ; main clause ; adverb clause of time.

3. Main clause ; noun clause in apposition ; adverb clause of result.

4. Adverb clause of purpose ; main clause ; adjective clause.

5. Adverb clause of condition ; noun clause in apposition ; main clause.

[1] Ridiculous ?   Yes, but why rend fine poetry ?

REVISION PAPER 3

1. Read the following passage carefully, and then answer the questions on it below.

MARTIN (*a wealthy bachelor and an employer of labour*). *I have every reason to think that I am heavily overtaxed.* You fathers are let off much too lightly. *You pay very little to the State so that I can have the privilege of paying for the education of your children.* Why should this be imposed upon me? *How can I possibly benefit from money that is spent on other people's children?*

LAWSON (*the father of five children*). When they leave school, they come to work in your factory. You benefit from their skill.

MARTIN. But they have no skill. They know nothing about my trade when they come to the factory. Surely the school ought to teach the children something about mat-making: *then* I could save much wasted time, and they could have higher wages right at the beginning.

LAWSON. You say you derive no benefit from their education. They appreciate the value of order and discipline, not perhaps a rigidly strict discipline, but enough to make them defer to authority. But for this they might become thieves or poachers in your woods and fields. Education gives you security.

MARTIN. I already pay quite sufficient in rates and taxes for the police to protect me. It is fear, not education, that keeps people honest.

LAWSON. It seems that you would prefer to have your labourers ignorant so that you could pay them even lower wages.

MARTIN. How can you say that I pay my men poor wages? Have you ever bought anything from me? What do you think——

LAWSON. Don't get heated. I made no mention of *poor*

238

wages. Change the subject. We're nearly in the station, and the train's on time for once. Didn't I hear that your nephew has just gone to Oxford?

MARTIN. Yes. He's to finish off a sound, general education.

LAWSON (*as he alights from the train*). I was just wondering if that will include mat-making.

(*a*) Trace carefully the course of this conversation and arrange your statement of it so as to show quite clearly how the last point reached is developed from the first. Write in your own words, and try to keep within the limit of 150 words.

(*b*) Which remarks in the above dialogue seem to be irrelevant? State why you consider them to be off the subject.

(*c*) Turn into reported speech the passage beginning ' How can you say . . .' and ending '. . . if that will include mat-making.' Avoid any ambiguity.

(*d*) Divide the sentences in italics in Martin's first speech into main and dependent clauses. State clearly the functions of each subordinate clause.

2. Read the following lines carefully. They are taken from a poem by Edmund Waller and were published in 1686.

> The seas are quiet, when the winds give o'er ;
> So calm are we, when passions are no more :
> For then we know how vain it was to boast
> Of fleeting things, so certain to be lost.
> Clouds of affection from our younger eyes
> Conceal that emptiness which age descries.

(*a*) Give *briefly* in your own words the substance of these lines.

(*b*) Explain in some detail the point of the metaphor in the last two lines.

3. Express the following passage in your own words :—

Learning is like a river, whose head being far in the land, is, at first rising, little, and easily viewed ; but, still as you go, it gapeth with a wider bank ; not without pleasure and delightful winding, while it is on both sides set with trees, and the beauties of various flowers. But still the further you follow it, the deeper and the broader 'tis ; till at last it inwaves itself in the unfathomed ocean ; there you see more water, but no shore—no end of that liquid flowing vastness.

This passage is figurative. Show, at each stage of the river's course, how the simile helps to make clear the thought expressed.

4. Correct or justify the syntax of the following sentences, giving reasons :—

   (*a*) The characters of Ariel and Caliban differ from each other as black from white.

   (*b*) Hardly had the men begun to lay the new pipe-line when the whistle went for lunch-time.

   (*c*) The enforced delay and inaction was very irksome.

   (*d*) I most certainly object to you being here.

   (*e*) In reply to your invitation we will be pleased to accept.

  (*f*) It is a long time since we have had either an invitation for a dance and cabaret show or even to afternoon tea.

5. Analyse into clauses, and comment on the functions of the words and phrases italicized :—

> But if reduced subsistence *to implore*,
> In common prudence they would pass your door.
> Unpitied Hudibras, your *champion friend*,
> Has shown how far your charities extend.
> This lasting verse shall on his tomb be read,
> ' He shamed you *living*, and upbraids you dead.'

6. Analyse the following passage into clauses, stating clearly the nature of each clause :—

Three of the principal railway companies which had been in despair so that for years there had been no development now stated that they would soon be paying substantial dividends as a large influx of business was expected from the new mines that were beginning to flourish in the far West.   *London Chamber of Commerce.*

7. Analyse into clauses, and comment on the functions of the words and phrases italicized :—

Although the position of the lost treasure ship has not been located, all members *of the expedition* know *that* progress has been made *which* has amply justified the expense the committee has borne since 'H.M.S. Spreadeagle' first noticed her *sinking*.

8. Comment on the literary qualities of the following extract from *The Plagues of Athens*, by Bishop Sprat (1635-1713).

> Upon the head first the disease
> Like a bold conqueror does seize,
> Begins with man's metropolis,
> Secures the Capitol, and then it knew
> It could at pleasure weaker parts subdue.
> Blood started through each eye.
> The redness of that sky
> Foretold a tempest nigh.
> Then down it went into the breast,
> There all the seats and shops of life possest,
> Such noisome smells from thence did come
> As if the body were a tomb.

9. Construct sentences in which the main and dependent clauses appear in the order indicated.

(a) Adverb clause of manner ; main clause ; noun clause as object.

(b) Main clause ; adjective clause ; noun clause as object of a preposition.

(c) Main clause ; adverb clause of comparison ; adjective clause.

(d) Adverb clause of cause ; adjective clause ; main clause.

(e) Main clause ; noun clause as complement ; adverb clause of place.

APPENDIX

TABLE OF TENSES

Infinitive : To Write

	Present	Past	Future
Simple .	I write *I wrote*	I wrote	I shall write (you, he) will write
Continuous	I am writing *I am writing*	I was writing	I shall be writing (you, he) will be writing
Perfect .	I have written *I have written*	I had written	I shall have written (you, he) will have written
Passive Voice	It is written *It is written*	It was written	It will be written

Notice

The *Continuous* tenses are formed by some part of the verb *to be* and the *present participle*.

The *Perfect* tenses are formed by some part of the verb *to have* and the *past participle*.

Passive Voice is formed by some part of the verb *to be* and the *past participle*.

Only the simple tenses of the passive voice are given.

The tenses

' should write ' ; ' should be writing ' ; ' should have written ' ;

are spoken of as

Future in the Past	*Future in the Past Continuous*	*Future Perfect in the Past*

1. Find out what name would be given to the tense I ' should have been writing.'

2. Write out the Passive form of all the Active tenses referred to above.

INDEX

243